ABOUT THE AUTHOR

Mark Williams was born in 1952 and educated at Stockton-on-Tees Grammar School and St Peter's College, Oxford. Between 1979 and 1982 he was Lecturer in Applied Psychology at the University of Newcastle upon Tyne, and from 1983 to 1991 was Research Scientist at the Medical Research Council's Cognition and Brain Sciences Unit in Cambridge. From 1991 to 2002 he was Professor of Clinical Psychology at the University of Wales, Bangor, and, in 1997, founded its Institute of Medical and Social Care Research. In 2003 he returned to Oxford for a Wellcome Principal Research Fellowship, and is now Emeritus Professor of Clinical Psychology and Fellow of Linacre College in the University of Oxford, an Honorary Fellow at St Peter's College and at Bangor University, and Honorary Canon of Christ Church Cathedral. In 2009 he received the Stengel Award from the International Association of Suicide Prevention for 'outstanding contribution to the field of suicide prevention'. He is a Founding Fellow of the Academy for Cognitive Therapy, a Fellow of the Academy for Medical Sciences and a Fellow of the British Academy.

His other books include *The Psychological Treatment of Depression* (1984, 1992); *Cognitive Psychology and Emotional Disorders* (1988, 1997 with F. Watts, C. MacLeod and A. Mathews); *Mindfulness-based Cognitive Therapy for Depression* (2002; second edition 2013, with Z. Segal and J. Teasdale); *The Mindful Way Through Depression: Freeing Yourself from Chronic Unhappiness* (2007, with John Teasdale, Zindel Segal and Jon Kabat-Zinn); *Mindfulness: A Practical Guide to Finding Peace in a Frantic World* (2011, with Danny Penman); *Mindfulness: Diverse Perspectives on its Origins, Meaning and Application* (2013, with Jon Kabat-Zinn); and *The Mindful Way Workbook: An Eight Week Program to Free Yourself from Depression and Emotional Distress* (2014, with John Teasdale and Zindel Segal). He has contributed to TV and radio broadcasts, including BBC2's *Heart of the Matter*, Radio 4's *Science Now* and *All in the Mind* and PBS's *Science Friday.*

PRAISE FOR *CRY OF PAIN*

'At the beginning of this volume Mark Williams says "this book aims to help people come to a deeper understanding of the suicidal mind". Readers will conclude that he has achieved unqualified success in this ambition. The understanding he provides ranges, for example, from social to biological explanations, from psychiatric to genetic influences, and from historical attitudes and laws to current dilemmas, including euthanasia, assisted suicide and suicide bombers. Overriding the wide-ranging explanations for suicide, the author gradually explains the psychological theories of suicidal behaviour for which he and his colleagues are renowned. This leads on quite naturally to therapeutic and prevention initiatives.

Readers of this book, be they clinicians, researchers or lay persons, will put it down with a greatly enriched understanding of the many factors which may lead a person to thinking or acting on suicidal thoughts. The author deserves the utmost praise from those of us working in this difficult field for providing this highly accessible and engaging account of the tragedy of suicide whilst, at the same time, leaving readers with a sense of optimism about the opportunities to prevent suicide and to help those at risk.'

Keith Hawton, Professor of Psychiatry and Director, Centre for Suicide Research, University of Oxford

'*Cry of Pain* is a wonderful book that provides a highly readable, original and compassionate account of an issue that we sometimes find it difficult to talk about. It bridges the gaps between a number of perspectives: the lay and the professional; the personal and the societal; the psychiatric and the social. It comes up with what is essentially a unified theory of suicidal behaviour. This book will be of interest to those in health and other caring roles, as well people who suffer suicidal ideas, and their families. Professor Williams makes the statistics and research on suicidal behaviour highly accessible but this is no dry textbook – it contains very helpful messages about the causes of suicide and, ultimately, very hopeful messages about its prevention.'

Professor Nav Kapur, Professor of Psychiatry and Population Health, Centre for Suicide Prevention, University of Manchester, UK

'Anyone who has read the work of Professor Mark Williams or attended his presentations will expect a book that is clearly written and accessible, sympathetic and compassionate. This book undoubtedly lives up to those expectations.

Cry of Pain starts with a brief history of suicide and relates this to contemporary society. Professor Williams then takes a multi-disciplinary look at suicide, and the causes of attempted suicide, which is very helpful for the general reader. It courageously deals with the topic of rational and assisted suicide before discussing the suicidal mind and the extent to which suicide can be prevented. Throughout, it presents the statistical evidence clearly and logically. The book concludes by looking at therapy, particularly cognitive therapy and mindfulness, topics that Professor Williams has devoted a great deal of time to in recent years. From the perspective of one who works with those bereaved by suicide, I can see much value in developing this approach to support the suicide-bereaved.

This book should be on the shelf of everyone studying the topic of Suicidology and I would also strongly recommend it to the suicide-bereaved.'

John Peters, M. Suicidology, Volunteer, Survivors of Bereavement by Suicide

CRY *of* PAIN

Understanding suicide and the suicidal mind

PRO AMS

PIATKUS

First published 1997 under the title *Cry of Pain* by Penguin Books
Second edition published 2001 under the title *Suicide and Attempted Suicide* by Penguin Books
This updated and expanded edition published in Great Britain in 2014 by Piatkus
Reprinted 2014

A CIP catalogue record for this book is available from the British Library.

ISBN 978-0-349-40281-9

Typeset in Sabon by M Rules
Printed and bound in Great Britain by
Clays Ltd, St Ives plc

Papers used by Piatkus are from well-managed forests and other responsible sources.

MIX
Paper from responsible sources
FSC® C104740

Piatkus
An imprint of
Little, Brown Book Group
100 Victoria Embankment
London EC4Y 0DY

An Hachette UK Company
www.hachette.co.uk

www.piatkus.co.uk

To Phyllis, Rob, Jen and Annie

CONTENTS

	Acknowledgements	xi
	Introduction: The Suicidal Process and the Cry of Pain	xiii
1.	A Brief History of Suicide	1
2.	Suicide in Contemporary Society	24
3.	Suicide: A Psychiatric or a Social Phenomenon?	44
4.	Attempted Suicide	64
5.	The Causes of Attempted Suicide	79
6.	Rational and Assisted Suicide, Euthanasia and Martyrdom	101
7.	Psychodynamics, Biology and Genetics	123
8.	The Suicidal Mind: Defeated and Trapped	139
9.	Mind-lock: Why the Past Obstructs the Future	161
10.	The Media as a Catalyst for Suicidal Behaviour	176

11. Can We Prevent Suicide? 187

12. Healing the Pain: Therapy for the Suicidal Mind 209

13. Concluding Thoughts 228

Notes and References 237

Resources 267

Index 273

ACKNOWLEDGEMENTS

In preparing this new, 2014, edition, I wish to acknowledge the help and support of Catherine Crane, Thorsten Barnhofer, Bergljot Gjelsvik and other colleagues at Oxford, Keith Hawton, Helen Bergen, Sue Simkin, Danielle Duggan, Silvie Hepburn and Melanie Fennell; also, Rebecca Crane and Sarah Silverton at Bangor University, with whom I have collaborated in exploring how mindfulness-based interventions might help suicidal people. I am grateful to Professor Rory O'Connor and Professor Andy MacLeod who have worked with me over many years in developing the ideas expressed in this book, to my colleagues in the British Isles Suicide Research Network, especially Nav Kapur, David Gunnell, Jonathan Evans, Glyn Lewis, Allan House, David Owens, Ella Arensman, Steve Platt and Paul Corcoran, and to Alan Apter, Annette Beautrais, Lanny Berman, Kees Van Heeringen, Diego DeLeo, Bob Goldney, Murat Khan, Lars Mehlum, Brian Mishara and Mort Silverman and many other colleagues in the International Association for Suicide Prevention, and especially Vanda Scott who has been an incredible source of support for our work at Oxford. Thanks also to Sheila Crowley at Curtis Brown and to Judith Longman for support throughout the publication process, and to Anne Lawrance at Piatkus. All of these wonderful people may never know how much their enthusiasm has made this edition possible. I am deeply grateful to them all.

Mark Williams, Oxford, December 2013

INTRODUCTION: THE SUICIDAL PROCESS AND THE CRY OF PAIN

There is much that presents a real and often tragic puzzle to be solved by family and friends, by physicians and other professionals involved with someone who has committed or attempted suicide. 'Why did they do it?' '*How* could they do this?' 'Why did they not see there was help available?' 'Why this?' 'Why now?'

For therapists and clinicians, and for scientists who want to find any understanding that will help those who are vulnerable and their families, there are also puzzles that often seem unsolvable. What is it that causes someone to end his or her own life or to harm themselves? Is it down to a person's temperament – the biology of their genes – or to social conditions? Could suicide be caused by what has been learned over a lifetime in a way that points to a psychological explanation? What provides the best clue to a suicidal person's thoughts and behaviour? Each type of explanation, seen in isolation, has its drawbacks, so we need to see how they may fit together to give a more complete picture.

The large growth in interest during recent years in the subject of suicide and suicidal behaviour may be due, first, to the rapid increase in suicides by young people (particularly young men) between the mid-1970s and 1990s. Although the same period saw a decrease in the numbers of older people committing suicide (traditionally the most vulnerable group), the change in rates meant that many more suicide victims had taken their lives 'at the prime of life'.

Second, there has been an increased wish within many governments to challenge healthcare systems to meet targets to improve the health of their populations. Suicide rates are seen as a visible and quantifiable aspect of the mental health of a nation.

Third, interest in suicide has been fuelled by a renewed debate, especially in the United States, about medically assisted suicide and rational suicide (self-deliverance). When Derek Humphry's book *Final Exit* was published in 1991, with its matter-of-fact, detailed discussion of the best way of ending life, it sold more than 500,000 copies in its first year. These are issues and debates in which both public and professionals are interested.

In the main, two types of book are written in response to this increased interest: the first is written for the mental-health professionals; the second for suicidal people, their families or for suicide 'survivors'.[1] Of all the books which proved useful to both the professional and lay communities, Erwin Stengel's *Suicide and Attempted Suicide*[2] became a classic. Written originally in the early 1960s and reprinted several times, it gave the main facts and figures together with sufficient interpretation to help the reader understand something of the mind of those who feel suicidal. The book separated suicide from attempted suicide, but in its revision Stengel included an extra discussion about the 'appeal function' of attempted suicide.

Having mentioned the idea of 'appeal' – the 'cry for help' – in the early editions, Stengel then had to work hard to counteract a fundamental misunderstanding. People thought that he meant that non-fatal suicidal behaviour was *only* an appeal, only manipulative, when he had meant to imply that such behaviour had an appeal function, in the same way that physical illness has an appeal function – i.e. other people will change *their* behaviour to try and help the person. In this sense, he says, 'the appeal effect of a suicidal act may be the greater the less it was intended'.[3] However, the scene was set for a misunderstanding for many years. Even now, many suicidal acts are dismissed as 'mere' cries for help, as if the motive to communicate distress was incompatible with a serious attempt to end life, and as if the self-damaging act did not represent a mental-health problem which needs to be taken seriously.

So the 'cry for help' idea, though originally intended to be a neutral theory about suicidal behaviour, has outlived its usefulness. It still leads to misunderstanding. First, it has contributed to a widening of the gap between how people understand non-fatal suicidal behaviour (self-harm) and death by suicide. Second, it is almost always used pejoratively, or at least to imply that a certain suicidal act was not so serious but 'merely' a cry for help. Those who work closely with people who feel suicidal and sometimes act on such feelings know that such behaviour is never 'merely' anything.

This book gives an alternative perspective. Suicidal behaviour is most often not a cry for help but a *cry of pain*. This idea is intended to capture the way in which an act can communicate something without communication being the main motive. It is like an animal caught in a trap, which cries with pain. The cry is brought about by the pain, but in the way it communicates distress, it changes the behaviour of other animals who hear it. And just like an animal which finds itself struggling, people who are suicidal have often been defeated by something that has happened to them. Even if there is no external evidence for such defeat, they *feel* themselves to be a loser, a failure, and responsible for the negative effects they are having on others. They come to the point where they see evidence of defeat and rejection everywhere. Periods of struggle against such feelings are punctuated by periods of inactivity and despair.

The slide into helplessness can occur irrespective of psychiatric diagnosis. Attempts to control such despair by struggling, trying to shut it out with alcohol or drugs or brooding about it only make the feeling worse, so the sense of defeat, inescapability and being trapped gets worse as well. This only adds to existing and very real problems that come from failures to deal with 'external' problems in living (family, job and relationships). Suicide and self-harm (non-fatal suicidal behaviour such as overdosing or self-cutting) arise from mental pain that is felt to be intolerable.

The distinction thus drawn with earlier ideas about the 'cry for help' is quite deliberate. Suicidal behaviour may be a cry for help in a minority of cases, but mainly it is 'elicited' by the pain of a situation with which the person thinks and feels they cannot cope – a cry of pain first, and only then a cry for help.

Yet decades after Stengel wrote his clarification, and almost twenty years since the first edition of this book appeared, the 'cry for help' idea is still repeated as a comment that dismisses and disregards some of the most vulnerable people in our community. Suicidal feelings and behaviour always need to be taken seriously. Although there are some grounds for maintaining the separation between suicide and non-fatal suicidal behaviour,[4] it is now widely acknowledged that differences may have been overdrawn. Yes, there are some distinctions, but the motivation for both completed and attempted suicide is complex and crosses the boundary between them. For example, anger and communication motives can be found in both, and even relatively 'low-risk' suicidal thoughts and feelings (which do not often lead to suicidal behaviour) may be dominated by the theme of escape and death, rather than communication.

This book aims to offer new perspectives on suicide and suicidal behaviour that can help us understand them better. There have been many developments in the field since Stengel's death. These include changes in the socio-demographic pattern of suicide deaths; knowledge about which social factors are most likely to produce changes in rates of suicide; a greater awareness of the strategies to prevent suicide (and their limits); more focus on the impact of the media on suicidal behaviour; and an understanding of the way in which depression and hopelessness may act as 'final common pathways' to suicidal behaviour. These developments are important, but they may be less so than a wholly new way of looking at the suicidal process. What defeats people is not an idea about themselves, the world or the future, but a profound sense that their mental pain cannot be tolerated a moment longer. Thus, the danger arises not from the initial urgency of suicidal ideas, but from what happens next: whether a person is able to meet their own suicidal thoughts and feelings in a way that does not make them worse, but allows them to pass in their own time.

The book aims to help people come to a deeper understanding of the suicidal mind. This includes those who are suicidal, their family and friends, as well as health and mental-health professionals to help them in their day-to-day clinical practice.

OVERVIEW

The chapters of the book will look at evidence from social, psychological and biological perspectives to see if there are common features that might shed light on suicide. In Chapter One, I will look at the suicidal mind from the perspective of history: how society has viewed suicide and the different historical reactions to suicidal behaviour – from extremely punitive to open understanding. This provides an essential background to understanding why, even despite more modern or enlightened approaches to suicide and self-harm, we still see a range of reactions to it, many of them hostile. In the last fifty years suicidal behaviour has shifted from being a matter for the police and law courts, to one for psychology and psychiatry. Chapter Two looks at what we know about the risk factors for suicide and Chapter Three asks whether suicide is better viewed as a psychiatric or social phenomenon. We will see that all the evidence points towards the importance of any factor that increases a real or perceived sense of being defeated and trapped.

Chapters Four and Five look at non-fatal suicidal behaviour and, once again, examine the links with the motivation for suicide. What used to be written off as a cry for help now comes 'centre stage', and new information showing that those who are most likely to be dismissed are more likely to die reinforces the view that such suffering can never be ignored.

Despite the evidence on defeat and entrapment, there are some circumstances in which people want to end their lives where this wish does not seem to be borne out of total despair, and we look at these examples in Chapter Six. In the case of assisted suicide, a person who is terminally ill seeks to have their loved ones or a caring doctor end their life. They say that since society now gives them the right to take their own life, this right is removed if they become physically incapable of executing it. They state a desire to exercise their rights and carry out their rational decision, now that their active life is over, to treat death as a 'good friend' rather than an enemy, and to have another person assist in their death. In Chapter Six we also consider the other major example of suicide in the apparent absence of despair: martyrdom, and its current manifestation in the 'suicide bomber'.

Chapter Seven returns to the more common reasons for suicide – hopelessness and despair – and shows how the very different perspectives of psychodynamics, biology and genetics converge on similar conclusions. Chapter Eight examines the sociobiology of entrapment. Here I draw on Paul Gilbert's seminal work in evolutionary psychology to see how defeat and entrapment arise from situations in our evolutionary past, focusing particularly on his idea of 'arrested flight', where an animal has been defeated by another, is desperate to escape, but escape is blocked. To me, this has always seemed to sum up the suicidal mind. The central idea of *Cry of Pain* is that although many factors contribute to suicide, it represents a reaction to a feeling of being defeated combined with a feeling of not being able to escape the consequences of defeat. Like the animal caught in a trap, the struggle to get free is followed by defeat and hopelessness.

In Chapter Nine we see how real events that create entrapment for animals are no longer needed to create the same feelings in humans. It is enough for our *memory of the past* to be biased in ways that prevent us from seeing anything but failure, and for this to be projected into the future, so we see nothing that will rescue us from our profound state of angst, restlessness and despair. What can then be set in train is a sequence of events that, unless interrupted, will lead to self-harm or suicide. There are also things that make the path from despair to suicide even more likely: the first is the influence of the media, which can act as a catalyst for those who are feeling despairing, and we'll consider the evidence for this in Chapter Ten; the other is the availability of the means by which people can harm themselves, and we look at this in Chapter Eleven. There we will read astonishing evidence from Norway, for example, showing that after people have seriously harmed themselves by taking overdoses their physicians prescribe *more* medication, rather than less. We'll see that there is overwhelming evidence that if we can find ways of preventing access to the means of suicide, the rate of suicide falls.

Relying on removal of the means of suicide is never enough, however. We have seen that a major contributor to suicide and suicidal behaviour is psychological: despair, hopelessness and the difficulty of tolerating such mental pain. Chapter Twelve examines the effectiveness of psychological approaches to suicide. The results have been patchy. But there is hope. Most promise is shown by those methods that help a person stand back a little to see more clearly the patterns of mind that repeatedly defeat them, and then help them take back control of their lives. Over the past two decades, I and my colleagues have been investigating whether we can train people to do this for themselves – not through standard talking therapy, but instead through inviting them to train their attentional capacities through mindfulness meditation. The idea is that defeat and entrapment arise and get worse when our attention is constantly hijacked by thoughts and feelings of failure and despair, and that, although we may be able to do little about these as they arise, we can do something about what happens next: if we try to suppress thoughts, they often rebound with greater force; if we ruminate about them, we can get more and more entangled in them. What mindfulness teaches us is how to strengthen our capacity to pay sustained attention in the present moment without being drawn into reliving the past and preliving the future. It teaches us how to respond to events without harsh judgemental reactions, starting by learning to be more self-forgiving when, as it inevitably does during meditation, the mind gets hijacked once again. This training takes some work, but it can bring huge relief not to have to struggle constantly with everything that the mind throws up.

Suicide is usually the most individual of acts, and I realise how difficult it is to try and draw conclusions that are general across a number of situations. Many readers whose lives have been touched by suicide or suicidal behaviour will, at many points, be able to think of exceptions to much of what is written here. Yet if we are to understand and help people in the future, there will need to be a dialogue between the general rule and the individual circumstance. This book is offered as a contribution to that dialogue.

CHAPTER ONE

A Brief History of Suicide

It was the early 1990s. A psychiatrist was talking about suicide risk in her patients. 'I can understand why some of my patients should want to kill themselves. If they really want to do it, there is nothing I can do,' she said. 'Even if I was able to stop them, would it be right to try? Many of them have enough insight to know how their illness has ruined their lives.'

Contrast this attitude with that expressed by Professor Gethin Morgan in a UK Health Advisory Service publication in the same year (1993):

> Those at risk of suicide come to us in our professional capacity to get help. They have already talked with relatives and friends and we may well be the last port of call. They watch us intently for our response. They are usually ambivalent about suicide and we have a responsibility to encourage the wish to live ... Anyone who has extensive experience in

> suicide prevention will know that things can improve in a most unexpected way even in the case of individuals facing what may seem enormous adverse odds. It is for us to assume that change for the better is always possible.[1]

So there is a disagreement about whether suicide is preventable, and also about whether, even if it could be prevented, such prevention would be morally justified. If suicide were sometimes a rational response to an unbearable situation, what business do psychiatrists and other mental-health professionals have in intervening?

These are not the only conflicts in attitudes to suicide. In fact, Western society's attitude to suicide throughout the ages has been at best confused, swinging between punitive severity and tolerant advocacy.[2] As I walked along the high street in Bangor, Wales, some time ago, someone thrust a leaflet into my hands. It was concerned with sin, mostly, but included a warning against the danger of a person 'becoming so discouraged to the extent of yielding to the horrible sin of taking his own life ... Through suicide the opportunity to repent is cut off and soul and body will be destroyed in hell.' To many, this will seem an extreme view from another age, yet it was only in the early 1960s that attempting to take one's own life ceased to be a criminal offence and became the province of the health service, rather than the courts. Since that time, several research studies seem to have shown beyond doubt that around 90 per cent of people who commit suicide were suffering some form of mental illness at the time they took their lives. However, it turns out that this is not a new idea.[3] We can see the same debates from the most ancient times, and it is to this history that we now turn.

ATTITUDES IN CLASSICAL AND MEDIEVAL TIMES

It is often thought that in Greek and Roman times there was a tolerance for suicide. However, many philosophers condemned self-destruction. Pythagoras, for example, compared suicides with soldiers who deserted their posts; Aristotle said a person should not commit suicide since such an act cancelled unilaterally his or her obligations to the state – the contract between a person and society. On the other hand, Stoic and Epicurean philosophers believed that suicide could be the right course of action in some circumstances, e.g. where there was terminal illness or unremitting pain. They also allowed that in certain cases it might be an act of nobility where it was an expression of political rights or values.

In the fifth and sixth centuries, attitudes to suicide shifted gradually away from more permissive Roman philosophical ideals and became more punitive. St Augustine thought the philosophical support of suicide abhorrent. However, the Christian Church has always had to contend with the difficulty that suicide is nowhere explicitly condemned in the Bible. Christian thinkers and philosophers have always had to resort to the commandment 'Thou shalt not kill'. Appealing to this commandment has difficulties of its own, since most Christian thinkers have wished to make an exception for people who kill as part of a just war. Clearly the commandment 'Thou shalt not kill', if taken as absolute in every eventuality, would prevent this sort of killing too. If killing could be excused in times of war, why were there no other circumstances in which the commandment could be set aside? And could not some of these be precisely those envisaged by the Stoic and Epicurean philosophers?

Because the Bible did not condemn suicide explicitly, Christian thinkers had to find other arguments. Thomas Aquinas argued that suicide was against the natural law. Since God was expressed in natural laws, suicide was a sin. We'll see later that other philosophers such as David Hume disagreed with this argument (see page 105). But adding weight to the Christian thinkers' condemnation of suicide was the popular belief in the demonic origin of self-killing. In the Middle Ages the view was encouraged that supernatural activity in the natural world was a relatively frequent occurrence: therefore, people who committed suicide showed evidence that they had been possessed by devils. The diabolical causes of suicide found many expressions in literature. One phrase repeated and elaborated throughout the Middle Ages was that of Egbert, an eighth-century writer, who blamed 'self-murder' on 'the instigation of the Devil'.

In England, 'self-murder' became thought of as an offence against God, against the King and against nature. Those who committed suicide were tried posthumously by a coroner's jury. If they were convicted as having murdered themselves, their goods, including all household items and money and debts owed to them, were forfeit to the Crown or the Crown's Agent. The result was that when someone committed suicide, especially if he (it was most commonly a man) was the head of the household, the family would be reduced to abject poverty.

In addition to these consequences, 'self-murderers' were denied Christian burial. Instead, their bodies were buried 'profanely'. The macabre ceremony surrounding such burials seems to have its origins in pre-Christian times. But the belief that suicide was a supernaturally evil act encouraged the desecration of the body of a person who had killed themselves. The individual was buried, often at a crossroads, naked and with a wooden stake through the body. The hole was then filled in, sometimes with the stake showing above the earth so that passers-by might be reminded of the awfulness of the circumstances of this death. The ceremony was carried out by officials of the parish, including the church wardens and their assistants, and the clergy did not attend.

As part of the posthumous trial for self-murder, the coroner's court had to decide whether it was really murder or not. The only mitigating circumstance was if it was found the person was insane. If someone killed themselves when mad or mentally incompetent in some way, they were not convicted. Instead of returning a verdict of *felo de se* (a felon of himself), the person was deemed to be *non compos mentis* (not of sound mind).

Despite the fact that committing suicide was considered a crime, during the Middle Ages very few juries actually brought in verdicts of *felo de se*. It was not that suicide was rare, but that juries, often consisting of local people who had sympathy with the family, were reluctant to see them become paupers. The Crown had little control over these local juries, and although from time to time attempts were made to tighten the enforcement of the law, this was rather sporadic. It was not until Tudor times that this aspect of social and legal life was more rigorously controlled.

THE TUDOR REVOLUTION IN ATTITUDES: GOVERNMENT AND FOLKLORE COMBINE

During the early sixteenth century, the government tightened up on a number of aspects of English law, enforcing its will where it had not done so before. The law about suicide was enforced using the Court of Star Chamber. This, the King's Council sitting in judicial session, tried (and succeeded) in many areas to enforce those laws where there was a direct financial benefit to the Crown and government. Since suicides considered *felo de se* meant that goods and households were forfeit, the Court of Star Chamber had a great deal of interest in ensuring that the verdicts were thoroughly carried out and the penalties exacted.

The struggles between local juries and the Court of Star Chamber continued, however. Local officials would often declare that the suicide victim had very few possessions. In one extreme case the total value of a person's possessions was declared to be precisely the value (to the last half-penny) of the person's debts. In this way, local coroners' juries attempted still to protect their fellow villagers and townsfolk from the excesses of central government.

The results of all the government reforms were reflected in what appears to be a dramatic increase in suicides, or at least those reported to the King's Bench. Around 1500 there was an average of 1 *non compos mentis* and 61 *felo de se* verdicts after suicide inquisitions each year. By 1600 these annual averages had risen to 873 *felo de se* and 7 *non compos mentis* verdicts.

The Tudor revolution in government was reinforced by the attitude of the churchmen, who continued to emphasise their belief that self-murder was an expression of despair brought about by the devil. Both Calvinists and non-Calvinists were equally vehement in their condemnation. For example, George Abbot, one-time Archbishop of Canterbury, declared that suicide was 'a sin so grievous that scant any is more heinous unto the Lord'. He was Calvinist, but the anti-Calvinist Lancelot

Andrewes was similarly explicit: 'It is worse than beastly to kill or drown or make away with ourselves; the very swine would not have run into the sea but that they were carried by the Devil' – a reference to the story of the Gadarene swine in the Bible (Mark 5, Luke 8).

In popular stories and in sermons the idea of Satan playing on a man's guilt and luring him to his death by abject despair is prominent. In morality plays, a point is often reached where the devil casts man into despair or 'wan-hope'. In John Skelton's *Magnyficence*, a character is persuaded by Despair that his sins are so bad that God will not forgive them. Despair urges him to suicide with the words 'ryd thy selfe rather than this lyfe for to lede'. The character Mischief appears, offering the instruments of self-murder: 'Lo here is thy knyfe and a halter, and all were go ferther, spare not thyself, but boldly thee murder.' The central character is about to use the knife against himself when Hope suddenly enters and urges him not to kill himself 'against Nature and Kynde'.[4]

In such a culture, suicide meant the struggle had been lost – the devil had won. In Christopher Marlowe's *Dr Faustus*, the devil instigates suicide more explicitly perhaps than in many other allegories. The Good Angel and the Evil Angel try to persuade Faustus to repent on the one hand and to despair on the other. Faustus cries, 'My heart's so harden'd, I cannot repent.' When Mephistopheles offers Faustus a dagger after he has yielded to despair, Faustus cries, 'Damn'd art thou, Faustus, damn'd; despair and die!'

There is little doubt that many of the people who tried to kill themselves or actually succeeded were suffering from severe depression. The fact that *non compos mentis* verdicts were not brought in for them cannot hide this, and in many cases the depression was clearly of psychotic proportions. A young Puritan, Nehemiah Wallington, imagined himself 'provoked by the Devil' to suicide and made eleven attempts. According to Nehemiah's own account, Satan showed himself in various manifestations: as a crow, as his sister, as a minister and as a disembodied voice. The disembodied voice immediately suggests auditory 'command hallucinations' of someone suffering from psychosis. But the pull to life turned out to be stronger than the pull to death, despite 'the temptation of Satan':

> Then Satan temted me again and I resisted him again. Then he temted me a third time, and I yielded unto him and pulled out my knife and put it neere my throat. Then God of his goodness caused me to consider what would follow if I should do so. With that I felle out a weaping and I flong away my knife.

As in contemporary accounts of 'reasons for living' versus 'reasons for dying',[5] the person who had suicidal thoughts would often stop themselves for these religious reasons or because of family. In the early seventeenth century an account is given of a woman whose husband had died and who was tempted to commit suicide, but found her love for her child saved her from doing so. But few such considerations made any difference in the case of someone psychotically depressed. John Gilpin, an ex-Quaker, reported that he was possessed by Satan. On one occasion his hand was carried to take up a knife which lay on the table. His hand was then carried with it towards his throat and a voice said to him 'open a hole there, and I will give you the words of eternal life' (a reference to St John's Gospel (6:68): 'Lord, to whom shall we go; you have the words of eternal life').

Such involuntary hand movements, whereby the limbs appear to be out of the person's control, are a feature of certain forms of brain damage.

During the sixteenth century there was little change in the overall attitude to the type of 'mitigating circumstances' that might be allowed by the coroners' courts. One might suppose that because melancholy was seen, as today, as the final common pathway to suicide, this would constitute enough grounds for a verdict of *non compos mentis*. However, the religious thinking of the time, combined with the popular belief that melancholy was a sign that the devil had taken over a person's soul, meant that society found it difficult to shake itself free from the conviction that suicide was the outcome of diabolical possession and not madness. The result was that fewer than 5 per cent of the men and women who committed suicide between 1485 and 1660 were judged to be *non compos mentis*.

Nevertheless, in the sixteenth century, as in other periods of history, a variety of attitudes can be discerned. The elements of more tolerant outlooks, later to become more general beliefs, can be found even where the zeitgeist was less accepting. For example, in Thomas More's *Utopia* people who were ill with incurable diseases were imagined to be able to kill themselves with the permission of their priests. This was considered, at least in pagan terms, to be a 'good and wise act', since the death of the person would put an end to torture, rather than to enjoyment. In those terms, then, it was considered a pious and holy act. It is not surprising that the intellectual elite of the country, influenced by the Renaissance emphasis on classical literature, should revisit many aspects of their more tolerant philosophies.

THE SEVENTEENTH CENTURY: GRADUALLY CHANGING ATTITUDES

During the seventeenth century a growing range of motives began to be imputed in the case of suicidal thoughts, feelings and behaviour. With this came an increasingly secular view of suicide as being caused by economic circumstances or psychological state of mind. After the mid-1600s coroners appeared much more ready to accept an alternative to the *felo de se* verdict. However, as is characteristic of a period of transition, no one could be certain that, should a suicide occur, there would not be a *felo de se* verdict, followed by the requirement to forfeit the deceased's goods. This is well illustrated in Samuel Pepys's diaries.

A businessman called Anthony Joyce, husband of Pepys's cousin Kate, tried to commit suicide by throwing himself into a pond. Pepys takes up the story in his diary entry of 21 January 1667:

> Comes news from Kate Joyce that, if I would see her husband alive, I must come presently. So I to him, and find his breath rattled in the throat; and they did lay pigeons to his feet, and all despair of him. It seems, on Thursday last, he went, sober and quiet, to Islington, and behind one of the inns, the White Lion, did fling himself into a pond: was spied by a poor woman, and got out by some people, and set on his head and got to life: and so his wife and friends sent for.

Joyce explained to Pepys that he had been led by the devil and that he had 'forgot to serve God as he ought'. However, it is interesting to note that Pepys himself believed the real reason for his suicidal behaviour was that his business had failed after losses sustained in the Great Fire. Here we see evidence of the increased secularisation of attitudes. But side by side with it another theme emerges.

Pepys goes on to give a first-hand account of the panic a suicide instilled in the bereaved family: panic that their goods would be forfeit (even though technically Joyce survived the suicide attempt for a few days). Pepys even agrees to hide some of the family's goods to prevent their being seized and some of the panic transfers to him. Finally, he uses his contacts in high places to avert the crisis:

> The friends that were there, being now in fear that the goods and estate would be seized on, though he lived all this while, because of endeavouring to drown himself, my cosen did endeavour to remove what she could of the plate out of the house, and desired me to take my flagons; which I did, but in great fear all the way of being seized; though there were no reason for it, he not being dead. So, with Sir D. Gauden, to Guild Hall, to advise with the Towne-Clerke about the practice of the City and nation in this case; and he thinks it cannot be found selfe-murder; but if it be, it will fall, all the estate, to the King. So I to my cosen's again; where I no sooner come but find that her husband was departed. So at their entreaty, I presently to White Hall, and there find Sir W. Coventry: and he carried me to the King, the Duke of York being with him, and there told my story which I had told him: and the King, without more ado, granted that, if it was found, the estate should be to the widow and children. I presently to each Secretary's office, and there left caveats, and so away back to my cosen's. When I come thither, I find her

> all in sorrow, but she and the rest mightily pleased with my doing this for them; and which, indeed, was a very great courtesy, for people are looking out for the estate.[6]

Shifts in opinion about suicide during the seventeenth century might not have been so absolute had they not been supported by shifts in the arguments from the intellectual elite of the country similar to those witnessed in More's writing a century before. Once again, the continued interest in classical philosophy, with its undertone of tolerance and understanding, was responsible. The momentum of interest in the humanism of the Renaissance, founded on a reverence for classical literature, philosophy and history, was maintained, involving an increasing influence by classical customs. This, in turn, revived interest in Stoic views which were more tolerant of suicide, and indeed recommended suicide as a right act in certain circumstances.

Yet the ambivalence to suicide continued. Even when a work was written that is celebrated as one of the greatest turning points in the thinking about suicide in the seventeenth century, *Biathanatos* by John Donne, its author dared not publish for fear of where his own arguments had taken him. This work explored the 'Paradox or Thesis, that Self Homicide is not so naturally Sin as it may never be otherwise'. The importance of this work is that Donne relied on theological analysis, rather than returning to classical literature. In this way he was able to undermine the arguments the Church had used for centuries. His arguments included the fact that, first, self-killing is nowhere forbidden in the Bible and that, second, many who have committed suicide in the history of the Church have been excused or seen as martyrs. Third, the reference to the sixth commandment, 'Thou shalt not kill', which St Augustine used, ignored the fact that on many occasions killing is found to be legitimate, e.g. in war, or in the execution of criminals. Donne criticises Augustine's arguments that biblical and early Christian suicides were permissible and poured scorn on the view that these acts were carried out by the secret command of God. This, Donne says, is mere supposition and cannot be considered a rational argument. Indeed, Donne goes further at one point to contend that one could see the death of Jesus of Nazareth as suicide.

Donne's treatise constituted an extremely rare set of arguments since most defendants of suicide of the time relied on classical literature. Even Thomas More, who had written *Utopia* envisaging that suicide would be permissible for humanists in that society, had not foreseen that suicide would be permissible for Christians.

By contrast, the Stoic view was that death 'unlocked the chains of suffering' and no law could forbid it. As the philosopher Montaigne put it, 'as I offend not the laws made against thieves when I cut my own purse, so am I nothing tied unto laws made against murderers, if I deprive myself of my own life'.[7] Far from imagining that suicide was against the natural law, writers relying on Stoic arguments argued that no one was obliged to live when his or her death might promote some greater good. In fact, they thought that suicide in certain circumstances was consonant with the natural law.

Yet John Donne was so worried about how *Biathanatos* would be received that he refused permission for its publication in his own lifetime. In presenting the manuscript to Sir Robert Ker, he commented that it was a book 'written by Jack Donne and not by Dr Donne', and it was finally published in 1647. It appears that Donne himself shied away from his own conclusions – not an uncommon occurrence. It was one thing to use arguments for the justification of suicide to undermine the state's wish to punish severely a person who took their own life; another to use arguments in such a way as to give the impression that suicide was an option implying that life could be ended lightly as an acceptable way of dealing with life's difficulties. Why such reluctance to publish? Donne was a poet, but also, as Dean of St Paul's, a pastor. As a pastor he may have had to deal with people bereaved by suicide, and may well have felt it cruel to be punitive. But the sensitive complexity of what is said as part of a private pastoral relationship does not transfer well into public pronouncement or public policy, a struggle that still affects the laws on assisted suicide to this day (see Chapter Five).

MADNESS AS ILLNESS

By the end of the 1700s, *felo de se* verdicts were as rare as the *non compos mentis* ones had been in the early Tudor period. The prevailing belief had become that suicide was either a product of rational choice or a medical calamity.

Once again, a case-by-case leniency exercised by individual courts confirmed the change. The coroner's jury became more and more reluctant to enforce penalties for self-murder. Two trends drove the change: growing resistance to a law which seemed too draconian, and a greater willingness to see suicide as the product of an unbalanced mind. Assisting the first trend against property forfeit was the increased belief, expressed by John Locke, that no government should interfere with a person's rights to private property. Government should not 'take to themselves the whole or any part of the subjects' property without their own consent'. Such beliefs had been confirmed and emphasised by the English Revolution of 1688.

Assisting the second trend towards mental illness as an explanation was the rejection of religious enthusiasm, whether Puritan or Catholic. Although it is likely that popular belief in supernatural forces continued (and still does), the intellectual elite gradually, during the Enlightenment, came to reject the belief in arbitrary supernatural intervention in the natural world. This gave way, in the case of suicide, to a medical interpretation which greatly influenced the middle-ranking men who served on coroners' juries. Now came a decisive shift in attitudes: signs of melancholy, previously taken as evidence that the person had 'given in to the devil', were found sufficient proof that a person's balance of mind was disturbed.

The increased tolerance for self-murder can be seen in various writers of the time. William Ramesay in *The Gentlemen's Companion* (1672) suggested that those who killed themselves, because they were frequently the victims of mental illness,

> should rather be objects of our greatest pity than condemnation as murderers, damned creatures and the like. For, 'tis possible even for God's elect having their Judgements and Reasons depraved by madness, deep melancholy, or somehow otherwise affected by Diseases of some sorts, to be their own executioners. Wherefore let's be slow to censure in such cases.

The suicide verdicts reflected these changing views: whereas fewer than 7 per cent of the suicides reported to the King's Bench were declared to have been *non compos mentis* in the middle of the seventeenth century, by the 1690s, around 30 per cent of suicides were thought to be so, and this proportion steadily increased over the next few decades into the eighteenth century. Forty per cent of verdicts were *non compos mentis* in 1710, and by the last third of the eighteenth century this had become the usual verdict. Indeed, in Norwich by 1770–1800, 100 per cent of the verdicts were *non compos mentis* – the verdict itself implicitly rejecting the folkloric and religious interpretations of suicide as a supernatural intervention by the devil and, instead, substituting a medical explanation which declared explicitly that the suicide was excusable.

One consequence of this change was that no more were *non compos mentis* verdicts used simply as a device for protecting some and not others. During the medieval and Tudor periods a person's social standing, his personality, his relationship with his neighbours and his survivors' claims on the sympathy of the local community all played a part in determining which verdict was brought in by the coroners' courts (as in the Pepys example – see page 10). Families of the rich who committed suicide were able to bribe the coroner or the jury, or perhaps more commonly could afford to bring in an expert medical opinion to certify that the person had undoubtedly been unbalanced at the time of death. Gradually, as coroners' juries became more reluctant to find the suicide guilty of *felo de se*, and more likely to bring a *non compos mentis* verdict, these differences and influences became less and less significant.

Despite these changes, the law of self-murder remained on the statute books: it was deemed necessary to discourage people from suicide (it was thought that it would cause a disintegration of society) and offered a means of condemning men and women who had committed suicide to escape punishment after being found guilty of an offence. In such cases, the rituals associated with self-murder were used as a way of stigmatising the dead for some offence committed previously. In 1790 *The Times* reported a story of a woman who poisoned sixteen inmates at the

Epworth Workhouse for whom she was responsible. Four of them died, and she afterwards overdosed herself fatally with the arsenic she had used. The coroner's jury was shocked by this crime and not only brought in a verdict of *felo de se*, but also ordered her body to be buried in the public highway with two stakes driven through it.

But this use of the *felo de se* verdict for extreme cases of the punishment of known criminals emphasises how much the culture had changed and how difficult and unusual it was becoming to bring in a similar verdict for suicides who had not committed such crimes. Increasingly, the suicide itself was not judged to be the crime. The coroners' juries judged the rest of the person's life, not the act of suicide.

THE SITUATION IN OTHER COUNTRIES

In the early days of the colonies in America, most colonies adopted the traditional English punishments though not all enforced the laws of forfeiture of goods (Pennsylvania and Delaware explicitly abolished it in 1701). After the Revolution, Maryland and New Jersey decriminalised suicide as part of their constitutions. Thomas Jefferson attempted to abolish forfeiture and argued against punishing suicide. He also pointed out that juries disapproved of such severity and it was therefore sensible to get rid of the uncompromising rules altogether.

The enforcement of laws on suicide in Germany, Spain and Italy is an unknown quantity, as few records remain. However, there is some evidence from France and parts of Switzerland. French law consisted of a collection of regional customs and codes, and different punishments were stipulated in different regions of the country. In some places penalties were worse than those imposed in England; in others they were mild. The major difference was that throughout France the laws against self-murder were applied very infrequently. In 1670 they were standardised in a law decreeing that every convicted suicide should forfeit his goods and be drawn on a hurdle to a profane grave. But interestingly, after this standardisation, the customs and laws were enforced even less often. By the time it took place, the growth in Enlightenment philosophies had begun to undermine the case for such punitive handling of suicide, and in 1770 in France the Rites of Desecration were abolished. Suicide was decriminalised completely twenty-one years later in 1791.

Switzerland, or at least the Swiss city states, Geneva and Zurich, were more rigorous in attempts to enforce regulations against self-murder. Their Calvinist regimes attempted to impose strict religious rules and customs. However, while suicides were often convicted, they seldom gave rise to severe punishment. As in France, by the time the authorities tried to reform the punishment of suicide, opposing trends had already moved towards the secularisation of suicide. The last example in Switzerland of dragging the corpse of a suicide victim through the streets occurred in 1732, and although the old law remained in force, as it did in France, until the early 1790s, the city officials in Geneva, for example, declared in 1735 that all suicides were insane and were to be spared punishment.

AMBIVALENCE WITHIN THE CHURCH

Although the Church had roundly condemned self-murder for most of its history, it did not actively participate in the rituals of desecration. It did not stand in the way either. Many of these rituals may have predated Christianity, and the fact that the Church did not object to them allowed them to continue. The Church did not say prayers for the dead and did not permit a Christian burial in consecrated ground for suicides. Of course, if somebody was found to have committed suicide because the balance of their mind was disturbed, there was nothing to stop Christian ministers from burying them in consecrated ground. However, even into the sixteenth and seventeenth centuries many conservative clergymen felt uneasy about such burials, even for those declared 'insane'. In the 1662 Book of Common Prayer, a rubric was added (not there in the 1549 and 1552 versions), saying that a clergyman could not bury in consecrated ground any 'who have laid violent hands upon themselves'. Whoever drafted the rubric failed to insert the word 'feloniously'. The rubric as it stood might exclude all people who killed themselves.

In the light of such confusion, clergymen looked for a compromise which they hoped would meet the private need without making a public statement. They allowed burial to be in churchyards, but buried such people on the north side of the church, alongside executed felons, excommunicates and unbaptised infants. This compromise had one unfortunate consequence. The north side of the church gradually came to be considered by local people as polluted, with the result that by the late eighteenth century, despite some churchyards running out of space to bury bodies, clergymen could not easily persuade families to bury relatives there. Families would rather dig up the bones of ancestors to make space for burial on the south side of the church. The Church was often relatively powerless to argue against popular superstition. But having been partly responsible for fostering such superstitions, it was perhaps not surprising that it became victim to them.

THE END OF THE CRIME OF SELF-MURDER

The UK Parliament did not abolish the religious penalties for self-murder until 1823, and did not abolish the secular punishments until 1870. Why it took so long to change these laws remains something of a mystery, although the main reason seems to have been the relation between the law on suicide and other criminal laws.

The problem of deterrence had been the main stumbling block: MPs thought that relaxing the law would cause people to kill themselves in larger numbers. In 1823, however, Parliament acted to repeal the custom of profane burial. Sir James MacIntosh in the House of Commons declared that punishing suicide was 'an act of brutal folly'. Although the Commons defeated MacIntosh's resolution, as soon as it had failed in its passage through the House T. B. Lennard introduced a separate bill to abolish the ritual penalties for *felo de se* and substitute the milder sanction of nighttime burial. He called the Rites of Desecration 'an odious and disgusting ceremony'. Such practices were useless as regards the dead and 'only tortured the living'. The bill passed with only one amendment to make it clear that this change in the law did not mean that clergymen were required to perform the usual rites over the bodies of suicides. Instead, the services they provided were left to their own devising. Some conservative clergymen resisted pressure to read the burial rites, and there is evidence that in the dying years of the nineteenth century the controversy among the Anglican clergy raged as fiercely as ever.

The provisions for the forfeiture of property for self-murder were repealed in 1870 as part of an omnibus bill that covered felonies of every kind. *Felo de se* is mentioned only once in the bill itself, and suicide was not discussed in the debates on the bill, presumably because forfeiture for suicide was such a rare event and no longer a current topic.

One interesting development which arguably allowed the law on suicide to change was the gradual emergence of a common-law crime of attempted suicide. In earlier centuries, suicide had been against the law, but it had not been a crime to *try* to kill oneself. During the 1700s, people who attempted suicide were sent to madhouses, jails or workhouses to prevent them killing themselves. However, during the nineteenth century there is evidence that, in London at least, people increasingly began to be arrested for 'attempting suicide'. By 1850 this 'crime' was recognised by the courts, and by the later part of the century people were arrested, and occasionally tried, for it.

In part this trend arose from the increase in police forces throughout the country. Previously there would have been very few officials who could have enforced such a law had it existed. But the rise in prosecutions for attempted suicide was also an answer to those who complained that the law of suicide punished the innocent (the family) and spared the guilty (the one who committed suicide). After about 1850, the law could be used to punish (and perhaps rehabilitate) would-be suicides.

The criminal status of suicidal behaviour did not end for the United Kingdom until 1961, when Parliament repealed the common-law felony of self-murder. Coroners and physicians subsequently no longer needed to attest that someone who killed him- or herself had done so when 'the balance of the mind was disturbed'.

CONCLUDING REMARKS

The history of attitudes to suicide could be interpreted as a journey from the darkness of ignorance and belief in the supernatural to the light of a modern and tolerant era. It is immensely more complex, however. While these attitudes have varied throughout the ages, and every age has seen a range of value systems brought to bear for an array of reasons, we have also seen that some in our own day would argue that suicide is a giving in to sinful despair brought about by the devil, as witnessed by the leaflet I mentioned at the start of this chapter. Ambivalent attitudes to suicide and towards people who harm themselves may partly reflect our failure to understand how someone is capable of taking this ultimate step. Part of us may respect or even admire their apparent control over when their life should end. Another part abhors it, for fear we might take the same route (rather like stepping back from the platform edge for fear we may be seized by the impulse to throw ourselves under a train).

Why does the idea of being under attack from an outside 'force' or 'devil' survive? One obvious reason is that a large proportion of society still believes Satan exists and influences human affairs. Additionally, the 'devil' vocabulary may persist because, for those who have been seriously depressed, it can feel as though they have been taken over by something outside themselves. The devil metaphor matches and gives shape to this inner feeling, even for those who would normally reject supernatural explanations of experience. In fact, one of the advantages of the metaphor is that it locates the source of the problem 'outside' the individual. In doing so, it contains the seeds of a less judgemental and more compassionate attitude to the one who is suffering. As we have seen from this brief history, such compassion has often been seriously lacking, just when it is needed most.

CHAPTER TWO

Suicide in Contemporary Society

Suicide is the most individual of acts; yet it happens too often for us to ignore the possibility that, when examined together, these individual acts may allow us to discern trends that will help us understand it better. If your life has been deeply affected by the suicide of a loved one, it can be painful to read about the statistics of suicide. Statistics can seem cruel and uncaring, as if a life or a death can be reduced to numbers. But if we wish to really understand suicide, there are some questions that can only be answered by taking account of entire populations: is the number of suicides on the increase or decrease – and in which groups of people? How is suicide related to gender, and to social class? What means do most people use? Are any trends limited to a single country – do suicidal trends respect national, cultural or ethnic boundaries? How is suicide related to socio-economic conditions? And what about unemployment and other such sources of stress – can we say definitively whether they affect the suicide rate, and if not, why not? If you don't want to read all these statistics, feel free to skip this chapter.

The French sociologist Émile Durkheim defined suicide as 'the termination of an individual's life resulting directly from a positive or negative act of the victim himself which he knows will produce this fatal result'.[1] But are such definitions useful in the real world of the inquest? Interpreting suicide statistics is often said to be difficult because they are inherently unreliable. 'Suicide' is a legal definition, so official statistics inevitably underestimate their number; the authorities have to be certain beyond reasonable doubt that death was caused by self-inflicted injury and that the deceased *intended* to kill him- or herself. One result of this definition problem is that passive methods of dying, for example, are less likely to be called suicide than active ones. Thus, drowning is called suicide in 54 per cent of cases, versus hanging in 98 per cent of cases. Another result is that a verdict of suicide may be less likely when a young person is involved. Coroners may, understandably, be reluctant to give a verdict of suicide where such a verdict would be so totally distressing to the family of the young person. A further limitation of statistics is that many countries do not report suicide rates. The World Health Organization collates these data, but not all member states return statistics reporting suicide rates. And even for those that do, we cannot be sure that the reported rates reflect the use of the same criteria to bring in a verdict of suicide. Surely, then, the data, even where available, are almost impossible to interpret?

Such a conclusion would be too pessimistic, however. Where there is insufficient evidence to justify the conclusion that a sudden death was suicide, the alternative is most likely to be an open verdict ('undetermined'). When these verdicts are examined, the sex, age and social-class profile of the deceased resemble closely the profile for people known to have committed suicide. Some researchers have therefore included such open verdicts in their statistics when trying to estimate the total number of people who kill themselves. However, research has shown that such trends are affected very little whether the open verdicts are included or excluded.[2] Further evidence for the reliability of suicide figures from country to country is that statistics largely agree on which sections of their populations are most at risk for suicide.[3]

INTERNATIONAL SUICIDE RATES

The data for suicide across different countries reporting to the World Health Organization can be found at http://www.who.int/mental_health/prevention/suicide_rates/en/ and on the website of the Oxford Centre for Suicide Research (http://cebmh.warne.ox.ac.uk/csr/statistics.html).

There are some important observations to be made. In every country but China, the suicide rate is lower for women than for men. Other gender differences become apparent when several years' figures are examined. For example, in many European countries the suicide rate in women has remained flat or decreased, while that for men has increased, most markedly in Ireland, Spain, the Netherlands, Norway, Belgium, France, Luxembourg, Denmark, Finland and Northern Ireland.

During the twentieth century the United States averaged a rate of 12.5 suicides per 100,000 population.[4] A high rate of 17.4 was observed during the Depression in 1932 and a low point of 9.8 in 1957. This rose again steadily to a peak of 13.3 in 1977, then dipped to 12.7 in 1987, and in recent years has been around 11 per 100,000 (17.7 in men, 4.5 in women in 2011). There have been changes in age distribution in the United States over this period: over the 1970s and 1980s the percentage of deaths by suicide by persons aged 15–24 years has increased, whereas the percentage of total suicide deaths by people over 45 years has decreased. In the USA in 1970 the median age of people who died by suicide was 47.2; by 1980 it was 39.9.

The number of suicides in England and Wales since 1911 for men and women shows the effects of the First and Second World Wars, when there were reductions, while there was a rise in suicides in the Depression between the wars (which peaked, as in the United States, in 1932). After 1945 the suicide rate rose steadily to a peak for both men and women in the late 1950s and early 1960s. Since that time a number of quite dramatic changes have taken place. First, the suicide rate in women has fallen continuously. Second, the suicide rate for men fell until the early 1970s, then started to rise. This was the first time in the twentieth century that suicide rates for males and females in the UK moved in opposite directions.

There was a particularly dramatic rise (75 per cent) in suicide rates among males aged 15–24 years from the early 1980s. Currently over 40 per cent of all suicides in the UK occur in males between the ages of 15 and 44 years, and this differs from previous times when the rates were much higher for older people. The situation by the end of the 1990s was that for men between 25 and 75 there was little difference in age-related suicide risk. Why this steep increase in young male suicides? One clue lies in the changing pattern of marriage and divorce. Divorced men have higher rates of suicide, so if the divorce rate rises, the suicide rate may rise with it.

METHODS OF SUICIDE

The methods by which people take their own lives reflect the availability of different means. In the United States firearms are used since they are widely available, and the various gun laws in different states make a difference to how much they are used in suicide. In the UK there have been changes over time. In 1970 the leading causes of suicide death were poisoning (31 per cent of males and 65 per cent of females) and hanging (23 per cent of males, 9 per cent of females). However, there were several changes between 1970 and 1990. In 1990 35 per cent of male suicides were due to vehicle exhaust, 31 per cent were hanging and only 14 per cent poisoning.

In women in the UK, there was a decrease between 1970 and 1990 in the numbers using poisoning (from 65 to 44 per cent) and domestic gas (reduced from 9 per cent to nil as non-toxic natural gas replaced coal gas). Instead, there was a switch to hanging (a rise from 9 to 23 per cent) and vehicle exhaust (a rise from 1 to 13 per cent). These trends suggest that while it used to be true that women used less lethal methods than men in their suicides, this difference is reducing.

More recent statistics show that during the 1990s there were further changes. The most significant was a drop in vehicle exhaust deaths, falling to 23 per cent of male deaths in the mid-1990s, and to 16 per cent in 1998. However, the proportion of men who committed suicide by hanging rose from 31 per cent in 1990 to 52 per cent in 1998. In addition, the increase in hanging continued for women too, with 31 per cent using this method by the end of the twentieth century. This trend continued between 2001 and 2011, with an increase in both the number and proportion of deaths by hanging in the UK.

FACTORS AFFECTING SUICIDE RISK

Over the years evidence has accumulated to show that the risk of suicide varies depending on a number of factors (for example, gender, ethnicity and the presence of physical illness). We shall consider each of these in turn.

Gender

In almost all countries in the world the rates for men exceed those for women by a factor of between 2:1 (Denmark, the Netherlands and Sweden) and 5:1 (Finland).[5] This sex ratio has existed from the earliest days. Historical data show that men have committed suicide at least twice as often as women in almost all samples of data that survive. In Europe, completed suicide seems always to have been an act more associated with men than women.

As we have seen, the pattern during most of the twentieth century, in which women's and men's suicide rates followed each other fairly closely (albeit at different overall levels), has now changed. The rates for women fell during the 1970s and 1980s, while those for men rose. The net effect was to reduce the overall figures for women over this period, but to leave the rates for men (taking all ages together) rising steadily.

Ethnic group

The suicide rate varies for different ethnic groupings: white people in the United States are approximately twice as likely to commit suicide as non-white people. This difference is particularly pronounced for the older age group. However, in the United States, Native American young people have a high rate of suicide, the highest rate being in those tribes undergoing the greatest and fastest cultural assimilation. In the United Kingdom, there have been reports that the suicide rate among Asian women is almost double that for other women of the same age, and although research has not yet established the reason, difficulties in resolving cultural clashes between social and family norms and expectations is a clear possibility.

Sexual orientation

It has been suggested that gay young people are two or three times more likely to complete suicide than other young people, comprising perhaps up to 30 per cent of youth suicides.[6] However, this is not backed by good evidence. The two studies that have been published (both US surveys) suggest much more conservative figures: that between 2.5 and 5 per cent of suicides are gay, and that these figures are not significantly different from the proportions one would expect by chance.

Religious affiliation

Rates vary according to religious affiliations. Many studies have found that any regular religious practice is associated with lower suicide risk, presumably because of the social network and sense of meaning it can provide in times of suffering. A number of studies have additionally found Catholics and Jews are less likely to commit suicide than Protestants: the Catholic countries of Spain, Italy, Portugal, Greece, Ireland and Poland have fairly low suicide rates. Yet there are other Catholic parts of Europe, such as France, where the suicide rate is relatively high, though the increased secularisation of France and reduced churchgoing (and consequent loss of social networks and sense of meaning) may be responsible.

Social class

Studies in the United States and Canada have found a strong association between differences in socio-economic status between communities (e.g. in proportion of substandard housing) and their suicide rates: the poorer the housing, the higher the rate. The exception to this trend is the poor areas occupied by a high proportion of African Americans, who have a lower suicide rate, most usually attributed to the strong social bonds within and between families.

Unemployment

Economic conditions have been studied many times, with some conflicting results. Studies have found that men who are unemployed are at two or three times greater risk of suicide death than the average. Many investigators therefore argue that suicide is one of the possible consequences of unemployment, and yet there seems to be a complex relationship between changes in unemployment levels and the suicide rate over time.[7]

National unemployment rates in the United Kingdom increased substantially at the end of the 1970s, stayed high until the mid-1980s, then declined until the late 1980s before beginning to rise again. Male suicide rates were at their highest between 1981 and 1990, at the time when unemployment rates were *lowest*. However, the relationship is not straightforward. Most unemployment is short term (under six months) and unemployment totals are net figures taken at a fixed point in time. This means that rates for unemployment never give the whole picture of the distress it causes. British sociologist Professor Stephen Platt has pointed out that the impact of unemployment depends on whether, say, an entire firm has been made unemployed in a community (in which case there may be some increase in social support – an ameliorating factor in suicide risks) or, by contrast, an individual is made unemployed, independent of others, which may be more of a stress factor.

However, the balance of evidence across the world shows that increases in unemployment *are* associated with increased suicides, especially among people of working age. A dramatic example of this has been seen in the recession of 2007 onwards. Across Europe the steady downward trend in suicide rates, seen before 2007, reversed very rapidly with the onset of the financial crash. The extent of this reverse differed from country to country: the 2008 increase was less than 1 per cent in the new Member States of the European Union, but in the old ones it increased by almost 7 per cent.[8]

Rural areas

Geographical region also plays a part in suicide rates across countries. In the United States the mountain regions have the highest overall rate and the same pattern holds for the UK. In a study with my colleagues Leslie Pollock, John Hollis and Patrick Vesey, we examined the suicide rates in Powys, Wales, one of the least densely populated areas of Europe. We found a suicide rate greatly in excess of the UK average (around 20 per 100,000). Looking closely at the data for a three-year period, we found that farmers or farm labourers accounted for 22 per cent of this figure, though they represented only 11 per cent of the population. We also examined whether it was the lack of access to primary-care services in rural areas that determined the high rates, but could find no evidence that the individuals concerned had visited their doctors any less frequently than happens in more urban areas. Rather, it appeared that the high rates could be accounted for by a greater availability of lethal weapons, with firearms used more commonly than the national average. A study by Keith Hawton and colleagues reinforces this conclusion:[9] between 1981 and 1993 there were 719 suicides or open verdicts of farmers in England and Wales. Firearms were used in 40 per cent of cases (compared with the national average of 4.3 per cent) and hanging in 30 per cent (compared with the national average of 23 per cent). Hawton pointed out how the easy availability of such lethal means was a critical factor in the high suicide rate within this community.

Imprisonment

A comprehensive study of suicides in twelve countries found that the suicide rates for prisoners were 100 per 100,000 compared to an average suicide rate of 21 per 100,000 in the general public,[10] and in England and Wales female prisoners are twenty times more likely to die from suicide compared to women of the same age group, a tendency which has remained stable over the last twenty-five years.[11] The high level of suicide among prisoners has given cause for concern, especially since many of the suicides in the under-45 age group are on remand, not yet found guilty of any crime.

Medical illness

There are several medical conditions that increase the risk of suicide. For example, among those with epilepsy the risk is four times that of normal controls, and for temporal-lobe epilepsy it is twenty-five times greater than controls. Cancer has also been associated with increased risk of suicide, being highest immediately following diagnosis and in those receiving chemotherapy. People with peptic ulceration have a high risk, probably because of the prevalence of alcoholism as a cause of the condition. With Huntington's there is a six-fold increase in the risk of suicide compared with the general population, both in those suffering from the disease and in family members who may also be at risk, but who have no overt symptoms as yet. People undergoing renal dialysis have been said to have a greater incidence of suicide compared with the general population, but there are not enough reliable studies to estimate the risk exactly. There is an increased risk in people who have spinal-cord injuries (a fivefold increase compared with the general population), and in those who have multiple sclerosis (a threefold increase for men and twofold for women). The risk of suicide in those who have AIDS was some thirty-six times greater than the general population in the 1980s, but this figure appeared to reduce to sevenfold during the 1990s.[12]

In many cases the fact that depression often occurs alongside physical illness increases the suicide risk. Medical illness can precipitate severe depression and, in extreme cases, can also produce an organic mental disorder leading to perceptual, cognitive and mood changes. In other cases the suicide appears to be a rational act where the person decides that the prospect of suffering and loss of dignity is intolerable. However, research evidence suggests that suicide in the physically ill very rarely occurs in the absence of psychological difficulties.

In fact, it is probably the effects of having a serious physical illness *per se* which is the important issue, rather than a particular diagnosis. The biggest contributors to hopelessness are likely to be whether an illness is life-changing or more chronic, and how much pain and entrapment are involved.[13] Another factor is that when people are in a lot of physical pain they are often prescribed a large amount of medication. This means that if everything becomes too overwhelming for them, suicide may be more likely simply because they have the means available in the form of the medication.[14]

It is important, therefore, for physicians and other health professionals not to ignore psychological problems that co-occur with physical illness. Depression associated with terminal cancer, for example, goes beyond sadness and includes a sense of worthlessness and failure which can make the person's experience seem unbearable.[15] Yet it is thought to be 'normal' and, as such, it therefore often goes untreated, despite the fact that psychological treatment can be very helpful in alleviating the depression.

Lifespan issues

In all countries suicide is extremely rare in children under twelve, but it becomes steadily more common after puberty, and the risk then increases with age. For older people to be more at risk of suicide appears to have been, until recently, the predominant pattern across all countries and cultures, though there is some variation in whether the increase is linear or has peaks and dips across the lifespan. The recent trend for older people to be less at risk and for younger males to be at greater risk has been widespread. But is suicide the same phenomenon in young adults as it is in older adults?

One factor explaining lifespan differences would be the increase in substance abuse which has occurred to a much greater extent in younger members of the population, and in young males in particular. Furthermore, there is some evidence that the most vulnerable young men are those from working-class backgrounds who have fewest employment opportunities – just the groups that have suffered the greatest rise in suicide rate over the past twenty or thirty years.

Different rates of medical illness across the lifespan might also contribute to variations between different ages. Illness is associated with 50 per cent of adult completed suicides, contributing more prominently for older adults. Medical illness in older adults contributes to suicidal risk in a number of possible ways. Depression may be worsened by the fact that the physical illness puts an increased burden on the fewer social supports that exist. There are also cognitive impairments often associated with ageing in general and with physical illness in older adults in particular. Finally, the use of certain medications to alleviate the physical illness sometimes lowers mood and impairs judgement.

Do different psychiatric disorders increase the risk of suicide at different stages in life? We shall see in the next chapter that the individuals most at risk are those suffering from depression and schizophrenia. Right across the lifespan, if these conditions occur together with particular personality traits such as impulsivity and aggression, and with alcohol and substance abuse, the risk is increased. However, there are changes over the lifespan in the particular combinations of these disorders. Adolescents who commit suicide tend to suffer from depression (and in some cases conduct disorders), though the depression is often hidden and recognised only after the event.[16]

Alcohol and substance abuse

Alcohol and substance abuse have been on the increase since the 1970s. One indication of the increase is the number of people each year who die from alcohol- or drug-related deaths (other than suicide). The data suggest that, since 1968, there has been a sixfold increase in drug-related deaths among men aged 15–24, and a fivefold increase for males aged 25–44. There are similar trends among women, but the rates are generally much lower. The data for alcohol show a similar pattern, with men aged 25–44 showing the largest increase in rates (more than fourfold between 1968 and 1990), followed by men aged 15–24. Once again, rates for younger women rose as well, but the levels were very low compared with those for men.

Alcohol and substance abuse represent major risk factors for suicide right across the lifespan. The prevalence of alcohol and drug abuse increases steadily from the age of 15 until about 45, after which it declines. The number of years somebody who completes suicide has typically been abusing alcohol is between twenty and twenty-five. This may be because, as alcoholism progresses, it erodes those factors known to protect against suicide: first, it destroys social supports; second, it destroys intellectual function through brain damage and brings about reduced health and increased incidence of medical complications; third, chronic alcoholism reduces personal control and increases helplessness. Since 60 to 70 per cent of patients with a diagnosis of alcohol problems have additional psychiatric diagnoses, however, it is possible that the substance abuse exacerbates the course of any psychiatric illness. Studies show that alcohol and drug abuse are most lethal when they occur alongside depression.[17] However, alcohol and substance abuse raise the risk of suicide as soon as the abuse starts. Substance abuse has been diagnosed in over one-third of young people committing suicide.[18]

THE RISE IN YOUNG MALE SUICIDE

In the 1990s the United States found itself with one of the highest suicide rates for young men in the world, and the question of why there had been such an increase in youth suicide became very pressing indeed. It appeared to parallel the increase in risk factors associated with suicide in young people: depression, conduct disorders and substance misuse. In addition, there were population effects such as that the proportion of youth in society was high, implying increased competition for opportunities (jobs and education). This is consistent with the finding that there was also a high youth suicide rate at the beginning of the twentieth century, when young people also comprised a higher proportion of the population. Other factors blamed have been the increased divorce rate, increased geographical mobility (with its consequent loss of important attachment figures), changes in family structure and decreased religious affiliation. However, some of the evidence for these remains patchy. The rise in the number of younger males committing suicide in the last few years has been almost universal, though the trend slowed again in many countries around the year 2000.

There are two classes of explanation. The first type sees the rise as part of an unexplained change in rates within a group of people born within a few years of each other, a *cohort* effect. The second type lays the blame at the door of prevailing social conditions, employment opportunities, drug and alcohol abuse, disempowerment. That is, it sees the change in rates as a *period* effect. Clearly there can be interactions between cohort and period effects, as where a certain cohort is exposed to an increase in the availability of some substance (e.g. illicit drugs). There is evidence of higher rates of depression, bipolar mood disorders and substance abuse for the generation born just after the war (the 'baby-boom' generation), which may explain some of the changes in the suicide rate. Let us examine this distinction between cohort and period effects more closely, as it potentially helps us understand suicide trends over the long term and prevents us making important mistakes in over-interpreting short-term changes in suicide rates.

Cohort and period effects

A number of studies in the United States, Canada and Australia have followed through the suicide rates for people born within a few years of each other. Each 'cohort's' suicide rate could then be compared with cohorts born at other times.[19] The results were striking. They found that if a cohort had a high suicide rate at a young age, then the increased risk of suicide continued throughout the life of that cohort.

Similar cohort data published by the Office of Population Census and Surveys in 1992[20] confirm the existence of a cohort effect in England and Wales. Men born between 1962 and 1971 have a higher risk of suicide than those born between 1952 and 1961, who, in turn, have a higher risk of suicide than those born between 1942 and 1951. Women born in the 1910s, 1920s, 1930s and 1940s show a gradually reducing rate.

What explains this cohort effect? Some studies have pointed to the size of a birth cohort: when a large number of babies are born during the same period, there is increased competition for resources, especially if they enter the employment market at a time of recession (as occurred at the turn of the twentieth century), and this results in higher unemployment and decreased access to educational opportunities for that cohort. Throughout their lives, more people in a larger cohort will be chasing whatever resources are available. The effect of the cohort size will depend upon the amount of resources. A large birth cohort will not always have this effect, if, by chance, there are sufficient resources to sustain its members at the important stage of their lives when they are first emerging into adult roles.

However, if the number of jobs in a country falls during a recession, then the effects are likely to fall disproportionately on those in the population who are members of the large cohort, whatever age it has reached: suddenly, too many people of about the same age will be chasing too few resources.[21] This is consistent with the suggestion that the reduced status of men caused by changes in employment prospects and family cohesion, together with the anticipation of diminished long-term roles as husband and parent, has produced a rise of alcohol and drug abuse in this sub-population that contributes to the increased suicide rate. Is there evidence to support this particular causal pathway?

Decreased family cohesion

It has been estimated that about half the increase in the number of men committing suicide towards the end of the twentieth century was likely to have been caused by the growing number of young men who are single or divorced.[22] However, since the reduction in young men getting married or having a stable relationship accounts for only half the increase, we must seek additional reasons for the change. A major piece of evidence about exactly which young people are becoming most vulnerable emerges from the finding that the increase in young male suicides is almost wholly accounted for by the increase in more working-class populations.[23] These are the young men who have been most exposed to the helplessness that comes about with reduced employment opportunities and in whom increase in misuse of alcohol and other drugs is most prevalent.

Changes in rates of depression

Part of the rise in young male suicide may also reflect changes in age-related depression over the twentieth century. People born more recently (since 1955) have the highest rates of depression across several countries[24] and people are becoming depressed at younger ages.[25] The cause of the change is unknown, but researchers into depression have come to similar conclusions as those investigating suicidal behaviour: that social and demographic changes such as the changing structure of families, social mobility and increased isolation, the growing gap between rich and poor, disengagement from the community and limited access to resources combine to explain the pattern of change. Both changes in rates of depression and in suicide have occurred in parallel with important changes in economy and in family structure over the past twenty or thirty years.[26]

Older adults' reduction in suicide: period or cohort effect?

Finally, could the trend towards lower rates in older people since the early 1960s be attributed to a period effect: has society found a way to protect older people from suicide risk during this period? Probably not. The current rates for older people – both men and women – are no lower than those for younger people; they are simply lower than the very high rates seen earlier in the twentieth century for older people. So the currently 'reduced' rates are largely attributable to the fact that the cohorts born since 1910 had more 'average' suicide rates throughout their lives compared to the very high rates of those born in the period 1870–1900 (i.e. those who contribute to the older age data in the suicide figures of 1946 onwards): it is not that we have done something to reduce the suicide rates for old people, but that we are seeing low-risk cohorts reaching old age. So the very high rates seen among some very old people (e.g. the over-85s) that remain despite the fall for other old people are simply due to the fact that they belong to the high-risk cohort born early in the twentieth century (1905–1915).[27]

CONCLUDING REMARKS

Returning to the questions posed at the beginning of this chapter and to summarise what the statistics tell us: is the number of suicides on the increase or decrease – and in which groups of people? It seems they are on the increase in most countries, but in men rather than women. This is particularly true of younger and middle-aged men, among whom suicide rates are rising. By contrast, the suicide rate is coming down in older people, a trend likely to be explained by the fact that a low-risk (or average-risk) cohort is reaching old age.

How is the trend related to gender, and to social class? The data of interest here show that the rise in young male suicide is almost wholly caused by an increase in working-class men – those most vulnerable to economic hardship in a recession, and most likely to abuse alcohol and drugs. Many studies show a bias, such that lower socio-economic groups are more vulnerable.

What methods do most people use? We have seen that outside China men use more lethal methods than women, though this difference is reducing. Do suicidal trends respect national, cultural or ethnic boundaries? While the methods used from country to country may vary (firearms being much more common in the United States, for example), the trends across virtually all Western nations are remarkably similar. Within each country, however, there are ethnic differences to be taken into account. African Americans are much less likely to commit suicide than Anglo-Americans, but Native Americans have a higher rate than either. Finally, unemployment is an important factor affecting the suicide rate, as the effects of the 2007 recession show.

The picture that emerges is that common to *all* the circumstances that create the conditions where suicide rate increases is a feeling of confusion, defeat and entrapment. Whether this is physical illness or unemployment, family breakdown or the alcohol and substance abuse that these can create (which also then causes more distress), we see different aspects of the same underlying process of helplessness and mental anguish. In the next chapter we examine how such entrapment can be compounded by psychiatric illness and social isolation, real or imagined.

CHAPTER THREE

Suicide: A Psychiatric or a Social Phenomenon?

'Suicide has been so closely associated with insanity only by arbitrarily restricting the meaning of the words.' So wrote sociologist Émile Durkheim in rejecting a psychiatric interpretation in his study of social causes of suicide in 1897.[1] Some hundred years later Susan Blumenthal, Chief of the Behavioral Medicine Program at the US National Institute of Mental Health, said: 'Over 90 per cent of patients committing suicide have a psychiatric disorder.' These authors appear to contradict each other completely about the significance of psychiatric disorders in suicide. Is the difference explained by the different eras in which they wrote? Do we have more data now that show Durkheim's analysis to have been wrong? That is possible, though it is worth bearing in mind that many prior to Durkheim concluded that 'insanity' was the most probable cause. At the end of the seventeenth century, to say someone committed suicide because they were 'insane' was one of the few ways of being non-judgemental, of showing compassion to the victim and care for the family (see Chapter One).

But Durkheim found an alternative way of being non-judgemental: suicide should be seen as a feature of society, not of the individual. He accepted that 'insanity' was sometimes involved as a cause of suicide, but rejected the argument that understanding psychiatric disturbance was the key to understanding suicide. Instead, he pointed to a number of 'social facts' about the incidence of suicide and its correlation with social integration and disintegration. Most famously, he pointed to anomie – the state associated with detachment from society – as a central feature of many suicides.

Many studies looking for a link between suicide and psychiatric disturbance have been done since Durkheim wrote his treatise. They seem to conclude that Blumenthal's proposition is correct, though this does not mean that Durkheim was wrong. Even if it proved to be that psychiatric disturbance precedes suicide in over 90 per cent of cases, its causal status would remain unclear. Mental illness may precede suicide because some circumstances drive people both to psychiatric breakdown and to suicide.

EVIDENCE FOR PSYCHIATRIC ILLNESS AS A CAUSE OF SUICIDE

Researchers have come to the conclusion that suicide is closely associated with psychiatric illness by using two methods. In the first, the researcher follows up people who have been psychiatrically disturbed in the past to see what proportion eventually die by suicide. Since the risk of suicide in the population as a whole is between 1 and 2 per cent, it can then be calculated how much greater risk this particular group carries. The second method is known as *psychological autopsy*. This involves careful interviewing of relatives and friends following a suicide, and asking questions about the mood and behaviour of the deceased in the period leading up to their death. The results from this method have been used to support the conclusion that the majority of suicides were suffering from psychiatric problems beforehand.

Early research showed that 70 per cent of suicides would have been diagnosed as suffering from major depression, 15 per cent from alcoholism and 4 per cent from schizophrenia or a schizo-affective disorder.[2] Later studies showed that one in seven patients hospitalised for major depression and one in ten with a diagnosis of schizophrenia or alcohol abuse die by suicide,[3] but even in these cases depression is almost always involved. So what is depression?

Depression

Depression as a normal mood state is a common experience. In minor depressive states, a person ruminates on negative themes. They feel resentful, irritable or angry much of the time, feeling sorry for themselves and constantly needing reassurance from those around them. Often, there is a variety of physical complaints that do not seem to be caused by any physical illness. As depression deepens, more symptoms become apparent. These include further emotional changes (feelings of extreme sadness and hopelessness); changes in the content or process of thinking (low self-esteem, guilt, memory and concentration difficulties);

changes in behaviour and motivation (feeling agitated or slowed down, reduced interest in social or recreational activities); and bodily changes (sleep, eating and sexual problems, loss of energy). If the depression is intense enough to include five or more of these symptoms for more than a two-week period and severe enough to impair a person's ability to function, it is called 'major' or sometimes 'clinical' depression. Twelve per cent of men and 20 per cent of women will experience an episode of such major depression at some time in their lives. At any one time, around 5 per cent of the population is suffering depression of this severity. Twenty-five per cent of these episodes of depression last less than a month; a further 50 per cent recover in less than three months. However, the depression can develop into a longer-term problem, with around a quarter being seriously depressed one year after symptom onset and one-fifth remaining depressed two years later. The lifetime risk of suicide in major depression severe enough to require hospitalisation is between 10 and 15 per cent, the greatest risk being associated with those whose episodes of depression last longer. The lifetime risk for people who have depression and have not been hospitalised is much lower, estimated at around 3 per cent.[4]

It has been shown that the population attributable ratio (PAR) for depression in serious but non-fatal suicidal behaviour (i.e. the proportion of serious suicidal behaviour that would be removed if depression were taken out of the picture) is 80 per cent.[5] Suicidal ideation is one of the most consistently recurrent symptoms of depression across episodes[6] and, combined with the high risk of recurrence of depression (accumulating to 90 per cent for patients with three or more previous episodes), makes treatment of patients who have experienced suicidal depression extremely important.

Alcoholism

Alcohol dependency can show itself in different ways: by regular excessive intake of alcohol on a daily basis; by regular excessive intake limited to weekends; and by periods of abstinence interspersed with extremely heavy drinking binges lasting weeks or months. The lifetime risk of suicide in alcoholics is similar to that of those depressed patients who are hospitalised – 15 per cent – with male alcoholics six times more likely than female alcoholics to commit suicide. The mean age for suicide in alcoholic patients is 47, following an average twenty-year drinking history.

Schizophrenia

Up to 1 per cent of the population suffers from a range of symptoms that are diagnosed as 'schizophrenia'. These include delusions, a disorder in the content of thought (e.g. the belief that one's thoughts are being broadcast from one's head, or being controlled by a dead person), ideas of reference (e.g. that events or people have a special and unusual significance, such as the change in a traffic signal or the expression on the face of a television newscaster meaning one has been chosen for a special mission). A second set of symptoms includes disorder in the form of thought. This may include the loosening of associations, in which ideas flow from one to the other without any apparent connection, sometimes to such an extent that speech is incomprehensible. A third set of symptoms involves disorders of perception, especially auditory hallucinations, in which (most commonly) the person hears voices speaking to him or her, often commenting harshly on his/her behaviour. Sometimes, and very dangerously, the voices command the person to carry out certain acts, including suicide. In a fourth set, there is often a change in mood, with normal expression of emotion being disturbed in one of two ways: either the mood is 'flat', with little sign of emotion, the voice and face remaining expressionless; or the person seems to have moods inappropriate to the situation, laughing or smiling at events or descriptions that would normally evoke sadness or pity. Finally, and unsurprisingly in the light of these other symptoms, the person may experience a disturbance in their sense of 'who they are'. There may be a disruption of the will, with a person finding it almost impossible to initiate any activity at all. In consequence, there is often major upheaval in a person's relationships with other people. The person typically withdraws, and becomes detached, though may sometimes cling to or get too close to others.

Schizophrenia may take many forms, so that some have suggested the term itself is meaningless, or that we should talk of 'the schizophrenias'. Others have maintained that as long as we realise the complexity of the disturbances, and that giving something a name does not really explain it, then continued use of the term is permissible. Several studies point to the fact that up to 15 per cent of patients with a diagnosis of schizophrenia (especially males) will end their lives by suicide, and in these cases it is the hopelessness that comes with the other symptoms that increases the risk.

Personality disorder

Personality disorder (especially borderline and antisocial personality disorder) carries an increased risk of suicide. 'Borderline' patients were originally so called because it was believed they lived at the edge between psychosis and neurosis. They have mood instability, a history of self-damaging acts and damaging relationships, chronic feelings of emptiness and boredom, intolerance of being alone and brief dissociative episodes, often associated with flashbacks of sexual abuse. Recent evidence suggests that between 4 and 10 per cent will eventually kill themselves. In antisocial personality disorder, although 46 per cent have some form of suicidal behaviour, the risk of completed suicide appears to be around 5 per cent.[7]

PROBLEMS WITH PSYCHIATRIC EXPLANATION OF SUICIDE: GENDER AND AGE EFFECTS

Despite these apparently strong relationships between psychiatric diagnosis and suicide, there are several reasons to look for other causes. One such is the gender difference: women are more likely to become clinically depressed, but men are more vulnerable to suicide (see Chapter Two). Neither can psychiatric illness explain the way such gender differences change with age – whereas female vulnerability tends to rise linearly but very slightly with increasing age, the male vulnerability rises markedly from ages 15–24 to 25–54, falls between 55 and 84, then rises again for the over-85s. This rise in the very old is most probably due to the fact that people born early in the twentieth century carried a slightly higher suicide risk with them throughout their lives (see discussion of cohort effects in older adults, page 42). The vast majority of older people, even those who are depressed, who have been bereaved, who are suffering from a medical illness or even those who are terminally ill, do not end their lives by suicide, however. This raises the question of what are the important risk factors in the older age group? The following have been identified: a history of poor adaptation to life's stress, vulnerability to loss and disruptions, loss of mastery and control, and cognitive impairment caused by organic mental disorder. Once again, we see the importance of people feeling trapped by what seems to them to be unbearable mental pain.

DURKHEIM'S VIEW OF PSYCHIATRIC CAUSATION

Before Durkheim the connection between suicide and psychiatric disturbance had been made many times. Some arguments had been relatively weak. Some had suggested that, even where no other symptoms of mental illness were present, the fact of suicide itself justified a psychiatric diagnosis. Suicide had been thought by some to be a disease in itself, *sui generis*, a specific form of insanity. In such a 'monomania' (a sick person whose mentality is perfectly healthy in all respects but one), suicide was argued to be the sort of behaviour 'not to be found in sane persons'. Émile Durkheim easily showed how this was a circular argument. To establish that suicide is caused by mental illness, we need to be able to say more than that suicide itself constitutes such a diagnosis.

Instead, Durkheim considered three types of psychiatric suicide. The first was *maniacal suicide* (caused by hallucinations or delirious perceptions), in which the person acts to escape an imaginary danger or to obey a mysterious order from on high. Today, such experiences would be associated with a diagnosis of schizophrenia. The second type was *melancholic suicide*, associated with extreme depression and exaggerated sadness. Such a state 'causes the person no longer to realise the bonds which connect him with people and things about him'. The third type was *obsessive suicide*, in which suicide was thought to be caused by no other motive, but only by a fixed idea of death; the person was tormented by the idea, since they were also aware that there was no reason to kill themselves, trying to resist the idea seemed hopeless, and the person, it was thought, sometimes simply gave up the struggle. Additionally, Durkheim pointed to the possibility of *impulsive or automatic suicide* – as unmotivated as obsessive suicide, but differing in that the idea comes suddenly with full force, 'not preceded by any intellectual antecedent' and with little apparent warning for themselves or others: the person sees a knife or walks near a cliff-edge, and the idea of suicide comes suddenly into mind. If the patient survives, they may say afterwards that they were not aware of or cannot remember any reason for their action.

In summarising the psychiatric suicides, Durkheim notes that all such suicides are either 'devoid of any motive' (obsessive and impulsive suicides) or are determined by 'purely imaginary motives' (maniacal and melancholic suicides). Where psychiatric disturbance itself explains the motivation, it does so by indicating how the illness acts to produce the behaviour either in the absence of motive or through the way it distorts the way the person views their world. Durkheim points out that 'many voluntary deaths fall into neither category; the majority have motives, and motives not unfounded in reality. Not every suicide can therefore be considered insane, without doing violence to language.'

DURKHEIM'S ALTERNATIVE VIEW – THE IMPORTANCE OF SOCIAL FACTS

Durkheim's main argument was that social facts have to be taken into account as realities external to the individual. Social institutions (families, churches, non-religious groups) were extra-personal forces, definite realities whose influence needed to be subject to scientific analysis – an argument that gave most impetus to the evolving science which would be called 'sociology'. (Durkheim was not translated into English until 1951.) The incidence of suicide was one such element: a reality explicable only by looking for links to other social facts about society. Each society was thought to have a 'collective inclination to suicide'. This inclination was found in the suicide rate within the society or sub-group and would not change while the character of the society or sub-group did not change. Thus, a certain number of suicides was to be expected in every society, and problems in the structure of society would lead to an increase in suicide rates. It followed that the more strongly any individual was integrated into a social group (e.g. close-knit families or religious groups), the less suicide was likely. Any changes in society that caused greater disintegration would increase the suicide rate.

Durkheim delineated three types of social suicide, to reflect the three categories of breakdown that might occur in the relationship between an individual and the society. In *egoistic suicide*, a person comes to have no concern for the community, nor any interest in being involved with it. This category includes people with physical or mental illness, together with those who suffer deprivation and bereavement. The result is a reduction in society's control, and weakened immunity against society's natural collective inclination towards suicide.

By contrast, in *altruistic suicide*, society has too strict a hold, and a person has too little individualism. Self-destruction is motivated by altruism, inspiring respect and admiration among other members of the group. The suicide bomber would be counted among those who commit altruistic suicide, as would religious 'martyrs' – Japanese samurai warriors who committed hara-kiri rather than fall into the hands of their enemies and kamikaze pilots of the Second World War. More controversially, those people who kill themselves because they are old or terminally ill, and do not wish to be a burden to family, friends or society, may be said to have committed altruistic suicide. However, it is often difficult to determine how much their sense of being a burden or that 'everyone would be better off if I were not here' arises from their depression, rather than from a clearly thought-out and tested set of reasons (see Chapter 6).

In *anomic suicide*, according to Durkheim, society has failed in its regulation and integration of its members. Changes in family structure, reduced employment opportunities, declining religious beliefs and practices, changes in marital codes – all were manifestations of anomie, resulting in disturbances of collective organisation. The result was a reduction in individuals' immunity against suicidal tendencies. In strict societies and subcultures, suicide rates would remain low because such integration of the individual with his or her social group would remain. Consistent with this idea, suicide rates have traditionally been low in Catholic countries, but have increased as these countries have gradually become more secularised.

EVIDENCE TO SUPPORT THE SOCIAL THEORY

Much of the data on suicide within and between populations is broadly consistent with the notion of anomie and societal disintegration as a major factor in explaining differences in propensity to suicide. A study of different areas around Bristol (UK) found the occurrence of non-fatal suicidal behaviour was highly correlated with deprivation (assessed by a number of factors, such as the proportion of people that own houses or cars, how many households are overcrowded, levels of unemployment).[8] Furthermore, the list of factors that increase the risk of suicide in those who have made a previous attempt makes the importance of social factors obvious: living alone; unemployed; from a broken home; men more than women; multiple attempts; not married; poor physical health; and infrequent use of health agencies. Although this is not true of everyone who commits suicide, and there are some who do so despite having none of these vulnerability factors, the picture that emerges is one of poor circumstances with few resources to sustain the individual. Most significantly, there is an obvious lack of other people to support the person. This is consistent with Durkheim's hypothesis.

In many countries, suicide is more common among those members of society most affected by economic downturns: semi-skilled and unskilled manual workers. It is more common in rural communities, where there is a special vulnerability to economic downturn (because of the possible loss of farms that generations of a family might have built up), combined with a mechanisation of farming that has seen decreased employment opportunities for many and increased social isolation of those few left.

Unemployment, whether in a rural or urban setting, appears to make suicide more likely. Even after controlling for social class, men aged 15–64 who are unemployed have a standard mortality rate greatly in excess of that of men in work. However, the relation between unemployment and suicide is complicated by two factors: first, the possibility that some may be vulnerable *both* to becoming unemployed and to suicide;[9] second, the fact that, in some cases of sudden unemployment in whole communities following the closure of factories, people may (at least for a while) feel more integrated with their community as they fight the 'common enemy'. However, such fellow-feeling may not offset the effects of economic hardship for long. Within individual families, increased depression in the former wage earner reduces energy levels. This can then be the cause of family friction as one partner accuses the other of 'not trying' to find employment. It is not uncommon to find single mothers talking frankly of how their unemployed (and now estranged) partner was a drain on the family's resources, especially if he had been spending money on alcohol or gambling.

Studies of how socio-demographic factors contribute to changing rates of suicide over time also confirm the main thrust of Durkheim's theory of anomie. Suicide rates in eighteen countries across Europe between 1960 and 1980[10] showed that *increases* were associated with: (a) reduction in the population aged 15 years and under, taken to be an indicator of the extent to which people were not living in family groups; (b) an increase in the percentage of the population aged 65 years and over, i.e. the age group that still had the highest rate in European countries at that time; and (c) an increase in women's tertiary education, taken to reflect changes in the family structure. Changes in suicide rate over the same time interval among 15–29-year-olds found some factors which overlapped with those of the earlier report, and some new ones, and more recent studies find a close link between financial hardship and suicide.[11]

The correlation between suicide and the divorce rate emerges from several studies. What is more questionable is whether this correlation will continue as divorce becomes more common and society develops more ways of dealing with and normalising single-parent families. For example, in the Netherlands the suicide rate among divorced people is tending to stabilise or decline.

CRITIQUES OF DURKHEIM: SOCIAL FACTS AND THE INDIVIDUAL

Durkheim has been criticised from various quarters. First, some have pointed out that he needed a better and more operational definition of social integration. Later sociologists have come up with clearer definitions of terms, e.g. of 'status' (a category of people with clearly defined roles). Thus, a person may have a variety of statuses and roles: within society (male, white), within the family (father, husband), within work (teacher, counsellor). In a similar vein, sociologists have much better definitions of 'social support' than those proposed by Durkheim.[12]

Second, he based his conclusions on studies of a Western society, and there is evidence that in other societies risk factors are different. For example, although the association between divorce rates and suicide holds for Western nations (the correlation for the United States has been found to be 0.78 for the 48 continental states), it does not hold for other countries. For example, the correlation between the divorce rate and suicide rate among the sixteen counties of Taiwan is an insignificant 0.05.

Third, Durkheim too readily separated melancholic from other depressive suicides. He allowed that many 'normal' persons who kill themselves may also be depressed and dejected, but maintained that they did not fall thereby into the category of melancholic mental illness. The difference, he suggested, was that in melancholy the person's depression was unrelated to their external circumstances, whereas in those he wished to call 'normal' the state of depression and the act of suicide had an objective cause. In this respect, Durkheim's analysis was wrong.

There is little evidence of such clear-cut differences between the various sub-types of depression.

Whereas it used to be thought that some depressions were 'reactive', caused by life circumstances, and others were 'endogenous', caused by biological factors ('endogenous' means 'originating from the inside'), research has shown that negative events and circumstances precede all types of depression equally often, and all types of depression have some biologically driven features. Even in depressions which follow directly after major loss or disappointment, there is evidence to show that, as the depression deepens, certain neurochemical pathways in the brain undergo a change, affecting a person's eating and sleeping patterns, energy levels and capacity to enjoy previously enjoyed hobbies, interests and social contacts. Such changes sometimes self-correct in time, and where they do not, antidepressant medication or types of psychotherapy that provide a structure within which the person can regain control over their moods have been found to help.

Nevertheless, the central thrust of Durkheim's argument remains true: we need to look for factors other than mental illness to explain why risk of suicide differs between individuals and between societies. The importance of social support cannot be overestimated in moderating the impact of other stresses. Not only is it important at times of stress, but people who have social support tend to adhere to the treatment suggested, and it is therefore no surprise that they respond better to it. With social support, people are more likely to take the opportunities given to begin to solve the problems in their lives, with or without the help of mental-health professionals.

However, understanding the social facts needs to be combined with understanding the individual circumstances in causing particular suicidal acts. Suicidal behaviour would be much more common than it is if individual circumstances had no role to play.

CAUSES: PSYCHIATRIC OR SOCIAL?

It certainly seems that suicide is closely associated with psychiatric disturbance. What, then, are we to make of Durkheim's scepticism about psychiatric illness, and how can we make sense of the equally compelling data linking suicide to social factors external to the individual?

Although psychiatric disturbance precedes suicide in many cases, it remains unclear whether its presence explains very much. Certainly, we can readily see that although up to 15 per cent of those who have been hospitalised for depression commit suicide, the majority do not. We therefore have to understand what is different about those who do commit suicide. Also, within the 15 per cent who do commit suicide, why did they choose that particular moment, when the difficulties from which they suffered may well have been with them a long time? Finally, there remains a proportion of people who commit suicide either as a catastrophic response to a negative event (usually a loss, or perceived loss), or as a matter of honour, or because they feel on rational grounds it is time to die. These cases are linked in the feelings of *uncontrollability* and feelings of *entrapment* they involve (we call this the *entrapment theory* of suicide).

Feelings of entrapment arising from inside a person are particularly damaging, yet are often ignored. Why? It may be because psychiatrists and psychologists often take account only of negative life events (such as bereavement, loss of job, marital breakdown) in explaining the onset of a psychiatric illness. Once the psychiatric illness has been diagnosed, however, the search for causes often stops. The illness has been explained. But this does not explain how the disturbance is maintained, why it sometimes lasts a long rather than a short time, or gets worse, rather than better. Occasionally, there are further negative external events that account for such prolongation. But we need also to take account of the negative effects of experiencing unpleasant psychiatric symptoms themselves: e.g. hearing voices that cannot be switched off, in schizophrenia; feeling constantly tired but unable to sleep, in depression; feeling at the mercy of craving, in alcoholism. Such uncontrollable stresses that arise from within are as likely to produce a state of helplessness as those that arise from outside. It is these that explain why psychiatric illness so often precedes suicide, and why most people who become psychiatrically ill do not commit suicide.

I suggest that the presence of mental illness does add significantly to the explanation of suicide in many cases, but, when it does, it does so only to the extent that the symptoms of the condition engender hopelessness. To state the hypothesis more strongly: *psychiatric illnesses carry an increased risk for suicide only to the extent that the person feels they cannot escape their symptoms*. For example, it is not the frequency of psychotic symptoms that predicts suicidality in schizophrenia, but how the person feels about having such symptoms: the extent to which the person feels *entrapped* by such symptoms.[13] The more someone feels trapped, the longer and more persistent will be the depression, and the greater the risk of suicide. Other predictors of suicide will all be elements that decrease a person's sense of control over external and internal events.

The evidence is compelling. In depression, it is the people who have been depressed longest, and who are, therefore, most likely to feel hopeless about recovering a normal state of mind, who carry most risk of suicide. Furthermore, retrospective analysis of suicidal behaviour in people who have been depressed in-patients, and of suicide in those who have previously attempted suicide, has found that the greatest risk for subsequent suicide was for those who showed the severest depressed mood, alcohol problems, long-term use of sleeping pills and long-term physical illness.[14] Finally, whereas attributing suicidal behaviour to the diagnosis of depression does not explain why the period immediately after discharge is the most vulnerable time, especially for men, such increased risk is more easily explained by the exacerbation of a sense of hopelessness brought about by the change in circumstances.[15]

Similarly in people with a diagnosis of schizophrenia, the suicide risk is particularly strong for those who feel hopeless, have suicidal ideation, fear mental disintegration, have made previous suicide attempts, do not adhere to treatment and experience many relapses in symptoms. Indeed, it is a *history* of depressive features (past use of ECT or antidepressants in treatment) which is an important predictor, not the *extent* of the schizophrenic symptoms (e.g. voices). This supports the view that it is not the voices themselves which increase the risk of suicide, but how the person feels about them. The external stresses with which patients with this diagnosis have to cope are well known: decreased job prospects, family disintegration, poor network of relationships. Entrapment theory would suggest that such events have most impact upon those who can compare current reality with what might have been.[16] Studies have found that most suicides in those with a diagnosis of schizophrenia are young males, functioning at above average level prior to the onset of the schizophrenia, but now unemployed. Those who previously had the most promising careers are at greatest risk – the contrast is, for them, the most stark. As in depression, any event that increases a sense of helplessness can increase the suicide risk, and change in circumstances is particularly likely to do so. This may include changing wards when an in-patient, or discharge from hospital. Each finding points away from the particular psychiatric diagnosis of schizophrenia *per se* as the factor that increases suicide risk and towards the increased helplessness and hopelessness such a disorder shares with other serious mental problems.

The link between suicide and helplessness in the face of feelings of entrapment in alcoholics is striking. Once again, discharge is a vulnerable time, often made worse by the fact that family contacts may well have broken down. Such people have vulnerable or fragile personalities and social problems that may have precipitated their drinking, but are then exacerbated by the drinking itself. Connected to this is the fact that alcoholic individuals who commit suicide are very likely to be either unmarried or divorced. Life events (especially loss events) are most closely connected to suicide in alcoholics, with 50 per cent having suffered loss of an important relationship in the year preceding the suicide (the figure for depressed patients is 20 per cent). Indeed, one-third of alcoholic suicides have suffered such a loss within *six weeks* of the suicide.

CONCLUDING REMARKS

The patterns in the suicide data reviewed in this chapter both confirm the significance of psychiatric illnesses and show how they combine with a psychosocial perspective in explaining suicide risk. Psychiatric diagnoses, especially depression, schizophrenia and alcoholism, act as markers of increased suicide risk. But suicide is not unique to any particular diagnosis. It arises from a *secondary* aspect of mental illness. In such mental states, the person experiences symptoms that can give rise to an inner turmoil that seems inescapable and uncontrollable. It is the combination of uncontrollable stress factors arising from sources external and internal to the individual that increases a sense of entrapment. The most potent preventative factor when such uncontrollable stress threatens to overwhelm the individual is the availability of social support from friends and family. When the suicidal feelings are too strong, however, even support of the highest quality will be ignored by the suicidal person; the hopelessness they experience includes extreme pessimism about whether anyone can help them, with tragic consequences.

CHAPTER FOUR

Attempted Suicide

'I have to admit that I am a failed suicide. It is a dismal confession to make, since nothing, really, would seem easier than to take your own life.' So wrote Al Alvarez in his book *Savage God*.[1] Alvarez knew first-hand what it was like to experience suicidal despair, and be driven to take the final step. The crisis took place on Christmas Eve ten years before he wrote these words. After a 'final, terrible quarrel' with his wife, she left to stay elsewhere for the night. Alvarez went upstairs to the bathroom and swallowed forty-five sleeping pills. Impulsive? In some senses, yes, but the act had been prepared for some time. His account illustrates, among other things, the premeditation of suicidal behaviour (he had been hoarding sleeping pills), the precipitation of the act by some 'final straw' and the unwillingness of the police to intervene in the late 1950s.

> I had been collecting the things for months obsessionally, like Green Stamps, from doctors on both sides of the Atlantic . . . hoarding them in preparation for the time I knew was coming. When it finally arrived, a box was waiting stuffed with pills of all colors . . . I gobbled the lot.
>
> My wife got back at noon, took one look and called the ambulance. When they got me to the hospital I was, the report says, 'deeply unconscious, slightly cyanosed, vomit in mouth, pulse rapid, poor volume'.
>
> I was still unconscious the next day and most of the day after that . . . During the afternoon of the third day, December 28, I came to . . . In a fog I saw my wife smiling hesitantly, and in tears. It was all very vague. I slept . . .
>
> At some point the police came, since in those days suicide was still a criminal offense. They sat heavily but rather sympathetically by my bed and asked me questions they clearly didn't want me to answer. When I tried to explain, they shushed me quietly. 'It was an accident, wasn't it, sir?' Dimly, I agreed. They went away.

Alvarez's experience raises many of the questions that need to be answered in relation to what is often called 'attempted suicide'. First, what proportion of people who think about harming themselves actually go on to do it, and what proportion of those who do, go on at some time in the future to kill themselves? Second, if ending one's life is not the only motive for such self-harm, what are the other motives? Third, how can one distinguish a failed suicide attempt (where the full intention was to end one's life) from self-harm intended to change some aspect of oneself or others?

DEFINITIONS

To answer the questions above, we need a clear definition of what we mean by 'attempted suicide'. Is all and any self-harm to be deemed an attempt at suicide, even self-cutting, or burning with cigarette ends? And what of the elderly woman who takes four sleeping pills, and telephones the physician in great distress? In this case the physician would be well advised not to ignore the behaviour, even though it represents no risk to life in the short term. Such a person may be used to taking half a sleeping pill to help her get to sleep at night, and therefore believes four such tablets (eight times her normal dose) will kill her. Turning a blind eye may be to miss someone who is extremely suicidal.

On the other hand, a young person who takes a hundred paracetamol may be at considerable risk of dying without medical intervention as a result of liver failure (especially if they have taken alcohol with the paracetamol), yet may at no point have thought of killing him- or herself. Indeed, the availability of large quantities of such lethal substances over the counter in the past has given the completely false impression of safety. Such a person can hardly be said to have been attempting suicide, though their risk of dying may have been greater than that of the elderly person who was at no significant risk.[2]

To overcome the confusion about the term 'attempted suicide', clinicians and researchers have, over the past twenty years, adopted various words such as 'parasuicide' or 'deliberate self-harm'. 'Parasuicide' was, for a time, the most widely used term for all such self-harm (whatever the explicit or implicit intention). The words used vary over time, but the most common terms in current use are 'deliberate self-harm' (in the UK this covers both what used to be called attempted suicide and medically less serious self-harm, such as surface cutting of the skin). In the US they have two categories: 'suicidal behaviour' and 'non-suicidal self-injury', the latter exclusively referring to superficial self-cutting or burning. The paradox of the US definition is that an overdose of any amount or stated intention *cannot* count as a non-suicidal act. This paradox is shown to be even more extreme when people who have been admitted to hospital after cutting themselves are followed up in the long term, when it is found that they are more likely to commit suicide than those admitted to the same hospital who had taken an overdose.[3]

For this reason, in this book I use *attempted suicide* and *deliberate self-harm* (DSH) interchangeably to refer to *an act with non-fatal outcome, in which an individual deliberately initiates a non-habitual behaviour that, without intervention from others, will cause self-harm, or deliberately ingests a substance in excess of the prescribed or generally recognised therapeutic dosage, and which is aimed at realising changes which the subject desired via the actual or expected physical consequences.*[4] The term 'parasuicide' may also be used.

The longstanding debate about what constitutes an accurate terminology to describe and classify suicidal behaviour is not simply a discussion about semantics. The terms that are used carry important assumptions about the phenomenon in question. At a very basic level, a pivotal issue is whether the large variety of types of behaviour involved in 'self-harm' is considered a problem that can be reduced by agreeing how to classify such behaviour, or whether the difference in types of behaviour and relative lack of a clear-cut diagnostic category is intrinsic to the phenomenon in question. For instance, the recent recommendations from American suicidologists to replace the term 'suicidality' with the more specific terms 'suicidal ideation', 'suicidal intent', 'suicide attempt' and 'suicide' may seem to provide much-needed order to the complex and multifaceted phenomenon of suicidal behaviour. In a similar vein, American suicidologist Mort Silverman[5] recommends adopting a biological disease model (i.e. the stages used to classify severity of cancer) to denote severity of suicidal behaviour. As clear cut as this may seem, it can give the impression that these 'specific' terms or stages are unambiguous, when in fact there is a wide variety of intention underlying self-harm.[6]

Classifications of suicidal behaviour are mostly attempts to operationalise the idea that suicidal behaviour varies in its seriousness. Clinically, this is often summarised by two characteristics of the most recent episode, i.e. the level of associated *suicidal intent* and the *lethality* of the self-harm in question. This is reflected in the distinction between 'suicide attempt' and 'non-suicidal self-injury',[7] and in the distinctions used frequently in clinical practice between 'gesture', 'ambivalent' and 'serious' suicidal behaviour.

Common to most classifications is that *lethality* is seen as a reflection of the 'true', underlying intent: whereas medically severe acts are considered serious (as reflected in the *a priori* assumption about underlying intent inherent in the notion 'suicide attempt'), acts of low medical severity are, in many cases, considered less serious and as predominantly being a means to bring about certain consequences other than death. A recent systematic review of health professionals' attitudes to suicidal behaviour demonstrated that they were significantly more sympathetic to medically severe self-harm than to acts of low lethality,[8] and another recent study showed that health professionals with longer training in psychiatry are more positive than those with little training.[9] Training and experience are important. Clinicians who are more competent in delivering Cognitive Therapy (in this case, for those with borderline personality disorders) are more effective in reducing risk of repeated self-harm in their patients.[10]

However, whether the actual medical risk reflects suicidal intent remains a controversial issue. Over a large number of cases there is sometimes a correlation between actual lethality and suicidal intent, but it is hugely difficult to infer degree of suicidal intent from the medical lethality in an individual case. Many suicidal individuals, including those having survived near-lethal episodes, say they want to live.[11] Findings from the Multicentre Study of Self-Harm in England showed that children and adolescents who presented to hospital following self-cutting were *more* likely to subsequently die by suicide than those admitted for an overdose.[12] The psychological experience of DSH needs to be teased apart from the physical consequences of the behaviour. This involves investigating dimensions of the *psychological* severity of an episode of self-harm.

One factor that has been suggested as accounting for the discrepancy between intent and lethality is a lack of knowledge about suicidal means.[13] Some people (especially those not used to taking pills) may believe that relatively few pills are lethal. The problem with this perspective is that it presupposes that choice of method is predominantly rational, e.g. had they known better they would have engaged in behaviour that was more aligned with their suicidal urges, and consequently that any discrepancy between intent and lethality is due either to lack of availability of suicidal means or lack of self-harm knowledge. However, as is evident from health psychologist Professor Rory O'Connor's research,[14] several other factors may determine the relationship between subjective experience of suicidal intent and actual enactment: impulsivity, access to suicidal means, ambivalence about self-harm and communicative aspects are all factors which can account for discrepancies between high level of intent and low lethality and vice versa. Actual medical severity would then be little guide to what may, in fact, be a very serious suicidal attempt. There is also, however, the obvious but often overlooked point that the correlation between actual physical lethality and intent is much stronger in cases where the person has an accurate perception of the lethality of their self-harm.

ATTEMPTED SUICIDE – HOW COMMON IS IT?

Defining attempted suicide is one thing, collecting data about it another. The lack of monitoring systems in many countries, as well as variation in the definitions used, makes it difficult to estimate accurately the prevalence of DSH. For a complete picture of attempted suicide rates and trends, we must rely on data from those centres and studies that have made special efforts to collect information over the years. Fortunately, these have presented a remarkably consistent picture.

A recent study within the WHO World Mental Health Survey initiative showed that 2.7 per cent of the population attempt suicide at some point.[15] Interestingly, rates for DSH did not correlate with those for suicide; that is, regions that have a high suicide rate did not necessarily have a high rate of deliberate self-harm.[16] A comparative study of eight European regions from 1989 to 2003 showed considerable variation in rates across regions and gender, with consistently higher rates for women than for men overall.[17] Findings from a WHO study of different European countries spanning ten years (1989–1999) found that DSH rates were higher for women than for men and more frequent in younger age groups.[18] (For the UK, further detail about the patterns of deliberate self-harm may be obtained from the latest publication of the Centre for Suicide Research at the University of Oxford: http://cebmh.warne.ox.ac.uk/csr/statistics.html.)

The Oxford statistics (which have been found to be representative of the entire UK) show that young women are more likely to harm themselves than young men (two-thirds are women and two-thirds are under 35 years of age). The peak age for women lies between 15 and 19 years, whereas the peak age for men lies at 20–24 years. Most people who attempt suicide are either single or divorced. The data also reveal that the majority are from lower socio-economic backgrounds. The rate for the 'highest' professional socio-economic groups, such as physicians, surgeons, lawyers, etc., is around 50 per 100,000 for women and 20 per 100,000 for men. This rate goes up over eight times for women and over twelve times for men in the least privileged socio-economic groups – those who work in jobs such as dishwashing or very low-autonomy manual occupations. How many will harm themselves again? Estimates over the years and from various centres have varied between 10 and 25 per cent, averaging around 15 per cent. Some go on to make more repeat attempts, so that in any sample of cases coming to hospital, around 44 per cent of both men and women have a previous episode of deliberate self-harm.

Suicidal ideas and suicidal behaviour

What proportion of people have *thoughts* about suicide at some point in their lives? Studies vary in their estimates, from very low (3.5 per cent) for those that merely ask about 'recent' thoughts, through 19 per cent (if the question is asked about the past year), to 53 per cent (if people are asked if they have *ever* thought of suicide).[19] Perhaps we should not be surprised that over half the world's population have had suicidal thoughts at some time in their lives – but that one in five has had such thoughts in the past year *is* surprising. Of these, only 1 to 2 per cent go on to harm themselves in some way, but when someone has harmed themselves once, how can we assess whether the person is at future risk of harming themselves again? The largest predictor of the future tends to be the past, in that previous history of self-harm predicts future episodes, and these are more likely to be medically serious if there are other indications of psychiatric disturbance and social isolation, as described in Chapter Three, leading to a sense of being trapped.

Different motivations for self-harm

It is clear that death is not always or even mostly the intended outcome of a 'suicide attempt'. If not, then what is the motive? Over half of those who have recently taken an overdose said they did not want to die at any stage, and of those who did say they wanted to die, many said there were other reasons, such as 'showing how much I loved someone'.[20] The most common reasons given for taking an overdose are listed in the box on page 73.[21]

Reasons for overdose

Ranked most to least commonly endorsed:

- The situation was so unbearable I had to do something and didn't know what else to do.
- I wanted to die.
- I wanted to escape for a while from an impossible situation.
- I wanted to get relief from a terrible state of mind.
- I wanted to make people understand how desperate I was feeling.
- I wanted to make things easier for others.
- I wanted to get help from someone.
- I wanted to show how much I loved someone.
- I wanted to try and get someone to change their mind.
- I wanted to try and find out whether someone really loved me or not.
- I wanted to make people sorry for the way they have treated me.
- I wanted to frighten someone.
- I wanted to get my own back on someone.

The most commonly endorsed reason is, 'The situation was so unbearable that I had to do something and didn't know what else to do', but this is often combined with others. This gives an important clue to what is going on in the mind of the person who is desperate – up against a 'brick wall' and feeling they just cannot cope any more – and it fits with the often-reported feeling that they didn't care whether they lived or died. They will, as it were, let the Fates decide. For many, it is more like Russian roulette than a considered act.

SUICIDAL INTENT

How can we tell if someone really intended to kill themselves? In the past, a number of terms have been coined to refer to people who, it is assumed, did not mean to kill themselves, such as 'gesture', 'manipulative' and 'cry for help'. These too easily assume that different motivations for deliberate self-harm are mutually exclusive, being either an attempt to communicate (gesture), to influence others (manipulation) or to die (suicide attempt).

Instead, it is important to build up a picture which incorporates a range of information, including details of the circumstances surrounding the episode (if necessary, obtained from relatives or friends) as well as the person's own report. The following issues need to be taken into account.[22]

External circumstances

1. *How isolated was the person at the time?* The further away from others a person chooses to harm themselves, the greater the intent.

2. *Was the act timed so that intervention was likely or unlikely?* Some clinicians believe that the highly suicidal person will calculate when to harm themselves so the likelihood of interruption is minimal.

3. *Were precautions taken against discovery?* Some people will lock doors, write notes saying they have gone away, travel to remote locations without telling of their whereabouts or book into hotels under other names, all to avoid discovery.

4. *Did the patient do anything to gain help during or after the attempt?* It sometimes happens that someone will have second thoughts, either just before or during a suicidal act, and telephone or tell someone what they are about to do or have just done. The highly suicidal person is less likely to do this.

5. *Did the patient carry out any final acts anticipating they would die?* Those with greater suicidal intent write wills, cancel regular orders, clear their desks, etc. in the expectation that they will die.

6. *Did they write a suicide note?* Although only 30 per cent of people who commit suicide leave a note, it usually indicates a high degree of suicidal intent.

Self-report

1. *Did they believe what they did would kill them?* As we've seen, people vary in how much they know about the lethality of suicidal acts, particularly overdoses. The amount of drugs taken has been found to correlate with suicidal intent if a large enough sample is taken,[23] although other studies have not found this to be the case.[24] Medical lethality is useful for

judging seriousness of intent where it is known the person who has taken the overdose is aware of the relative lethality of drugs. Otherwise, the person's own report about what they *thought* the outcome would be is the most important factor.

2. *Do they say they wanted to die?* Many studies show that over half of people who harm themselves say they did *not* want to die. High suicidal intent is associated with a clear indication that death was the intended outcome.
3. *How premeditated was the act?* Two-thirds of patients have not thought about it for more than an hour beforehand. The longer the idea of suicide had been in the mind, the greater the suicidal intent.
4. *Is the patient glad (or sorry) to have recovered?* The person who has harmed themselves and afterwards says they are sorry to be still alive is likely to have had greater intent.

Extrapolating from external circumstance and self-report

Taken together, these lists of external circumstances and self-report have been used to determine the degree of suicidality or suicidal 'intent'. Research has found that high suicidality, defined in this way, predicts future suicidal behaviour and future suicide.[25] One study found that 21 per cent of patients with high suicide intent later committed suicide.[26] However, there are important caveats. Some studies have not supported an association,[27] including some showing a disconnection between highly lethal methods (e.g. pesticides) and suicidal intent in young women with no pre-existing psychiatric history, commonly found in low- and middle-income countries such as China and Sri Lanka.[28] Moreover, many suicidal individuals, including those who have survived near-lethal episodes, report a will to live, indicating that the lethality–intent association is not straightforward.

Results have shown that people who harm themselves with high suicidal intent are more likely to have had previous episodes of self-harm, to be single or divorced and to live alone. However, they are no more likely to be depressed or personality disordered, no more likely to have had psychiatric treatment in the past and show no difference in the type of drug used in overdose or in whether alcohol was taken. By far the largest predictor is a chronic problem with alcohol abuse. Since chronic alcohol abuse itself puts a person at high risk of suicide, the joint influence of abusing alcohol and harming oneself with high suicidal intent should be taken as a very serious indicator that a person is vulnerable to suicide.

CONCLUDING REMARKS: ALVAREZ REVISITED

On the basis of the above descriptions, was Alvarez's deliberate self-harm a serious attempt on his life? Taking account of the external circumstances, the episode would have to be judged as of low suicidal intent. He took the pills in his own house on Christmas Day, after a row with his wife, making no attempt to isolate himself. The timing was more ambiguous in that his wife had just left to sleep at their flat for the night, but there is little indication that he believed she would not return the next morning. In any event, there was a house guest, who brought him a cup of tea in the morning, and his wife returned at noon. The house guest was able to bring the tea into his bedroom, so he had taken no precautions against discovery, such as locking the door. He did not act to gain help before or during the attempt, which might indicate high suicidal intent, but he had tried to contact his psychotherapist on Christmas Eve. When an immediate appointment was difficult to arrange, nothing was done. He made no final acts in anticipation of death, and did not leave a suicide note. All this seems to indicate low suicidal intent. Yet he very nearly died, so nearly became another tragic suicide statistic. This shows how difficult it is to judge suicide risk from apparent motives or circumstances.

Alvarez's internal *feelings* about what was going on indicate more suicidality than the external circumstances. He seemed to think the pills would kill him, seems to have wanted to die and had been hoarding pills for some time (indicating premeditation). Whether he was sorry he had not died is less clear. He does express disappointment, but not so much at being alive as from a sense of being cheated by death: 'Death had let me down.' There had been no moment of cathartic truth when the meaning of his life was revealed: 'All I got was oblivion.' He went on, 'As for suicide ... it is not for me. Perhaps I am no longer optimistic enough. I assume now that death, when it finally comes, will probably be nastier than suicide, and certainly a great deal less convenient.'

CHAPTER FIVE

The Causes of Attempted Suicide

We have seen how descriptions of suicide and suicidal behaviour emphasise that both are outcomes of a complex interplay of risk factors. However, this is a comparatively recent way of explaining the behaviour. As with modern epidemiology in general, theories about the cause of suicide and suicidal behaviour have moved from emphasising overarching, often *external* causal factors (e.g. medical illness, religious inclination) to relying, from the 1950s onwards, on ways in which different *risk factors* combine. Each risk factor may not be sufficient in itself, but together they contribute to the probability of suicide or attempted suicide – reflected in notions of people being at high or low risk. In this chapter, I will separate causal factors into a timeline, so we can understand the process from things that happened to someone a long time ago in their early life, to more recent events, to specific things known to trigger distress in the present.

LONG-TERM VULNERABILITY FACTORS

The *long-term vulnerability factors* include all those factors in the person's past or current relationships and living conditions which act as background to the shorter-term crises; for example, early loss by death or separation or other major traumas within the family, such as alcohol or drug abuse, mental illness, criminality or a sibling in a foster home.[1,2]

Parenting

Although there is an association between loss of parents (through death or divorce) and later suicidal behaviour, this does not imply that all cases have this in their background. Nevertheless, several studies suggest that poor parenting occurs unusually frequently[3] (such studies tend to use the Parental Bonding Instrument[4] – a questionnaire that measures how much people perceive their parents cared for them versus being indifferent or rejecting; it also assesses how much parents were overprotective versus encouraging independence). A recent review of parenting and suicidality studies concluded that the combination of low parental care and parental overprotection (termed 'affectionless control') was consistently associated with suicidal behaviour.[5]

Note that these studies are based on how it *felt* to have such parents. An interesting finding is that suicidal people perceived themselves as less *deserving* of care. They had poor self-esteem and placed a lower value on their own life. The curious combination of having parents who are perceived to have been more rejecting *and* overprotective is significant. Both can undermine the growing child's sense of autonomy and of being in control of events in his or her own life. Note however, that in all such studies, there are many people who have experienced loving parents, and yet for some reason find themselves feeling suicidal, and this is especially important to bear in mind as we turn to the next field – sexual abuse.

Sexual abuse

Several authors have suggested that a high proportion of suicide attempters have an even more acute disruption in early social relationships: they suffer sexual abuse. One study from the Netherlands examined the extent of sexual abuse in a sample of 158 female suicide attempters aged 20 years or older.[6] Fifty per cent reported having been sexually abused at some time in the past. The sexually abused women made their first suicide attempt earlier than the non-abused women: when they were 27 years old, on average, compared to an average age of 36 years. The abused women also had almost double the number of previous suicide attempts. Only 20 per cent of these women had been abused once; the majority had been abused repeatedly by the same or multiple abusers. For most, the first suicide attempt took place after sexual abuse. Although the majority of sexual abuse research focuses on women, men who have been sexually abused as children are also at increased risk of attempting suicide.[7]

Particularly worrying is the finding that women who have been abused have a much greater probability of multiple suicide attempts later. More sexually abused women (48 per cent) make further suicide attempts than women with no history of sexual abuse (29 per cent) and those who have been abused by a family member are at particular risk.[8] No difference has been found between those who had been the victims of child sexual abuse (under 16 years) and those first abused when 16 years or older. Similarly, and somewhat surprisingly, there was no difference in the pattern of suicidal behaviour between those who had had one sexual-abuse experience and those who had been abused multiple times. Neither did the history of sexual abuse affect the characteristics of the suicide attempt – for example, the method used or the reasons given to explain the suicide attempt or even the suicidal intent.

This is an important finding. It undermines the argument that a suicide attempt by a woman with a history of such sexual abuse is a 'cry for help' – the view that people with a history of such experiences come to believe that only an extraordinary measure such as a suicide attempt will gain them attention. The Dutch study did find that women who had been sexually abused had, as others had found, poor relationships with people around them, problems with achieving a sense of fulfilment from their lives and more problems in integrating with others.

The fact that these women also predict (accurately) that they will be suicidal in the future is worrying for those interested in reducing suicidal behaviour. The pattern they show is consistent with the pattern of learned helplessness, where a person believes there will be nothing they can do to achieve control in their life in the future or to stop traumatic things happening to them. Even if small unpleasant events happen in their daily lives, they are likely to explain these in terms of *stable* factors (something that won't go away) and *global* factors (something that affects all areas of life). For example, if they get into an argument with a friend, they are likely to believe it was caused by their long-term difficulty in sustaining a relationship with that person, and this same problem in sustaining relationships will also affect their relationships with everyone else, including future boyfriends and girlfriends, future employers and so on. In future stressful situations this pattern of attribution is likely to produce an overwhelming sense of helplessness and hopelessness, even when there might have been something the person could have done.

SHORT-TERM VULNERABILITY FACTORS

The *short-term vulnerability factors* include all those factors in the current situation which put an additional burden on the person's coping ability in the month prior to an attempt. Whereas both suicidal and depressed patients have an increased incidence of unpleasant life events compared with controls, the suicidal group suffers a steep increase. Interpersonal conflict is particularly common.[9] Additionally, there is a greater incidence of physical illness (especially in women). Given the preponderance of sources of physical and emotional stress, it is not surprising that over half of attempters, including three-quarters of adolescent attempters, contact some helping agency (most of them the GP) during the month before they attempt suicide.

Investigators have also found an increase in disturbance in relationships and work during this phase. Both male and female attempters report equivalent levels of relationship difficulties, though more males than females report significant work difficulties.

Employment status

A large study has shown that unemployed men are less likely to be married and less likely to live with their family; they are more likely to be of a lower social class, to have been given a diagnosis of abnormal personality, to misuse drugs, to be in trouble with the police and to have a criminal record. This has important implications for studies that have found a relationship between unemployment and deliberate self-harm. A recent review of all published research suggests that the risk of suicide increases the longer the duration of unemployment, with risk greatest in the first five years.[10] While the increase in *suicides* in England since the 2007–8 recession is thought to be attributable, in part, to rising unemployment,[11] the link between unemployment and *self-harm* is more uncertain. Unemployment is undoubtedly an important additional stress on people, but we must be careful to be sure that the link between unemployment and self-harm is not caused by other factors (e.g. drug abuse) that predict both unemployment and attempted suicide.

Substance abuse

In an earlier study of predictors of suicide in 15–24-year-olds, substance abuse emerged as a key predictor of suicide following an earlier attempt.[12] Substance abuse is also associated with self-harm in adolescence.[13] Habitual abuse of alcohol and drugs provides the person with a readily available means of overdosing; it also decreases the sense of risk in doing so. Finally, the abuse can affect judgement, so that normal ability to solve problems (which may already be impaired in this group) becomes even more damaged. Substance abuse thus makes more likely the transition from suicidal ideas to actual behaviour.

PRECIPITATING FACTORS

Precipitating factors are those events which occur in the few days prior to the attempt. Disharmony with 'key other' people in the person's life is the most common event; disharmony with relatives, anxiety about work/employment, financial difficulties and physical pain or illness are other reasons. One study assessed the negative life events experienced within forty-eight hours of a suicide attempt in 110 adults and found that interpersonal events – especially those involving a romantic partner – were particularly common.[14]

Special dates

Days in the calendar that are special for some are likely to be the most difficult for others; when everyone else appears to be enjoying themselves, those who are depressed and hopeless are at their most vulnerable. We have already seen how suicidal feelings are sensitive to interpersonal disruption – boyfriend/girlfriend disputes are one of the major precipitating factors, for example. Putting all this together, one might predict that a date such as St Valentine's Day, 14 February, will be a time of particular vulnerability. In fact, one study has shown this date to double the number of attempted suicides.[15] Furthermore, the proportion of cases that were adolescents/young adults (aged 12–20) was 45 per cent on 14 February, but only 17 per cent (the UK national norm) on 7 February.[16] However, the rate of deliberate self-harm around Christmas goes down, rather than up, despite a lowering in mood for some and an increase in alcohol-related problems.[17]

Public events

The death of Diana, Princess of Wales, on Sunday, 31 August 1997, was, for many people in the United Kingdom (especially those who had not lived through the wars of the twentieth century), one of the most tragic public events they had experienced. In the week following her death the number of suicide attempts rose by 44 per cent (especially in women, where the increase was 65 per cent).[18] Even more striking, in the four weeks following the funeral, deaths due to suicides and open verdicts rose by 17 per cent (34 per cent in women, and especially in women aged between 25–44 years, where the increase was 48 per cent).

WHY DO EVENTS HAVE SUCH A CATASTROPHIC EFFECT?

Events involving a key person, such as arguments with a spouse or partner, are very common immediately preceding attempted suicide. Such events are particularly associated with suicidal feelings in the context of any ongoing difficulties in their relationship. Relative to others, suicidal individuals have (or feel they have) weak social support systems. When asked, they report interpersonal situations as their chief problems in living. The family background may be disturbed and current living conditions fraught with difficulties. Yet, when such people come for help, they often blame themselves. It sometimes seems as though the very act of seeking help confirms to them that everything is their fault. Why else, they think, would they need help?

Someone who has undergone long-term adversity, such as sexual, physical or emotional abuse, may suffer from a number of psychological difficulties. Not all who have experienced such adversity will have severe difficulties later, and there may be some who do have psychological difficulties that have not been brought about by a problematic past. But the association between such difficulties and suicidal behaviour is well established and very little added stress may be needed to precipitate suicidal ideas and behaviour.[19]

We may note, once again, the message from the research – that it is not necessarily the stresses themselves that increase the risk of self-harm, but how people relate to them: some cope by seeing emotional upheavals as situations they can solve or as passing events that will fade in their own time. In the next section, we will see how difficult it can be, however, for those who are most vulnerable to stop themselves being overwhelmed by circumstances, both external events and internal reactions.

INTERPERSONAL PROBLEM-SOLVING

Difficulty in solving problems involving relationships is an obvious effect of past interpersonal problems, and also the cause of further problems. To investigate deficits in problem-solving, the most commonly used measure is the Means–Ends Problem-Solving (MEPS) test.[20] The MEPS test includes a number of different social scenarios; for each one people are given some initial circumstances in which a problem has to be solved (e.g. argument with boy/girlfriend) and a positive outcome projected (the friend likes him/her again). The task is to complete the middle part of the story, providing different ways in which the initial problem can be solved. The test is scored for the numbers and quality of 'relevant means' (problem-solving steps).

Using the MEPS test with psychiatric in-patients who had expressed suicidal ideas and a group of equally depressed but non-suicidal in-patients, one study[21] found that the suicidal patients were able to provide fewer than half the number of ways of solving problems. This result might have come about because the MEPS items did not fit these people's experiences, so the investigators also devised a modified test based on patients' personal situations, whereby patients were asked to provide a personal problem which had led to their being in hospital. Here, too, suicidal patients were more ineffective, their suggested ways of solving a problem often being irrelevant.

Even when suicidal people do come up with slightly more applicable solutions, these differ from the type of solutions given by others.[22] People who have made a suicide attempt are more passive (relying on others for solutions) and less active in their problem-solving than either people who have had suicidal thoughts they have not acted upon or non-suicidal psychiatric in-patients. Attempted suicide patients' solutions differ on a range of other qualitative aspects, including showing more avoidance and being less versatile.[23]

My colleague Leslie Pollock and I found that suicide attempters were poorer in problem-solving ability than matched psychiatric controls and this difference persisted despite improvements in their mood.[24] In recent research in Oxford, we have found that if someone has felt suicidal in the past when they were depressed, then, in the future, any mood disturbance can quickly reinstate the patterns of thoughts and behaviour that were linked with suicidal feelings. In particular, we have found that people's ability to solve problems effectively begins to deteriorate rapidly when mood begins to fall, especially in those who have been suicidal in the past.[25]

Given the increased number of stressful events known to precede a suicidal episode, the reduced ability to solve personal problems is especially challenging. An escalation in such stresses, combined with a reduced ability to think of steps to solve the problems generated, increases the likelihood of suicidal behaviour. As we saw in the previous chapter, the person feels they have run out of options about what to do to solve the problems in his or her life. This sense of having no options at all can arise very suddenly, with catastrophic consequences.

In suicidal adolescents, anger and the severity of initial suicidal behaviour predict repetition. Studies have shown where this anger may arise: repeated suicide attempts by adolescents are more likely if the young person has suffered loss of a parent and is living outside the parental home. Stress seems to be cumulative, building from early loss, through family disruption to interpersonal disputes occurring closer to the time of self-harm. Whether or not all such family backgrounds are this disrupted, it remains true that many suicidal adolescents view their family as disengaged and inflexible. However, it is difficult to determine to what extent this view arises from the depression, anger and hopelessness of an adolescent who is suicidal for other reasons. Adolescents often look at their own internal and external problems in ways that differ from the judgement of either their parents or a health professional. Adolescents may also believe that their parents and friends hold really high expectations for them and that if they fail to achieve these (often) unrealistic standards, they will have let them down. Rory O'Connor has found that among adolescents who score highly on this type of perfectionism, their risk of suicidal behaviour is increased.[26]

What is the basis for poorer problem-solving by suicidal

individuals? A possible clue comes from research on problems such people have in their memories of events from their past (see Chapter Nine). Patients who are depressed and suicidal tend to remember their past in a summarised, over-general way. For example, in response to a cue word such as 'happy', a suicidal patient might say, 'When I'm out with friends'. Note that their memory response does not single out a particular event. In contrast, non-suicidal people retrieve specific, datable events, such as 'Last Friday when I went out for a meal with friends'. Attempted suicide patients tend to recall a general description of a class of events. They stop short of retrieving a specific memory contained within that general description, though after further prompting often recall such an event. As we will see in Chapter Nine, getting 'stuck' at the stage of recalling a general category of events has implications for problem-solving, and can add to the sense of being trapped.

FUTURE-DIRECTED THINKING AND HOPELESSNESS

When people feel suicidal, they think about the future differently from when they are feeling okay. When they talk about the future, they use less elaborate descriptions. Furthermore, they seem to think less far into the future, and psychological testing reveals that they use fewer future-tense verbs when asked to finish incomplete sentences. Interestingly, suicidal individuals do not seem to spend time thinking of *negative* things that might happen in the future.[27] Instead, their thinking has a marked absence of any positive events they are looking forward to; it reflects a sense of hopelessness arising from the prospect of few positive events. Moreover, those who are suicidal have no difficulty in naming the sorts of things that other people are likely to be looking forward to, which may act to amplify the feelings of despair that they have when thinking about their own future.[28]

This hopelessness about the future plays a central role in suicidal behaviour. Many studies report that hopelessness is more closely related than depression to suicidal behaviour. People seem able to bear depression, so long as they are able to think the future might improve, but if they begin to feel hopeless, the risk of suicidal behaviour rises. If a person harms themselves on one occasion, the chance they will repeat the behaviour within the next six months is higher if they are more hopeless at the time of the first attempt. Even more worryingly, such highly hopeless individuals are at greater risk of completing suicide over the following ten years.[29]

But what is hopelessness? A study I conducted with research clinical psychologist Professor Andrew MacLeod examining the relative importance of positive and negative anticipation in hopelessness confirmed that attempted suicide patients were less able to think of future positive events, but showed no difference from controls in being able to think of future negative events. Importantly, we also found that this problem with thinking of positive things in the future was just as true for the immediate future (the next day and week) as for the long-term future (a year and ten years). The fact that highly hopeless people lack short-term plans, as well as the long-term means to achieve their goals, is important for therapy. Anyone would feel overwhelmed by hopelessness that stretched far into the future, and it may be helpful to realise that the same blankness about the distant future also affects the sense of what will happen in the next few days.

Trying to find some small specific thing to look forward to over the next few days may feel more doable than thinking of larger goals over the next few years.

Further research by Andrew MacLeod and colleagues has replicated this finding, and shown that the inability to imagine positive things that may happen in the future is not simply due to the presence of depression in attempted suicide patients.[30] More recently, Rory O'Connor and colleagues found that positive future thinking was a better predictor of recovery in the months following a suicide attempt than Beck's Hopelessness Scale (a commonly used assessment tool that gauges a person's level of hopelessness about the future) or measures of anxiety and depression.[31]

REASONS FOR LIVING

Some years ago an American professor of psychology, Marsha Linehan, and her colleagues developed a Reasons for Living inventory.[32] (Some of the main items from her scale can be seen in the box on page 93.) Compared to both the general population and psychiatric controls, attempted suicide patients endorse fewer important reasons for living.

The importance of knowing about such reasons for living is that individuals may be very motivated to commit or attempt suicide, yet do not do so because they have reasons for staying alive. Reasons for dying may vary independently from reasons for living, and both need to be taken into account. There is particular danger when someone who has long been suicidal suddenly finds he or she has lost their reasons for living (e.g. their children, partner, religious faith).

Reasons for Living

- Survival and coping beliefs: *'I still have many things left to do'*
- Responsibility to family or friends: *'It would hurt my family too much and I would not want them to suffer'*
- Child-related concerns: *'I want to watch my children as they grow'*
- Fear of suicide: *'I am afraid of the unknown'*
- Fear of social disapproval: *'Other people would think I am weak and selfish'*
- Moral objections to suicide: *'My religious beliefs forbid it'*

Why do suicidal people have problems thinking about positive things that might happen in the future, which might give them a reason for living? An obvious answer is that poorer circumstances and reduced opportunities mean they do actually have less to look forward to. Poorer upbringing, stressful events, marital and family disputes, poverty and unemployment all feature in the lives of many such people. A poorer outlook for the future may be realistic in many cases. But our research has found that hopelessness adds significantly to the burden. Not everyone who has had such stress in their life is suicidal.

Work by psychologist Silvia Hepburn and colleagues in Oxford showed that positive future thinking is also very dependent on current mood. It seems that, for any of us, small increases in depression or sadness alter our view of the future, reducing our ability to come up with positive things that may happen. For those whose lives are also full of problems, this adds an additional burden.[33]

People differ widely in the extent to which their mind translates specific stress events into the general feeling that nothing can be done – a sense of helplessness that goes much wider than the original situation. It is the over-generalisation from one situation (that may indeed have been impossible to do anything about) to others (that might be solvable) which is at the root of hopelessness. If a person feels that 'nothing can be done' about the second situation, they either take no action or they give up too early. There is then a self-fulfilling prophecy ('I said nothing would help, and nothing has'), which serves only to increase the sense of helplessness about any new situations.

The result is that such people may try to disengage from thinking about the future, but reluctant to let go, they have what Andrew MacLeod calls 'painful engagement' – a state where they have goals for the future, yet, despite believing those goals are not likely to come about, they are unable to let go of them because they believe they can never be happy without them.[34] In this state, they are less liable to become aware of any future possibilities for happiness or to make plans which could bring about positive events. So, whereas negative events appear to play a major role in the onset of suicidal feelings and hopelessness, whether people are able to anticipate positive events is important in determining how quickly they can recover from hopelessness.

When we think about the future, we also often think about the goals that we are trying to achieve and how, when we achieve them, we will feel good about ourselves. Rory O'Connor and colleagues[35] have shown that how we react when we realise that a goal is *not* achievable is related to suicidal behaviour. For young people, if they are reluctant to let go of these unachievable goals and at the same time they do not engage in new ones, their risk of repeat self-harm increases. For older adults, although they may have given up on unattainable goals, if they have not also engaged in new goals, they too are more likely to self-harm. If we are worried about someone, we should think about the reasons they have to live – what it is that 'gets them out of bed' each morning.

As part of her doctoral work at Oxford, psychologist Emily Hargus found that in addition to the reasons for living that Marsha Linehan had first described, many people say that what stopped them harming themselves when they felt suicidal was the sense that these feelings would pass, or that 'it was the depression speaking', so they found a way not to take it all so personally. This ability to 'stand back' and to take a 'decentred' perspective towards one's darkest inner thoughts and feelings may turn out to be a really important hallmark of those therapies that are most helpful in guiding people through difficult times and towards greater wellbeing and peace.

EMOTIONAL EXPERIENCE

There is a strong, convincing relationship between emotional experience and suicidal behaviour. Interestingly, the emotions typical of individuals who *attempt* suicide may be different from those of individuals who *die* by it. While both attempted and completed suicide are linked to depression, non-fatal suicidal behaviour appears to be related to anger whereas suicide may be more related to apathy or an absence of strong emotions. Attempted suicide patients are more angry, hostile and irritable compared to non-suicidal psychiatric patients and the general population, both before the attempt and after. Often, the relationship with close family, friends and partners has deteriorated into hostility, demandingness and conflict, especially in adolescence.[36] In contrast, persons who commit suicide seem to have been less angry, appearing apathetic and/or indifferent. Suicidal individuals appear unable to regulate their own emotional responses or experiences of emotional pain.

This does not mean that such suicidal behaviour is merely an expression of hostility or manipulation intended to harm or get back at others. For many, the very experience of intense anger, especially if it is ongoing and they cannot seem to control it, is painful and intolerable.

EMOTION REGULATION AND SELF-CUTTING

Self-cutting as a form of self-harm has often been dealt with separately, since people who harm themselves in this way have appeared to many clinicians to be a special group, and this form of self-harm has even been termed 'non-suicidal self-injury' to distinguish it from other forms of self-harm that are deemed to have greater suicidal intent. It used to be the case that people who harmed themselves by self-cutting were a small minority, accounting for about 10 per cent of hospital-treated self-harm episodes. However, a careful analysis of recent data from Ireland reveals that 14 per cent of self-harm in women, and 23 per cent in men, is self-cutting. Similar trends can be seen in the data from Oxford, where in 2002 self-injury alone was evident in 14 per cent of self-harm in women and 18 per cent of men, representing a substantial increase over previous years. Self-harm in the community is also common. Indeed, large-scale studies of adolescents suggest that approximately 10 per cent of 15–16-year-olds have self-harmed, most commonly by self-cutting, and the vast majority have done so in the past twelve months.[37] Adolescent girls are three times more likely to self-harm in this way than boys.

Although the cutting may not appear to be serious (and may even come and go as a temporary 'trend' in high schools), repeated attempts to self-harm in this way may be associated with other personality problems: impulsivity, instability both in emotion (especially anger) and in interpersonal relationships (experienced as very intense). Individuals concerned are extremely sensitive to stress, especially that arising from interpersonal problems, and are particularly prone to look for any signs that others are abandoning them, reacting to the situation as if the abandonment were already complete.

In fact, to call such behaviour 'non-suicidal' is misleading, since there is a strong association between such 'non-suicidal self-injury' and suicidal behaviour: over a third of people who self-cut say that they had engaged in such behaviour while actually experiencing suicidal thoughts.[38] Even more importantly, for those who cut themselves seriously enough to attend hospital, there is a high risk of eventual suicide.[39]

If such unstable emotion and relationships dominate the person's life, they may be said to have a 'borderline personality disorder'. The 'borderline' category refers to those who show impulsive self-damaging behaviour, unstable and intense interpersonal relationships, inappropriate and intense anger, problems with the experience of self (frequent crises of self-identity), extremely unstable emotions, chronic feelings of emptiness or boredom and intolerance of being alone. They are desperate to have company, but may treat their companions with so much intensity (clinging alternating with anger) that they are left alone again very soon. Their physically self-damaging acts often occur after (or during) dissociative states (e.g. out-of-body experiences, experienced very negatively).

In the most extreme cases, all sense of self (of being a voluntary agent, having personal memories and a body) disintegrates. In the resulting 'out-of-body' experience, the scene is viewed from another angle, as observer rather than as participant. Experiences of alien control, and of hallucinations, may also occur following extreme or long-lasting stress associated with such a failure to control emotion that it simply escalates catastrophically. Such experiences occur for the first time spontaneously under extreme stress (such as sexual abuse, often found in the background of the most severe cases). Once such a dissociative experience has occurred, however, the threshold for the recurrence of such a phenomenon is lowered: it can be reactivated under conditions of future (and often lesser) stress.

People who cut themselves often report that the cutting is the only way they know to stop the intense feelings they are experiencing. One adolescent girl said it felt as if her head would explode unless she did something to stop it. She knew that cutting would stop it and put her back in touch with herself and her body. But what explains the catastrophic escalation of emotion that often precedes self-cutting? To understand this we need to understand that negative emotion often results from breaking the rules one has set for oneself.

Consider the situation in which a person has been punished in the past for the expression of emotion. In relatively mild cases, this occurs every time a parent tells a child to 'pull yourself together'. The child may learn the lesson, 'It is shameful to display your emotions.' Or, in the most extreme case, a similar thing may happen in sexual abuse by an adult, where a child has been threatened with punishment if he or she becomes upset. In both the mild and the severe case, there is conflict between the expression of emotion and its suppression in order to avoid future punishment.

In later life, when the person experiences emotional turmoil, the very fact of feeling emotion is breaking one of their rules. But breaking the rules causes more emotion, which then leads to attempts to suppress it. The result is a rapid escalation of negative emotion arising from such a feedback loop: the expression of emotion itself violates a goal ('do not feel or show emotion'), but the consequence of violating any goal is increased emotion. This leads to people *feeling* upset, but telling themselves they *should not feel upset*. Notice again how the escalation of the intense emotion and the entrapment that it creates arise from the way someone *reacts* to early signs of emotional disturbance. The attempt to stop feeling something backfires, and makes more 'adhesive' the very thing that the person wants to get rid of. Telling oneself 'I should not be feeling like this' is one of the 'invalidation strategies' that maintains the very emotion it is designed to abolish, identified by Marsha Linehan in her treatment of people who suffer from 'borderline' symptoms. Linehan has also developed a number of specific strategies for dealing, in a non-harmful way, with the escalation of emotion for those who feel the urge to damage themselves as a way to escape emotional intensity. As part of her therapy, she may advise a patient to hold an ice cube in each hand until it melts. The pain of the cold ice is often sufficient substitute for self-cutting, but without the physical damage.

CONCLUDING REMARKS

Several psychological factors contribute to increased risk of non-fatal suicidal acts, often by adding to the burden of already stressful lives. Suicidal behaviour is associated with poor problem-solving ability, particularly a struggle with active problem-solving, and with difficulty in recollecting events from the past in sufficient detail to help solve current interpersonal crises. It is also associated with hopelessness, the inability to imagine future positive occurrences (even for the next day, never mind the following weeks, months or years). Finally, those who are prone to feel suicidal have trouble regulating their emotion, and it is particularly tragic that such difficulty may partly arise from the attempts to control emotion which then backfire.

CHAPTER SIX

Rational and Assisted Suicide, Euthanasia and Martyrdom

The last few years of the twentieth century and the first few years of the twenty-first have witnessed a radical shift in attitudes to life and death that has had a great impact on society's view of suicide. Increasing secularisation in some parts of the world has led to greater tolerance of assisting suicide as a legitimate means to end a life that is felt by the person to be over. In contrast to growing secularisation, escalating religious fervour in other groups across the world has led to a resurgence of the use of suicide as a weapon of war, calling it martyrdom. In this chapter, I will explore both tendencies. We start with assisted suicide and euthanasia, taking up the story in the 1990s when changes started to gather pace.

EUTHANASIA AND ASSISTED SUICIDE

In the United States the state of Oregon was one of the first to allow assisted suicide. The legal change had been the result of a long-fought battle in the courts. A state referendum in 1993 had been narrowly in favour of allowing assisted suicide, and in 1994 the state agreed to allow it. The proposed move caused a great deal of controversy, and the decision was blocked. The law did eventually change in 1997, and the 'Death with Dignity Act' was passed. This allowed patients of sound mind to request a prescription for a lethal dose of medication. Two doctors must confirm a diagnosis of terminal illness with no more than six months to live. Two witnesses, one a non-doctor unrelated to the patient, must confirm the patient's request. The patient must also be notified of alternatives to assisted death, including hospice care. The request must be repeated after fifteen days. In a 1997 case, the Supreme Court ruled that no right to assisted suicide exists, but that states could decide whether to allow assisted suicides to take place. During the first six years after the Oregon law took effect, 171 Oregonians died by doctor-assisted suicide.

Agreeing with the move towards such a change, a 47-year-old man suffering from AIDS said, 'Whose life is it anyway? It should be between me, my God and my doctor.' Elsewhere, a woman who two years previously had been told she would not live argued against the measure. She was now well again, but said that at the time she was so depressed she would have asked a doctor to end her life.

The Catholic Church in the state vigorously opposed the change in the law, and continues to campaign against it. It argues that it is putting the weak and the vulnerable at risk.

Developments in this area are occurring at some speed. Responding to increasing liberalisation of the state laws in the USA, Esther Fein of the *New York Times* posed a stark question: 'Will the right to die become the duty to die?'

Let us look more closely at the arguments for and against.

The word *euthanasia* (from the Greek words *eu* and *thanatos*) literally means 'easy or (gentle) death'. It was declared unethical by the World Medical Association in 1950, and to understand why we have to see its background. Two forms of euthanasia are normally distinguished. The first is *compulsory euthanasia*, or 'mercy killing', done without the consent of the person concerned, and mostly applied to grossly deformed children. For example, a Dutch gynaecologist in 1994 admitted killing a three-day-old girl at her parents' request. Her brain was only partly developed, she had spina bifida and partial paralysis, her limbs were malformed, and the doctor judged that she faced a life of constant pain.

The usually cited problem with this is that it constitutes a 'slippery slope' and violates the fundamental right to life, this being backed up by religious people's belief in life as God-given. However, a distinction is often made between an analgesic and lethal dosage of pain relief. An *analgesic dose* may have the unintended effect of shortening life, but a *lethal dose* has the direct intention of shortening life (the ethical doctrine of 'double effect' allows the first, but not the second).

The second form of euthanasia is *voluntary euthanasia*. Here, a person of sound mind asks that their life should be ended in the event of their becoming a victim of irreversible illness. Advocates (e.g. the Hemlock Society in the United States or members of Dignity in Dying in the UK) maintain that, with safeguards, the law should permit it and people should be supplied with the means to take their own life or a doctor should be authorised to end their life, provided the request is made before witnesses.[1]

The difficulty here is the assumption that we have the right to decide over our own life or death absolutely. The argument from these groups suggests that we 'own' our own lives. This argument has a long history.

Historical background

In 1695 Charles Gilden, searching to justify the death of his friend Charles Blount, attempted to put Blount's death in the context of Stoic philosophy and dealt head-on with some of the classical arguments against suicide. Whereas Aristotle had argued that self-killing injured the state and was illegal even when no decree specifically forbade it (see Chapter One), Gilden denied that society had the right to stop a man killing himself any more than it could rightfully prevent him emigrating. 'Now if I can leave any one particular Body Politick I have the same right to leave another and so on through all those of the World, and then by consequence I offend not, if by my Death I take myself away from all.'

Pythagoras' view was that men were put on earth like soldiers at their post. It was therefore 'desertion' to end one's own life. Gilden points out that, first, a simile is not an argument, and, second, the simile is inexact since soldiers enlist willingly in the army in which they serve. Human beings do not choose to be born.

In the Middle Ages, Thomas Aquinas (1225–74) said that God had instilled in humans an instinctual desire to preserve their own lives. Thus, suicide violated natural law. Gilden argued that this was not so – rather, that suicide was consistent with 'the precepts of Nature and Reason'. Human nature cannot desire the continuance of pain and suffering, so a life of such pain should be allowed to be ended. To end one's life in such circumstances is, therefore, a greater good than self-preservation. It cannot therefore be contrary to natural law.

The case against suicide eventually lost its power to stop the inexorable march of change towards the secularisation and medicalisation of suicide. The arguments of the philosopher David Hume in his essay 'On Suicide', written in the early 1750s, were particularly telling. The essay was suppressed and Hume was forced to withdraw it from a print run of the *Five Dissertations* in which it was to appear. Nevertheless, it did circulate and proved to be a robust statement of the secular view.

Hume argued, first, that inasmuch as one believed in the providence of a Deity, this 'providence appears not immediately in any operation, but governs everything by those general and immutable laws that have been established from the beginning of time'. Second, human life and death do not depend on God, but rather on 'the general laws of matter and motion'. Third, it is not valid to argue that men and women are 'owned' by God, since people come into being through natural processes of reproduction. God no more owns us than do our parents. Fourth, people who commit suicide cannot break the laws of nature since all our powers (including those that empower us to take our own lives) are natural faculties. So even employing them to kill oneself, one cannot 'encroach upon the plan of his providence or disorder the Universe'. Finally, Hume conceded that humans display a 'natural horror of death', but this does not thereby imply that such horror represents a 'general law of matter and motion'. Although such a horror might explain why suicide is not more common, it does not have the authority that natural-law theorists such as Aquinas implied.

Hume was consistent with other thinkers of the eighteenth century who wished to base their ethics on social rather than religious grounds. In this respect he needed to meet head-on the argument that somebody who commits suicide commits a wrong act because they let down society. Hume argued that 'a man who retires from life does no harm to society; he only ceases to do good; which, if it is an injury, is of the lowest kind'. The important calculation is to balance the good to society against the harm the suffering person sustains by continuing to live. Where the suffering person has grown so infirm as to become a burden to society, Hume concludes that suicide is a service which has benefits: 'resignation of life must not only be innocent, but laudable'.

What would Hume, as an empiricist, have made of the evidence which has now emerged about the aftermath of suicide? In many cases, suicide appears to have such a devastating effect on the survivors that, if it were only the balance of suffering one were examining, one could conclude that suicide was not ethically justifiable. By confining the argument to people undergoing unbearable suffering, one may, to some extent, clarify the ethical dilemma for the individual, but this does not clarify whether suicide is justified when other people's feelings are taken into account. People who are suicidal seem to have severe tunnel vision, imperceptible to themselves, in which they cannot see the awful consequences of their action for others. But in the case of most assisted suicide, it is suggested, these awful consequences are avoided: the person decides to seek help to ensure a better and more peaceful death at a time of their own choosing, with the permission of their closest families.

Nevertheless, anxiety about assisted suicide has a long history. Indeed, we might say that the field of medicine was founded on the need to separate life-enhancing treatments from more superstitious beliefs that would allow the person to die in some circumstances. Physicians are taught to cure and to relieve suffering. The Hippocratic Oath states that physicians will use treatment to *help* the sick according to ability and judgement, that they will *never* use it to injure people or wrong them. Psychologists are taught to help people find their way through the intolerable burdens of living. But we have no ultimate power to prevent our patients and clients harming themselves. In most cases the law will not require people to accept medical or psychological treatment against their will. Provided a sufferer has received information from a physician and can give informed consent, there is no legal obligation on a person to accept medical treatment.

Legal support for assisted suicide

The Netherlands has led the world in allowing doctors greater freedom to decide. In 1995 television audiences throughout the world were able to watch a Dutch doctor in a television documentary, *Death on Request*. Dr Wilfred van Oyjen said that he helped people with such a 'good death' three or four times a year. The film featured a man who had developed Lou Gehrig's disease, which brings about incurable degenerative wasting of the muscles. His feet and legs became paralysed first, then his right shoulder and arm, then his face. He and his family realised that, unless some decisive action was taken, he faced death by suffocation, as the weakening muscles of his chest finally collapsed.

His requests for euthanasia were repeated as the guidelines in Holland prescribe (a voluntary, well-considered and lasting request to die). The guidelines also prescribe that there must be no other solution acceptable to the patient, that the time and manner of the death must not cause unnecessary suffering to others (such as next of kin) and that the doctor must prescribe and administer the right drugs. Dr van Oyjen is one of those who feel it would be letting his patient down to refuse such a request.

This contrasts with the situation in the United Kingdom, where it is accepted that doctors often use the 'doctrine of double effect' to deal with situations of unbearable suffering. This permits doctors to use drugs in sufficient quantities to relieve suffering, even if that hastens death, so long as they do not intend to kill. According to Dignity in Dying (formerly the Voluntary Euthanasia Society, Exit), one survey of British doctors showed that 50 per cent had been asked by a patient for help to die. Of these, one-third said they had complied.

This is not ethical, according to Dr van Oyjen. Such surreptitious euthanasia can take several weeks, and is dishonest. It also means that the patient can die in delirium brought about by huge doses of morphine. 'I am giving people the possibility to make choices. What kind of quality of life, and death, do they want? Death is not always awful. With a good doctor, death can be faithful, like a good friend.' Perhaps most importantly, the doctor can choose the right moment, when he judges that the patient and their family are most at peace with the ending of life. Dr van Oyjen will take hours, days if necessary, waiting for the right moment after the decision has been taken. He feels it essential to get close to the family if a 'good death' is to be brought about.

When the arguments are expressed in this way, they seem very compelling. And despite the fact that many people still say that assisted suicide is either intrinsically wrong or socially undesirable, all over the world the legal frameworks are being put in place that allow it to take place.

In the United States, two states have followed Oregon and introduced similar legislation: Washington State in 2008, Vermont in 2013. Others, however, remain more doubtful. In 2004 and 2006 the California State Legislature considered whether to go down the same route, but decided against. In Massachusetts, Michigan and Maine, voters have voted against assisted-suicide proposals. Legislation to legalise the practice has also failed in Hawaii and Wyoming.

There are several European countries where 'assisting a suicide' is not on the statute books as a crime: Switzerland, the Netherlands, Belgium, France, Germany, Sweden and Finland. In England and Wales it remains illegal for anyone to aid someone to take their own life under any circumstances (with up to fourteen years in prison as the penalty), but the courts have a history of being lenient. In December 1994 the courts decided not to prosecute a man who had administered a lethal dose of morphine to his terminally ill wife. In this case the Voluntary Euthanasia Society (now Dignity in Dying) was careful to distance itself from supporting the man. They pointed out that there was no evidence that the wife had agreed to her life being ended in this way. In November 2004 the High Court in England allowed a man to take his terminally ill wife to Switzerland where the organisation Dignitas advised her on how she could take her own life. Although this is legal, the Swiss at that time expressed concern about nationals from other countries coming to Switzerland to do something that would be illegal in their own countries. The debate continues, and many cases of UK nationals going to Dignitas have resulted in police investigations, but none of these (at the time of writing – 2013) has so far involved any criminal charges. Data from the Dignitas clinic shows that over 1000 people used it between 1998 and 2009, with over 50 per cent (563 people) coming from Germany, 134 from the UK and 112 from Switzerland itself.

In the UK in 2010 Debbie Purdy, who has progressive multiple sclerosis, won her legal battle for guidance over whether her husband would be prosecuted if he took her to Dignitas to die. The Director of Public Prosecutions for England and Wales stated that although assisting suicide remained illegal, if those assisting were acting from wholly compassionate motives, then in practice no prosecution would follow. The guidance laid out a range of issues to be taken into account when deciding whether or not to prosecute, such as whether the victim had reached a 'voluntary, clear, settled and informed' decision and had the mental capacity to do so. All cases would still be investigated by the police, and if there was any evidence that the person had been pressurised or encouraged in any way to commit suicide, or if there was any evidence of a history of abuse against them, a prosecution would be likely.

Arguments against euthanasia and assisted suicide

The arguments still go on, and it is important that all sides are heard. This section considers some of the arguments against assisted suicide.

Consent

Some people make a distinction between euthanasia and assisted suicide. Euthanasia usually means that someone else (such as a physician) takes deliberate action, such as an injection or withdrawing medical treatment, to end a person's life. Assisted suicide usually refers to someone else providing the means – e.g. medicine – to allow a patient to end their *own* life. Of course, in cases where someone's illness or condition physically prevents him or her from taking action, the two definitions merge.

One argument against euthanasia is that a terminally ill patient may not be in a state, at the point near death, to be able to withdraw consent. Suppose someone were to agree, before witnesses, family and doctor that, in the event of breakdown of bodily function, active steps should be taken to end their life. Once they have deteriorated, how could they ever withdraw that consent should they change their mind? The right (at any time) to withdraw consent from or change one's mind about a medical procedure is seen by many to be paramount. Yet, with the very weak, this right may be denied because of their frailty.

Slippery-slope arguments

The World Medical Association's decision in 1950 to declare euthanasia unethical was made on the grounds that it would undermine trust between patient and doctor, and between patient and family, just when they are at their most vulnerable. For every time a doctor assists someone to die to ease their burden, or that of their families, there arises the possibility that someone, somewhere, will seek the death of someone for the wrong reasons. This is the slippery-slope argument, which asserts that a small change to allow assisted suicide would have wider and undesirable consequences. The first of the two most often cited undesirable consequences is where old and infirm people are seen as a burden on their families – even more urgent at a time when there is much in the news about elderly people being a drain on society because of increased life expectancy.

It is not possible to speak of general policies of euthanasia without this being raised as a specific issue in many individual households. Talk of euthanasia in a household where there is an older relative could fuel talk about them being a burden. In an article on euthanasia,[2] the prominent campaigner for assisted suicide Derek Humphry quoted Richard Lamm, ex-governor of Colorado, who made a speech about the rationing of healthcare costs, suggesting the elderly took more than their fair share. Humphry quotes Lamm to show that economics will force this onto the public agenda sooner rather than later. But many would consider that where economic considerations are brought in is when the euthanasia argument is at its weakest.

The second most often cited undesirable consequence is that people who are depressed will make what appears to be a rational request to end their life. In a controversial case in 1994 in the Netherlands, a doctor assisted a woman to die who appeared, by all accounts, to have been depressed. This raised an important issue. People may consider it is never justified to assist the suicide of someone who has a condition, a symptom of which is itself a wish to die. Nevertheless, the Dutch Supreme Court in 1994 ruled that, in exceptional cases, physician-assisted suicide might be justified for patients with unbearable mental suffering, but without physical illness.

Are such slippery slopes likely to occur? Those who argue against euthanasia say the slippery slope is already taking place in the Netherlands. By 2013 about 2300 people were opting to die by assisted suicide in the Netherlands each year, out of a population of around 17 million. Guidelines issued for doctors are being overstepped, opponents claim, second opinions are regularly abandoned, and when a euthanasia death is reported, there is rarely an investigation. Indeed, those who oppose euthanasia allege that many euthanasia deaths are not recorded even on the death certificate, all evidence in these matters falling under the control of the physician. This, it is suggested, does not provide satisfactory safeguards against abuse. A study of these issues in 1997 attempted to estimate the number of assisted suicides in *psychiatric* practice in the Netherlands. Over 500 psychiatrists (over half of all psychiatrists in the Netherlands) participated in the study. Thirty-seven per cent (205) had received requests for assisted suicide during the period of the study, though the majority had not complied. Their study concluded that around 320 requests were being made each year, and these resulted in between two and five assisted suicides being carried out.[3]

No man is an island

Another argument against 'rational suicide', assisted or not, is the 'no-man-is-an-island' argument (it is ironic that the quote comes from a meditation by John Donne, who believed that suicide was justifiable and argued so strongly in *Biathanatos*.)

One version of this argument is that by ending our life we deny our family and society the opportunity to fulfil their duty of care to us. Another version is more simple: those who would justify committing suicide on the grounds that their life is their own property are failing to take into account that each of our lives is shared by parents, brothers and sisters, partners, children, neighbours and friends, colleagues at work and so on. Not to take account of their reactions to our death, or, worse, to make assumptions (e.g. that they would be relieved of a burden) without checking, is hardly to take a 'rational' decision.

Research shows how suicide affects family, friends and community in enormous ways. It can be the worst of all deaths in its impact on survivors: it causes grief they may never resolve and creates guilt in a way no other death does, even raising the risk of suicide in others. Families are put under tremendous strain as they seek to come to terms with the death, each family member trying to do so in his or her own, often lonely, way. A truly rational approach to self-killing or assisted suicide must take account of all these things. If a person says, 'But no one would mind if I ended my life' or 'People would be better off if I died', then it would not be appropriate to call it rational unless they have checked whether their beliefs are true.

Rational versus depressive suicide: Arthur Koestler

Perhaps the most difficult dilemma is to distinguish between those who ask for suicide because they are depressed, and those who ask for it when 'of sound mind'. Take one often-cited example of someone who decided rationally to kill himself: Arthur Koestler, who died by suicide with his wife Cynthia in 1983. Because he was vice-president of the Voluntary Euthanasia Society and wrote a preface to its publication *Guide to Self-deliverance*, he is commonly said to be the paradigm case of rational suicide.

Yet in his own prolific writings he shows that he suffered much from depression, punctuated by bouts of mania. His uncle had committed suicide, and in his autobiographical book, *Arrow in the Blue*, he tells of his own troubled life.[4] He was an only child, born when his mother was 35 years old. She was very possessive, yet capricious in her moods. There were often abrupt changes from effusive tenderness to violent temper. He talks about being tossed from 'the emotional climate of the Tropics to the Arctic and back again'. Plagued by guilt and often feeling he deserved to be punished, he felt bewildered and rejected, and suffered suicidal depressions and recurrent suicidal fantasies. He attempted suicide twice, once at 29 years old by coal gas, and a second time in prison in Lisbon by an overdose.

At the end, suffering from leukaemia and Parkinson's disease, he killed himself and his wife did likewise. However, one week before they did so, Cynthia told a friend that Arthur was having hallucinations. Cynthia herself had a family history of suicide, her father having ended his own life when she was 10 years old. It is also clear from her writings that she had seriously contemplated it herself before. In a seminal paper in 1986[5] Professor Robert Goldney of Adelaide University points out the irony that, had Koestler owned a copy of the *Guide to Self-deliverance* in the 1930s, the world would have been denied the vast majority of his writings.

Rational and irrational: can a distinction be made?

Joseph Richman, Professor Emeritus at the Albert Einstein College of Medicine, New York, argues that to drive a wedge between rational suicide and other forms of suicide is illusory.[6] All suicides have features in common. There is usually evidence of a crisis, of loss and separation; there is the role of others. To make a dichotomy between the sick and the healthy obscures the issue. When there is a crisis around illness, loss and death, all unresolved problems and conflicts of the ill person come to the fore and can be seen as overwhelming.

Many believe that being terminally ill is itself sufficient reason to want to die. The terminally ill find that their depression is often seen as natural and therefore goes untreated. Yet, while deep sadness is natural, depression is more than sadness. It brings with it a sense of guilt, of being a burden, of worthlessness and a feeling of failure. Further, the person often believes that no one will want to see them in their condition, so there is no point in contacting anybody. They may feel guilty about things they have done or about situations or relationships that remain unresolved, and the depression will ensure 'it is not worth' trying to resolve them.

Is there a role for therapy here? The evidence suggests there is. People can, in fact, overcome their depression even within the context of a terminal illness – evidence the hospice movement has been citing for some years.[7] Do people seeking assisted suicide need a psychotherapist? Proponents of rational suicide discourage people from seeking help on the grounds that they are not mentally ill. This is probably right, but you don't have to be crazy to see a therapist any more than you have to be stupid to go to school.[8]

All wishes to die represent in some degree a problem perceived as insoluble except through death. In that situation one needs to respect a person's autonomy. But personal autonomy should not be confused with isolation and loss of social cohesion. How can we judge whether or not someone is in control of their own actions? Depression leaves little room for argument. We know it affects chemical pathways in the brain and results in a lack of energy, lack of pleasure and lack of interest in social activities and social contacts. It also results in recurrent thoughts of death or suicide. Compounding this is the sense of hopelessness that occurs in many depressions: a foreshortening of the future and an inability to see anything to look forward to. Depression therefore leaves little choice. It pushes the person, impels them to certain actions. It is not open to reasonable argument.

Proponents of rational suicide say that people have chosen this option and are not depressed. In that case they must expect to be able to discuss realistically the pros and cons of their actions. They must also expect that their reasons will be questioned. The major presupposition that each of us has an overall right to decide on our own life can be questioned, and only where the full social and family context is taken into account can it ever be justified deliberately to shorten a life.

MARTYRDOM

The definition of martyrdom is closely tied to the group that shares the belief of the one who dies, as has become tragically clear following September the eleventh 2001. A suicide bombing by an Islamic fundamentalist may be called martyrdom by his or her own group, but to everyone else it is merely terrorism. Each group, religious or political, has its martyrs. They differ in a number of respects from the types of suicide so far considered.

Most people who commit suicide are depressed when they do so; they see death as the end to their suffering. One of two feelings usually predominates in the mind of the person who is suicidal in this depressive sense, and both stem from hopelessness. The first is that they have been abandoned by everyone; the second is that they are a burden to everyone, especially to those they love. Contrast this with suicide bombers who believe they are martyrs. They see hope, and believe in a cause. Although there are many different contexts for martyrdom, all martyrs believe that by their death they are bringing about some combination of the following gains: advancing a cause by inspiring members of their own group; harming the enemy; delivering others from suffering (but not suffering that has been caused by them, as in depressive suicide); and gaining entrance to an afterlife.

In this sense, martyrdom is a paradigm of Durkheim's altruistic suicide. These people kill themselves because they are totally submerged in their groups. Death for them is a duty. They are seen as making heroic sacrifices for the group or its leadership. In altruistic suicide, the individual's life is not their own property; their own goals of behaviour emanate from the external source, the group.

Is there a distinction between the suicide bomber and others who put their lives at risk (such as those who join the army) for what they believe in? There seems to be a continuum between altruistic suicide and other forms of altruism, in which a person risks his or her life for their group and is prepared to accept death as the unavoidable consequence of performing some act of bravery, charity, justice, mercy or piety. The difference is that, in the latter cases, the person does not will their own death. If there were any other way, they would take it.

Are suicide bombers, 'martyrs' to their own cause, psychiatrically disturbed – or is it simply belief in a cause that drives them on? Altruistic suicide is not performed through madness – the person, as far as we know, is in full possession of his or her faculties. Indeed, it would not have the impact it clearly does on the group if it were suspected that the person was mentally ill.

Is martyrdom always associated with religious faith? Belief in a deity is clearly an important component of some acts of martyrdom in that it provides a moral context. Most martyrs moreover have a belief in an afterlife, even when the belief in a god is not conventional. Those who took part in the mass suicide in Jonestown, Guyana, in November 1978, led by Jim Jones, believed in reincarnation. But they also believed that the revolutionary principles they stood for would achieve immortality through their deaths. Jones said, 'We are not committing suicide;

we are committing a revolutionary act.' The followers of David Koresh had also planned a mass suicide, with hand grenades, if he died during the battle with law-enforcement officers at Waco, Texas. One witness at the inquest said that following Koresh's death, 'We were all to be translated ... come out of our bodies and go to heaven.'

But not all the deaths that occurred or were planned in these contexts were suicide. Some people in Jonestown were murdered. Other suicides there appear to have been not so much altruistic as fatalistic. Many were malnourished as a result of a poor diet, and their emotional disturbance was heightened because the community thought it was under attack. In a chilling parallel, a witness from Waco said that if any follower had been afraid of killing themselves, another could do it for them with a shotgun.

Similar stories of suicide bombers being brainwashed into carrying out their missions, and coming to their senses before they activate their bomb, are becoming more common. In Afghanistan in January 2012, a thirteen-year-old boy was told that the bomb he was going to wear would only kill Americans, but that God would spare *him*. At the last moment he suddenly realised that this was not true, and gave himself up. Despite this, we need to take account of the fact that throughout history there have been instances of people being prepared to die a martyr's death for a bigger cause. The most famous cases are the kamikaze.

The kamikaze

Learning about the mind of the martyr seems impossible since they are not here to study. However, there are some 'wartime martyrs' who, though they volunteered to die, escaped death: Japanese kamikaze (literally 'divine tempest') pilots who survived when their planes were shot down on their way to a target in the Pacific and were awaiting recall to another suicide mission when the war ended.

By the last year of the war, the US Navy thought itself invincible in the Pacific, but the kamikaze shook its confidence. So keen were the young Japanese pilots to participate in this 'spirit of the Samurai' that some signed their papers in their own blood to try and increase chances of selection. By the end of 1944, over 500 kamikaze missions had been flown against the US Fleet, but Japan was still losing. A new elite, 'The Thunder Gods', was formed to pilot aircraft equipped with large missiles. These turned out to be too cumbersome and the pilots were shot down before they could reach their targets. The Thunder Gods were therefore asked to undertake a different sort of mission: to take ordinary planes and crash them into the fleet.

On 1 April 1945 the United States invaded Okinawa, and on the 6th, after an ominous silence, the US Fleet was attacked by up to 350 planes at a time. By the end of June, after about 2000 kamikaze missions, 36 Allied ships had been sunk, and ten times as many damaged; 500 Allied personnel were dead and 4800 wounded.

What was the motivation of the kamikaze pilots? By the accounts of those who remain, and their officers who assigned them, they had an attitude to death characteristic of many martyrs. First, they believed that obedience gave meaning to self-sacrifice. They had come to the point when to give up one's life for one's country was the highest honour. Second, they believed they were not going to 'die' at all; their souls would go to Yasakuni, a special place for those who die fighting for their country – a special place also reserved for the Emperor. As one said, 'Even if you did die, you felt you would still be alive to describe it.' The widows of these men paid their respects and went to honour their 'god-like' husbands.

But it wasn't always quite so straightforward for the pilots. People who interviewed them subsequently found that a different, more sombre mood sometimes emerged. Some appear to have brooded about their death, complaining that the waiting went on for ever. Others said it felt as if they were being sentenced to death. Still others questioned whether they had been in their right mind when they volunteered. They rejoiced for the camera, but harboured doubts off camera. They dealt with such feelings by reattributing any emotions to things other than the fear of dying. One pilot said that at the time he'd find himself crying in the night, but not because he was frightened. He couldn't say he really ever knew why he was crying. Perhaps it was because most kamikaze pilots never reached the age of twenty.

CONCLUDING REMARKS

Can suicide be rational? There is little doubt it can. Durkheim argued strongly in favour of this in 1897, and there is no reason to disagree. Many endorse the aims of those societies that promote euthanasia and assisted suicide as a rational, compassionate end to life. Many others have no difficulty accepting that there are situations, as in wartime, when there is a very thin line between those prepared to put their lives at risk for the good of their country and those who go out on a suicide mission. The picture that emerges is one of ambivalence in the face of death. Even with strong cultural support, religious beliefs and even legal support, there is no guarantee that the end of life will be easy to contemplate with equanimity. For those wishing to support their loved ones at the end of life, and to care for those who seek to take active steps to end their lives, there is a need for enormous patience, openness and compassion from the rest of us, whatever the circumstances, and whatever is finally decided is the right thing to do.

CHAPTER SEVEN

Psychodynamics, Biology and Genetics

There is no one reason why people kill themselves. Suicide is the final common pathway for many human problems. But there are also biological factors, and some of these may have a genetic component. I shall now build upon the discussion of psychiatric, social and psychological perspectives on suicide and attempted suicide to review psychoanalytic and biological perspectives.

PSYCHOANALYTIC PERSPECTIVES

The starting point for psychoanalytic work on suicide and attempted suicide is Freud's 1917 paper 'Mourning and Melancholia', the aim of which was to draw a comparison between severe depression and the normal experience of mourning following loss. In suicide, the life instinct is overcome by more powerful forces, leading to a reaction that is an even more extreme form of the self-deprecation found in depressed people. Mourning is a normal means of coping following loss of a loved person (the 'loved object'). (If you are new to psychoanalytic literature, it may be helpful to know that the word 'object' refers to a person or an internalised image of a person.) However, people who have lost others on whom they depended too much for their own sense of self (a 'narcissistic object-choice') find the experience of loss impossible to tolerate. The anger of normal grief is, for these people, a rage of murderous proportions. Identification with the lost object (internalisation) means that the object that is to be murdered becomes part of the ego.

> If one listens patiently to a melancholic's many and various self-accusations, one cannot in the end avoid the impression that often the most violent of them are hardly at all applicable to the patient himself, but that with insignificant modifications they do fit someone else, someone whom the patient loves or has loved or should love ... So we find the key to the clinical picture: we perceive that the self-reproaches are reproaches against a loved object (individual) which have been shifted away from it on to the patient's own ego ...
>
> There is no difficulty in reconstructing this process. An object-choice, an attachment of the libido to a particular person, had at one time existed; then owing to a real slight or disappointment coming from this loved person, the object-relationship was shattered. The result was not the normal one of a withdrawal of the libido from this object and a displacement of it on to a new one, but something different ...

> it was withdrawn into the ego. In this way, the object loss was transformed into an ego loss.[1]

Since outwardly directed reproaches towards the lost object are not possible, they turn into self-reproaches and the wish to harm oneself. When the rage is sufficiently intense, it will lead to strong urges towards self-destruction.

> If the love for the object – a love which cannot be given up though the object itself is given up – takes refuge in narcissistic identification, then the hate comes into operation on this substitutive object, abusing it, debasing it, making it suffer and deriving sadistic satisfaction from its suffering.
>
> It is this sadism alone that solves the riddle of the tendency to suicide which makes melancholia so interesting – and so dangerous ... No neurotic harbours thoughts of suicide which he has not turned back upon himself from murderous impulses against others ... The ego can kill itself ... if it is able to direct against itself the hostility which related to an object and which represents the ego's original reaction to objects in the external world.[2]

In a later discussion of suicide, Freud introduced the concept of the death instinct (Thanatos). He defined this as a drive, commonly seen in nature, to reinstate the former state of affairs, the return of all organic or living matter to its inorganic, unorganised state. This view sees life as a preparation for death, with the death instinct as a drive to its end. Freud used the concept to explain why the super-ego develops such harshness towards the ego in melancholia.

> We find that the excessively strong super-ego which has obtained a hold upon consciousness rages against the ego with merciless violence, as if it had taken possession of the whole of the sadism available in the person concerned. Following our view of sadism, we should say that the destructive component had entrenched itself in the super-ego and turned against the ego. What is now holding sway in the super-ego is, as it were, a pure culture of the death instinct, and in fact it often enough succeeds in driving the ego into death.[3]

At times Freud expressed uncertainty about the status of the death instinct he had invoked, saying he did not know how far he believed in it and would not seek to persuade others. However, he continued to find it a useful idea, eventually changing the concept of masochism from being simply the opposite of dominant aspects of sadism to a primary instinct in its own right; a basic drive towards subjection and submission, and in the most extreme form a drive to embrace death. (Chapter Eight will show how many of the same ideas have emerged in sociobiology.)

Later psychoanalytic writers have built upon Freud's observations. Menninger asserted that every suicide had three elements: the wish to kill (originating in the death instinct), the wish to be killed (originating in the super-ego's masochistic need for punishment) and the wish to die (originating in a relatively fundamental desire to return to the womb). Such approaches emphasise the aggressive nature of suicide, but careful attention to the fantasies of suicidal patients shows that aggressive impulses are not always the most prominent.

Patients speak about a wish to join a dead relative with whom they identify strongly. These reunion fantasies are not readily explained simply on the basis of self-directed aggression. They appear to result from libidinal rather than aggressive wishes, pleasurable rather than masochistic fantasies. Other patients have fantasies about rebirth following their own death, a rebirth they can hasten by destroying this self (compare the examples of martyrdom in Chapter Six). Still others appear to be looking for a sense of mastery, or even omnipotence, over an impossible situation, and their death is the only element in life that they feel they have retained control over. Some believe they will still, in some sense, be present after their death to 'see what happens next', and, in a spirit of revenge that is sometimes present as part of suicidal thoughts, able to experience pleasure in the distress their death might cause others. The inconsistency between death as escape into oblivion and a continued existence in which the pain of others can be experienced is not apparent to the suicidal person in their confusion.[4]

Object-relations approach

Freud had suggested that suicide was an attack on the love-object, now lost, that had been internalised. Child psychoanalyst Melanie Klein extended these ideas, suggesting that the person was motivated by the wish to preserve the good aspects of the internalised object (now a valued part of the self).[5] The inwardly directed attack was therefore aimed mainly at the bad part of the object. Since aggression mainly arose from the death instinct, there was a danger that such destructive forces might destroy a good object.

Early in a child's development, they are in a symbiotic relationship with their mother and the child's idea of self and of mother are not yet differentiated. Later there will come inevitable separation and individuation, where self and object are differentiated. What happens if this transition is not completed satisfactorily? One outcome might be that the person will tend to become involved in relationships where the other party is not treated as a separate and unique individual, but as part of the self. This choice of friend or partner has been called 'symbiotic object-choice', corresponding to the 'narcissistic object-choice', in Freud's writings.[6] Suicide, according to this analysis, involves not only ridding the self of bad internal objects, but recreating the connection with the earlier 'symbiotic mother' of pre-individuation infancy.

The hypotheses about suicidal behaviour that invoke fantasies about return to infantile dependence on the mother have been extensively developed by attachment theorists. According to Bowlby,[7] infants respond to even brief separations with distress, and if such separations and returns are not predictable or controllable, there develops a style of anxious and insecure attachments. These styles, resulting from the breakdown of the reciprocal interaction between child and primary care-giver, may persist, and can even affect the way the child, when grown up, relates to his or her own children.

Secure attachments in infancy are the primary means by which the child learns to regulate his or her own emotions. In the absence of mature self-regulatory structures, such children come to depend too much on others, or ideas about others that have been internalised, for comfort. They will become over-sensitive to abandonment; vulnerable to crises of aloneness which give way to self-contempt and murderous rage. Suicidal behaviour in this context can be seen as an interpersonal act, an (albeit maladaptive) means of procuring attachment, signalling distress to others in the environment and punishing them for their actual or perceived rejection of the person.

American psychoanalyst John Maltsberger summarises the sorts of ideas about death that might be apparent in the suicidal person:

- Suicide is a gateway leading into a dreamless sleep (nothingness).
- It will effect a reunion with someone or something which has been lost.
- It will be a way of escaping from a persecutory enemy, interior or exterior.
- It will destroy an enemy who seems to have taken up a place in the patient's body or some other part of him- or herself.
- It will provide a passage into another, better world.
- One can get revenge on someone else by abandoning him or her or by destroying his or her favourite possession (one's own body), and one can then watch him or her suffer from beyond the grave.[8]

An underlying theme is the idea that one's body is a prison from which suicide promises an escape – particularly true of those who suffer physical pain. Maltsberger advises therapists to assess the extent to which their suicidal clients have lost the capacity to tell whether or not their own body is a part of themselves: 'Do they feel at home in it and take it for granted as an integrated self aspect, or do they experience it as an alien cage in which they are confined, a cage belonging to, or even identified with, someone else?' This facet of the psychodynamics of suicide takes us a long way from simply seeing such death as an expression of anger turned towards the self. Importantly, it builds bridges to other approaches to suicide by raising the theme of suicide as a response to the inability to escape. Inescapable stress has biological consequences, which might be triggered by stress that is *believed* to be inescapable (which introduces psychological mechanisms).

BIOLOGICAL APPROACHES

> From the brain, and from the brain only, arise our pleasures, joys, laughters and jests, as well as our sorrows, pain, grief and tears ... It is the brain which makes us mad or delirious; inspires us with dread and fear, whether by night or day; brings sleeplessness, mistakes, anxieties, absent-mindedness, acts that are contrary to our normal habits. These things that we suffer from all come from the brain, including madness.

So wrote Hippocrates, who lived between 460 and 377 BC. He had, as this quote from his book *On Sacred Disease* shows, an approach to mental disorder that feels very modern.

To understand the possible role of the brain in general and suicidal depression in particular, we need to understand the role of neurotransmitters. Neurons (nerve cells, of which there are billions in the brain) typically consist of a cell body, dendrites (finely branched structures connected to the cell body) and axons. Electrical impulses are transmitted from one neuron to another by means of neurochemicals which bridge the gap at the point of contact between one cell and the next (the synapse). Across this synaptic gap, or cleft, neurotransmitters such as dopamine or norepinephrine travel, released from one neuron and triggering an electrical impulse at the 'receptor' of the next neuron. Brain scientists have so far discovered over fifty different types of neurotransmitter, each of which may act alone or in combination with others to serve different pathways in the brain.

One is at once able to see a number of ways in which the delicate balance of brain activity could go wrong. First, there may be too much or too little neurotransmitter present at the synapse. Second, the receptor of the 'receiving' neuron may be too dense or too sparse, so that even a normal amount of neurotransmitter has too much or too little effect. Third, there may be other neurochemicals that may block or excite the action of another, either inhibiting the neuron from firing as it should or facilitating its action.

For many years it has been believed that depression is associated with a depletion of certain neurotransmitters. Most interest has focused on norepinephrine and serotonin. A reduction of the activity in brain pathways which rely on these neurochemicals may be responsible for the changes in appetite, sleep and energy levels in depression. Antidepressant medication was thought to work by making more neurotransmitter available at the synapse, by blocking the reabsorption ('reuptake') into the presynaptic neurons. This relatively simple theory has always had a number of difficulties, the major problem being that the action of the antidepressant in blocking reuptake is relatively quick, but antidepressants take ten days to two weeks to have their therapeutic effects. Another problem is that more careful measurement of norepinephrine has shown it is not reduced in depressed patients, and may even be increased in some.[9]

Interest has therefore shifted away from simple ('too little neurotransmitter') theories to consider instead the changes that take place in the density and sensitivity of the receptors – how well these are able to respond to the amount of neurotransmitter available. Such changes at the receptor site take longer, and may explain why antidepressants take so long to begin to alleviate depressed mood. It is now believed that antidepressants alter the complex interaction between different inhibitory and facilitatory pathways.

In suicidal behaviour, the neurotransmitter serotonin has been thought to be involved. Evidence comes from a number of sources. Low levels of the product of the metabolism of serotonin (the 'metabolite', 5-HIAA) have been found in the cerebrospinal fluid (CSF) of suicide attempters, when measured after a lumbar puncture. Asberg and colleagues found this was true of people who used more violent means to harm themselves, consistent with parallel findings that reduced levels of serotonin or reduced metabolism of serotonin (not the same thing) are found in violent offenders – those who take their anger out on others.[10] Low levels of 5-HIAA in the cerebrospinal fluid are associated with suicidality and impulsivity both on behavioural and self-report measures, in depressed people and in patients with personality disorder, schizophrenia and alcoholism and in impulsive violent offenders.[11] This has given rise to the suggestion that serotonin affects tendencies to act with impulsive aggression, rather than being associated with the direction of such aggression. Studies suggest that the serotonergic involvement is with trait (permanent predisposition), rather than state (transient, situation-specific), features. Thus, some people have a lifelong tendency to behave in an impulsive way. Then, if depression produces a further temporary lowering in brain serotonin, there will be increased tendency to act impulsively in response to negative events.

If violent suicide is associated with abnormalities in the

serotonin pathways in the brain, might this be detected at post-mortem? Establishing the facts remains extremely difficult. The method by which someone has died (overdose, carbon-monoxide poisoning) can affect the physical state of the brain at death, and the delay before post-mortem also affects the chances of discovering subtle differences between suicide victims and controls. Error can also creep in through factors such as abnormal diet or drug and alcohol use.

However, most researchers agree that some sort of association between serotonin function and violence (either internally or externally directed) exists.[12] Relevant to this is the finding that murderers have a suicide rate several hundred times greater than people of the same age and sex who have not committed murder, and that people found guilty of violent and impulsive crimes, such as arsonists, have low serotonin levels and a very high incidence of violent suicide attempts. Crimes that are premeditated are not so closely associated with low serotonin levels, emphasising once again the importance of impulsivity.[13] Of course, all these groups tend to share other psychosocial risk factors, such as early loss, disrupted family background, alcohol and substance-abuse problems. What has not been established yet is whether biochemical studies have accounted for variance in the suicide statistics that cannot be accounted for in these other ways.

The fact that biological findings have crossed diagnostic boundaries (serotonin involvement is associated with violent suicidal behaviour in depressed people, those with a diagnosis of schizophrenia, alcoholics and those with a personality disorder) implies that suicidality should be assessed and treated in its own right, rather than relying on the treatment of the psychiatric disturbance in which it occurs. Another advantage of the biological approach is that it would provide a means by which genetic influences might have their effects. It is known that family history of suicide is associated with more serious and more thoroughly planned suicide attempts in men,[14] and this seems to suggest a role for genetic causation. It is to this that we now turn.

GENETIC INFLUENCES

Suicidal behaviour is more common in the relatives of completed suicides, suggesting a genetic component, but people related to each other commonly share much more than genes. They also share a similar environment, with all its stresses and difficulties. Furthermore, if a suicide has occurred in a family, there is the possibility of later imitation, and a feeling that the family is 'tainted' with a suicidal history which makes other members more likely to see this type of death as a way out of difficulties they themselves encounter.

Since identical twins share the same genetic make-up, such twins should be more alike with respect to suicidal tendencies than non-identical twins. In the past the evidence was contradictory, but further research is clarifying the picture.[15] One study found that identical twins had a concordance rate for suicide of 13.2 per cent (the percentage of twins who show the same behaviour as their other twin), compared with a concordance rate of 0.7 per cent in non-identical twins.[16] The balance of evidence favours higher concordance rates for suicide in identical twins.

A major single gene effect is unlikely. More likely is the combined effect of many genes which leads to an increased risk of suicide, but needs environmental triggers. These other effects are likely to outweigh the genetic effects. Most twins were 'discordant' with respect to suicidal behaviour (i.e. that is, one twin committed suicide, but not the other). Also, most of the suicides in the twins who were concordant (i.e. both committed suicide) had psychiatric disturbances known to be associated with suicide. If genes are involved, it remains to be seen whether what is inherited is a suicide gene (most unlikely) or a predisposition to psychological disturbance.

The studies most likely to be helpful are those that look for adoptees who commit suicide in later life. It is then possible to tease apart biological from environmental influences by looking at the suicide rate in biological versus adopted relatives. A study in Denmark identified 57 people who were adopted and later committed suicide, and studied the suicide rate in their adoptive and biological parents, siblings and half-siblings (269 relatives in all).[17] They selected a control group of people who were adopted, but had not committed suicide and studied a total of 269 of their relatives too. The incidence of suicide in the biological relatives of the control group was 0.7 per cent compared to an incidence of 4.5 per cent (6.5 times higher) in the biological relatives of those who committed suicide. In the adoptive relatives of both controls and suicides, there were no suicides at all. Further study of the sample showed that whereas depression (unipolar and bipolar) was higher in the biological relatives of the suicide victims, the highest incidence of suicide was in relatives of those who had a diagnosis of 'brief affective reaction', a term given to brief emotional disturbance often including an impulsive suicide attempt precipitated by a stressful life event. This gives a clue to what the genetic predisposition might be, adding weight to the idea that it is the inability to inhibit an impulsive reaction to stress that is involved. Such a personality predisposition crosses the boundaries between different types of psychiatric disorder.

Depression, schizophrenia, alcoholism or personality disorder might all have been candidates as carriers of a genetic loading for suicide, since they all carry an increased risk of self-harm behaviour. But the fact that suicide does not discriminate between the diagnoses throws doubt on this possibility. I have suggested that it was not the diagnosis *per se* but an individual's perception of their symptoms as aversive and uncontrollable that was important.

The next generation of research on serotonin is likely to have to address several pressing issues. What is the effect of chronic stress on the serotonergic system and on impulsivity? What is the relationship between alcohol and impulsivity? Alcohol disinhibits a person and makes them act in a more dangerous way, but also lowers serotonin. It remains unclear whether this disinhibition comes from the serotonergic effect, rather than the disinhibiting effect of alcohol itself. It is possible that alcohol's effect on impulsiveness is simply short term, whereas that of serotonin is longer term.[18]

In 2003 Caspi and colleagues published a study in the journal *Science* that examined a large cohort of young people in Dunedin, New Zealand, looking at how frequently they became depressed or suicidal in their mid-twenties. They found that some were genetically vulnerable to depression (showing a difference in the gene controlling the transport of serotonin in the brain), but even these people did not become depressed or suicidal unless they experienced a serious negative event in their lives. It seems as though the genetic vulnerability needed to be 'switched on' by stressful events.

The 1990 conclusion of American neuroscientist Seymour Kety still stands:

> We cannot dismiss the possibility that the genetic factor in suicide is an inability to control impulsive behaviour, while

> depression and other mental illness, as well as overwhelming environmental stress, serve as potentiating mechanisms that foster or trigger the impulsive behaviour, directing it toward a suicidal outcome. In any case, suicide illustrates better than any of the mental illnesses ... the very crucial and important interactions between genetic and environmental influences.[19]

CONCLUDING REMARKS

A common theme emerges from both psychodynamic and biological approaches to suicide: the theme of escape from a situation that is seen as inescapable in any other way. From the dynamic perspective, the roots of this inescapability are to be found in the type of attachments formed early in life. In some theories, these are seen specifically as over-narcissistic, but it is common ground between many of these theories that loss or threatened loss of important relationships later in life produces an intolerable feeling of abandonment and interpersonal failure. Loss at any stage in life produces a mixture of protest, anger, anguish and despair. Such loss is associated with biological changes, and the serotonin system in the brain may act as an important link in the chain of events connecting uncontrollable events with impulsive and aggressive responses, whether directed at others or at oneself.

Neither psychodynamic nor biological theories make a clear distinction between impulses that drive someone towards suicide as an option, on the one hand, and factors that remove the obstacles to such behaviour, on the other. A wish that one could escape a hopeless life situation or escape one's mental anguish might provide sufficient push towards suicide, but it is equally important to understand the factors that take away the usual reasons for living or remove the barriers to dying. One such barrier might be the fear of death. We have seen how this can be reduced by a feeling that death might not be the end and by repeatedly imagining, or thinking about, a suicidal act, or even by repeated attempts that slowly build the courage to go further, as American academic psychologist Thomas Joiner has suggested.[20] Fear of death might also be reduced by exposure to real or fictional accounts of suicidal behaviour in books, magazines, television and radio, and we will return to this possibility in Chapter Ten. But first, we will look more closely at the theme that has emerged throughout the book: that suicide and suicidal behaviour arise when a person feels defeated by their life circumstances, and can see no way out.

CHAPTER EIGHT

The Suicidal Mind: Defeated and Trapped

In the United Kingdom each August teenagers receive their final examination results from schools and colleges. The grades obtained are usually critical in determining whether they are able to go to the college or university of their choice. One year, when the Advanced level (the end-of-school public examination) results came out, a talented pupil from a village in Norfolk killed herself. She felt that her grades (a B, a C and two Ds) were not good enough to win her a place on the physiotherapy course she'd hoped to do. On the day she collected her results, she told friends she wanted to be alone, but then let herself into her cousin's empty cottage and hanged herself.

What can explain such a rapid escalation of suicidal depression? She was popular and talented, had hobbies and appeared happy-go-lucky. It particularly surprised people since she had fought back after a riding accident two years before in which she broke her back, and seemed to be a survivor. Hindsight in such cases can be very deceptive, and it is unwise to imagine that such a rare event might have been predicted. At the same time, several commentators suggested that her case should signal a danger that the education system had become too dominated by a league-table culture that emphasised academic performance as the sole criterion of success. The example of Japan was thought to be another warning.

The high rate of suicide among teenage students in Japan is often linked to the highly competitive nature of the education system. Pupils as young as twelve often attend cramming schools in an attempt to improve marks so that, eventually, they will win a job with a top company. A further consequence of such a dominance–subordinance environment is the high rate of bullying, or *ijime*, between pupils. Such bullying is often the actual precipitant of a suicide. During the 1990s, the government in Japan became increasingly concerned about bullying in the education system, which was being under-reported by schools, who feared criticism for allowing it to occur. Meetings took place against the background of the suicides of two 13-year-old boys. One of them, from Nishio, in the prefecture of Aichi, had hanged himself. He left a four-page suicide note giving details of the beatings and extortion he had suffered for over a year. He had been repeatedly dunked in a river until he feared he would drown, and forced many times to give money. 'These days they bully me so hard and demand large sums of money although I have none. I can't stand it any more.'

The Education Ministry was forced to admit that a large part of the problem stemmed from the highly competitive nature of the education system. In a special report in December 1994 it called on teachers to be more aware of pupils' stress levels and competition between them in examinations. Little guidance was given, however, as to how teachers might assess whether students were suffering in this way.

The use of exam success as the sole criterion of self-worth produces individuals who feel ashamed of their 'weakness' and trapped by their apparent failure, especially in those who are perfectionists. The feeling of humiliation acts as a barrier to sharing the fear of failure with peers or family, and is exacerbated by feelings of loneliness, and each mood feeds on the other in a vicious spiral of despair.

An added issue in the current milieu in many countries is bullying through the internet. This takes various forms. One particularly vicious type involves young people being persuaded to give secret information or share intimate photographs with people they have met through social networking sites, who then threaten to embarrass them by sharing the information or pictures. Even the threat of such humiliation has been enough to cause young people to kill themselves.[1]

Fear of shame and humiliation is illustrated by another situation that has come to light. Around fifty suicides in the United Kingdom each year are people found shoplifting and awaiting a court appearance. Most often they had no financial need to shoplift. There is, for them, an overwhelming feeling of shame and humiliation. If the case comes to court, the verdict will often reflect the judgement that the person is suffering a psychological problem that needs psychological intervention rather than punishment but many commit suicide before that verdict can be reached.

Interpersonal disputes can involve combinations of the same emotions. A woman in her mid-forties in East Anglia in the UK took a massive overdose soon after she discovered that the man she planned to marry a few weeks later (having lived with him for several years) had unilaterally cancelled the arrangements. Without her knowledge, he had sent notes to all the guests to say the wedding was called off. He visited her in hospital, but only to tell her to collect her stuff, which he had left in suitcases on the front doorstep. Her overdose was not lethal, and she lived. But her crisis threatened to last for some time, and while it did so she remained at serious risk of further suicidal behaviour.

Knowledge of brain function is not all we need to explain such behaviour. We need to understand what environmental and psychological 'signals' bring about biological changes in brain function, and, in turn, what effects such biological changes will have on the way we think and act. For example, psychosocial stress is a critical factor in bringing about biological changes. Long-term stress in both animals and humans can have profound effects on patterns of endocrine and neurotransmitter function. There is increasing evidence that repeated stress in life can bring about changes in messenger RNA and DNA, and there is a renewed interest in mapping the downstream effect that such changes can then have on psychological function.[2]

Depression can be seen as the response to the long-term threat posed by constant frustration and disappointment, by the loss of people, things and status. Such frustrations and losses may result from constantly being put down by society or receiving insufficient help or support. In considering how we can explain suicidal behaviour in a way that takes full account of biological, psychological and social processes, a helpful starting point is ethology. Ethology is the study of animals in their natural habitat. The approach has been influential in such important theories as that of Bowlby on attachment. There are a number of different ways in which animals and humans respond normally to losses: by energising behaviour to try and secure rewards in other ways; by switching to alternative sources of reward; and by giving up. These can become distorted in catastrophic ways that cause the individual to believe he or she is trapped, and to begin to think of ways of escaping. I have suggested throughout this book that suicidal behaviour is best seen as a cry of pain – a response elicited by this situation of entrapment – and only secondarily as an attempt to communicate or change people or things in the environment. It is time to go into more detail about how this happens.

In the sections that follow, I will suggest that biological, psychodynamic and social aspects combine to help explain response to entrapment and threatened entrapment. In particular, I suggest that all of us are sensitive to signals from our social environment that indicate threat to our 'rank' within a group and our acceptance as an integral 'part' of it. Events that seem to us to threaten our rank or group membership are seen as signs that we are a 'loser' or an 'outsider'. Like the woman whose wedding was cancelled, we perceive ourselves to have lost a battle and our self-esteem is radically reduced, triggering evolutionarily old biological patterns in the brain. This produces further hypersensitivity to social information and ruminative brooding about what we can do to restore things, resulting in a vicious circle that appears to confirm our worst fears. In the early stages, an intense period of activated 'reactance' is shown, in which we protest against the threatened loss or rejection. It is at this stage that, for some, 'low-intent' suicidal behaviour may occur. In the later stages of response, we may slide into complete despair and apathy, and serious attempts at suicide may occur. Occasionally, however, a person may experience a catastrophic increase of suicidal impulses in response to loss or failure, and an unexpected suicide occurs. In what follows, I shall examine theories from animal as well as human behaviour to give a wider perspective on defeat and entrapment.

CONSERVATION-WITHDRAWAL

The Australian psychiatrist Robert Goldney was one of the first to take an ethological approach to suicidal behaviour, employing Engel's ideas[3] about 'conservation-withdrawal'.[4] This refers to a biological system which responds to stress by reducing activity, raising barriers against stimulation and conserving energy: a sort of hibernation. This pattern may follow a prolonged period of heightened arousal where the organism has attempted to cope by over-engagement and overactivity. When the organism falls into the state of conservation-withdrawal, the behaviour that is visible in the social group has a signal function – warning others of a loss of supplies and of exhaustion. The intended outcome is to 'ensure the supply' and 'retain the object'.

This, Goldney notes, has striking parallels with the reports of those who take overdoses: they want to escape; they do not know whether they want to live or die; they cannot stand the pressure any longer. Many have pointed out how people can see a connection between death and sleep, and this can be found in the reasons people give for suicidal acts.[5] They want to 'pull the bedclothes' over their heads, or 'go to sleep for a long time'. The fact that drug and alcohol abuse and suicidal behaviour often go together can be linked to the innate mechanism of 'conservation-withdrawal'. Substance abuse also represents an attempt to react to the stresses of life by shutting out all external stressors. When such attempts to bring about temporary oblivion with alcohol and drugs fail, then other mechanisms for conservation-withdrawal come into play. The fact that alcohol and other drugs can reduce the fear of the possible negative consequences of any behaviour, when applied to suicidal acts, renders them all the more likely.

Many suicide attempts can thus be seen as a wish for temporary relief. The attempt may represent a conservation of energy, a raising of the barriers to the outside world, or at least an attempt to re-exert control over it. Although the idea of conservation-withdrawal fits in some respects, it seems to apply best to the later stages of response to uncontrollable stress, when the individual has given up hope, become despairing and apathetic. It does not capture the more active, 'protest' aspects of some suicidal behaviour, which, I shall argue, arise at an earlier point in the process.

AN EVOLUTIONARY APPROACH

Recent research helps us to go into more detail about the types of biological mechanisms that may be involved in depression and suicidal behaviour. This has been drawn together by Professor Paul Gilbert,[6] who suggests we look to the animal kingdom for hypotheses about the evolutionary primitive mechanisms that might influence human behaviour. He is particularly concerned to explore the concepts of defence and safety.

People differ widely in what they find threatening: the fear of a physical illness such as a heart attack; the fear that others will criticise them; the fear of being overwhelmed by emotion when describing past trauma; the fear that people will find out one's weaknesses. Gilbert suggests that defence and safety may be fundamental psycho-biological organising systems that guide the development of interpersonal schemata and strategies. Non-threatening environments promote creativity, cooperation and affiliation. Threatening environments inhibit flexibility and exploration, producing more stereotyped, automatic responses. This has implications for suicidal behaviour, and how it is linked with inflexibility in cognitive processes such as memory and problem-solving. The most important 'unsafe' environment for most humans, however, is not exposure to predators or physical harm, but exposure to unfavourable social comparison. Thus, we need to explore further the evolutionary significance of social comparison in determining rank and status within social groups.

The animal kingdom shows many examples where social groups survive because of the smooth operation of social processes – for example, when sexual partners are chosen and when potential rivals are excluded. An important aspect is rank and status within a social group that shares the same territory. High-ranking individuals explore more, have more erect posture and are less timid than low-ranking individuals across a number of species. Changes in rank can bring about changes in biological systems (e.g. in levels of testosterone), but, more importantly for understanding depression and suicidal behaviour, in levels of the neurotransmitter serotonin. What evolutionary function do such systems have?

Such biological systems seem to be involved in regulating fights and challenges in a group by establishing a hierarchy. It is important for an animal that is likely to lose encounters not to compete continually, so expending valuable resources in challenges that cannot be won. On the other hand, some contests may be worth fighting. The ranking determines who is likely and who is unlikely to be beaten. A large number of signals are used by animals to communicate challenge, attack and submission. Submission, when triggered, involves a menu of behaviours indicating that no further threat to the victor is intended. Further challenges are inhibited by this mechanism. Neither party need waste further resources on establishing relative rank. Furthermore, the signalling that goes on in animal groups means that they may not actually have to fight it out.

Out of this research comes the study of analogous behaviour in humans. Although such extrapolation has to be done with extreme care, the analogy between observations of social groups in animals and humans is justified so long as it is used to set up *hypotheses* rather than coming to *conclusions* about human behaviour. How best to proceed? We can observe that humans appear sensitive to and make rapid judgements about one another's rank and status. The social comparison process may be done on the basis of the size of another person's house, the make of car they drive or the quality of their clothes. Social biologists refer collectively to these attributes, when observed in animals, as resource holding potential (RHP).

Ritual encounters between two members of the same species result in comparison of relative RHP, and the loser will back off. As the hierarchy becomes established, the amount of fighting reduces. Gilbert suggests that the human equivalent of RHP is self-esteem. Self-esteem is an estimate of one's ability to secure important goals such as a desired job or partner. It is damaged by unemployment, by failure in love and by aggression from others, as in school by bullies or in the home by family members who use psychological or physical violence.

Dominance hierarchies have evolved through stages. First, they were territorial, where fighting was designed to create space for territorial ownerships. Subsequently, territories gradually dissolved and success in the dominance hierarchy became associated with other forms of social success. This results in the fact that, today in humans, rank is often (though not always) influenced by things such as perceived popularity, beauty, talent, etc. Gilbert maintains that when individuals lose rank, the defensive systems of escape and avoidance become activated. Importantly, while the means of acquiring rank and status may have changed, *the feeling when one loses has not.*

Being 'in' with the group

In addition to helping to establish rank by looking for signs of RHP, social comparison can also judge the extent to which one is succeeding in gaining favourable attention from other members of the group. Unlike RHP, which is to do with ranking, this is concerned with judgements about *sameness* v. *difference* from the reference group. Gilbert calls it Social Attention Holding Power. It conveys status by *attractiveness*, rather than by aggressive displays of strength over weakness. It is concerned with receiving signals that one is attractive to others and/or needed by them.

In clinical practice, one may observe two types of problem when individuals are over-concerned with whether they are liked by or useful to others. First there are those who appear to be sustained exclusively by *receiving* attention from others. They are sensitive to any signs that these sources of attention may be under threat of being switched off. They feel abandoned when this happens, and are likely to become demanding of others' attention, seeking reassurance that they are still loved. In therapy, they may say, 'No one really loves me,' or 'All my friends are sick of me.'

Second, there are those who appear to be sustained by their ability to *give* attention to others and be needed by them. People who seek helping roles in various organisations may fit into this category. They are often held up as examples to the group, as people who 'can't do enough for others'. They are welcomed by most groups they join, since they often appear to have boundless energy. There is little wrong with this except when 'being needed by others' is the sole source of their satisfaction in life. If so, they become vulnerable when other members of the group or family make it clear they no longer need their help. In this case, the person may feel depressed, for they know no other way of relating to people other than through helping them. When depressed, they do not doubt that others love them, but rather they say, 'I am a burden to others,' or, in the most extreme cases, 'They would be better off without me.' Their 'black and white' (dichotomous) thinking makes them conclude that there are only two possibilities: either they are a help to others or they are a burden to them.

Social comparison and helplessness

Whether attempting to compare resources for ranking using RHP or to evaluate the extent to which one fits in with the group (the amount of Social Attention Holding Power), the effects of social comparison run deep. It is the comparative effect – not the absolute effect – that governs the amount of stress or depression. During the Thatcher/Reagan years politicians used to answer the accusation that a large gap had opened up between rich and poor by saying that although the rich had indeed become richer, the poor had little cause to complain since they had not become much poorer, if at all. However, this takes no account of the fact that people's mood and their psychological (and sometimes physical) health are determined by social comparison. Absolute levels of deprivation are higher in war, but cases of suicide and depression fall because all are perceived to be suffering together – social cohesion goes up. Similarly, absolute levels of deprivation are higher in underdeveloped countries than in most Western countries, but levels of suicide and depression are not.

Once a society has achieved a certain level of economic well-being and been able to remove most large-scale threats to life expectancy, such as infectious diseases, it is not absolute levels of poverty and employment which are important in physical and mental health, but distribution of inequality.[7] It is the conclusion that compared to others, one is a failure, unwanted or powerless, which increases vulnerability to emotional distress.

Involuntary subordination: feelings of defeat

Paul Gilbert draws an important distinction between voluntarily giving up and moving on and involuntarily being defeated.[8] In the latter case, the individual is trapped and feels they have no alternative. Involuntary subordination is an important aspect of depression, which may arise from a person being forced to be subordinate and take a submissive role. This takes us back into social rank theory. The dimension of rank (whether one is dominant or subordinate in a group) may be more significant in the cause of depression than previously thought. When depressed, people seem to feel an increased need for recognition and prestige. They worry about how they are succeeding in relation to others, evaluate themselves as inferior or second rate, feel weak and ashamed about such weakness. As we've seen, the usual summary term for such a constellation of symptoms is 'low self-esteem', which sums up the sense of subordination, the perception or reality of negative social comparison.

The value of the concept of involuntary subordination is that it sums up what many see as the cause of increased depression in women relative to men: that it is often a consequence of enforced subordinacy. To protect themselves (and often their children), women are forced to take a submissive role, increasing self-blame so as to reduce the likelihood of counter-aggression from their partner. Consistent with this, researchers found that women being abused by their partners blamed themselves for their partners' violence. However, this was only true if they were asked about it while still in the relationship. Asked after they had moved out of the relationship, they blamed their partners. So far as we can see, their self-blame while still in the relationship felt genuine to them; they were not consciously telling lies as a protective strategy. In a context where one partner is criticised and disempowered, an evolutionary primitive inhibitory system comes into play and this system gives rise to the symptoms we know as a depressive state.

Such an evolutionary primitive mechanism may come into play even if there is only the *perception* of low status, failure and weakness. A person may be pursuing unrealistically high goals, so their perfectionism itself may give rise to the perception that they are failing, weak or subordinate. They feel they have failed, then feel trapped by such failure, since there seems no way out of their situation. Occasionally, a single failure can activate these depressive mechanisms very suddenly with devastating effect, as we see in the cases of school 'failure' and suicide reported at the start of this chapter. Suicide following bullying is an example of the more long-lasting stress of being trapped giving way, eventually, to this most extreme form of escape.

ENTRAPMENT: THE PROBLEM OF 'ARRESTED FLIGHT'

By the word 'entrapment', I mean anything that stops an animal or human from getting away when it wants to flee. One striking example from the animal world of the consequences of entrapment is the behaviour of birds when establishing their territories. If birds meet within a disputed territory, they engage in aggressive displays. One wins, the other loses. The loser flies away to find another territory. Note that in this case, although it has been defeated, because it can escape it suffers few ill effects from its encounter. But if this meeting occurs in a limited territory – say, in a cage or other circumstance from which the defeated bird cannot escape – it is a different story. Here is one early description of what happens in this case:

> Its behaviour becomes entirely changed. Deeply depressed in spirit, humbled, with drooping wings and head in the dust, it is overcome with paralysis, although one cannot detect any physical injury.
>
> The bird's resistance now seems broken, and in some cases the effects of the psychological conditions are so strong that the bird sooner or later comes to grief.[9]

Note, first, that the 'depressed' behaviour occurs in the absence of physical damage. Second, it is striking that the defeat itself is not sufficient to trigger the response. If the bird can escape to another territory, it shows no ill effects. It is the *combination* of defeat and the lack of escape (entrapment) that is needed for the reaction to occur (what Gilbert calls 'arrested flight').[10]

I suggest the sense of *entrapment* is central to suicidal behaviour. In the case of the A-level student with which this chapter began, there was an unpredicted and sudden surge of such feelings of 'no escape'. In most cases, however, the entrapment is a longer term state, first because external causes of stress are themselves long term (e.g. the person is trapped by bullying peers or partners). But it may be prolonged also because the person has grown up in an environment where he or she could exercise very little control, where others had all the power, so the person has learned over a long time period that the only possible response option is to submit. The person is thus extra-sensitive to social threats, and their world constantly seems to present fewer alternatives for action, whatever the reality. The result is long-term demobilisation, a biological state involving chemical changes.

The depressed suicidal person effectively 'takes themselves off the list' of those who might threaten the more powerful. This is akin to the low-risk, low-gain strategy of some animals – one that involves internal inhibition of any behaviour that would appear to challenge those higher in the dominance hierarchy. The downturn into depression may involve the activation of these inhibitory mechanisms of 'no challenge'. At the extreme, they are associated not only with reduced aspiration, but also abnormally low aspiration: feelings of worthlessness, uselessness, powerlessness; and lack of interest in engaging in any social behaviour that might involve taking even minimal risks. Depression is the biological assignment of 'loser' status. It signals to oneself and others that one is not prepared to take on challenges or fight for resources.

The benefit in the animal kingdom is that the risk of losing fights is minimised, but in the case of bullying in human societies, in schools or armed services or prisons, the competitive nature of the institution appears to encourage the bully to continue to torment the subordinate long after the weaker one has given up. The inhibitory mechanisms designed to protect the loser from further losses fail to work.[11] At such times, the risk of suicide is increased.

Cry for help or cry of pain?

With this understanding of how defeat and entrapment combine, we can see more clearly why suicidal behaviour is best seen as a cry of pain – an understandable reaction to unbearable distress – and not merely a 'cry for help' that is only communicating distress.[12]

This acknowledges that the motivation for suicidal behaviour is complex. Most suicidal behaviour, whether the outcome is fatal or not, has some element of the Janus face – mixed feelings about the will to live and the will to die. As we know, even within the general population, many people have at some time felt suicidal. Given that the lifetime risk for clinical depression is 20 per cent, and that suicidal feelings are a common accompaniment to such depression, it makes little sense to dismiss those who actually harm themselves as not serious, or to dismiss the pressure to escape that the person feels.

Suicidal behaviour can have a communication outcome without communication being the main motive. The behaviour is elicited by a situation in which the person feels trapped. As with the animal caught in a trap that cries in pain, the fact that the behaviour affects that of other members of the species does not mean that the *only* motive for the cry was to seek help.

Some self-harm may not be motivated by a wish to die, but most shares with suicide the wish to escape from an otherwise unbearable situation. The difficulty many authors have got into is to define completed suicide as the core behaviour that needs to be explained, and attempted suicide as its pale reflection (with 'cry for help' being used to explain only self-harm and never suicide). Instead, if one defines *entrapment and helplessness in the face of actual or threatened loss* as the basic dimension, it becomes easier to see that *all* self-harm falls somewhere along the same continuum, whatever the outcome. Such feelings of being trapped are fuelled and maintained by biological and psychological changes. They appear completely impervious to intellectual argument, as Al Alvarez found:

> mere intellectual recognition did no good, and anyway, my clear moments were few. My life felt so cluttered and obstructed that I could hardly breathe. I inhabited a closed, concentrated world, airless and without exits. I doubt if any of this was noticeable socially: I was simply more tense, more nervous than usual, and I drank more. But underneath I was going a bit mad. I had entered the closed world of suicide, and my life was being lived for me by forces I couldn't control.[13]

Entrapment – evidence from history

One benefit of the entrapment model is that it helps to explain historical data. Take, for example, the increased risk of suicide that children and young people suffered in the late Middle Ages and early modern period. It appears the best explanation for this is the violence with which children were mistreated and the fact that such brutalised boys and girls had nowhere to turn. They therefore killed themselves to escape.

In their book *Sleepless Souls*, social historians MacDonald and Murphy give the example of a 12-year-old girl called Agnes Addam who went horseriding with a girlfriend in 1565 and dirtied her clothes.[14] She started to return home, but then seized with terror over what her father would do to her when he saw what she had done, she rushed into a pond and drowned herself. Another example, this time from 1729, is of a boy who threw a piece of glass at his brother and was so frightened afterwards, knowing he would receive a severe beating from his father, that he hanged himself in the outhouse. And there's a third example from around the eighteenth century of the 13-year-old son of a Hackney tradesman who was victim of a cruel practical joke: a girl hid her brother's new hat on overhearing their father threaten that if the boy lost it, he would be beaten within an inch of his life. When the boy found the hat was missing, he hanged himself for fear of the beating.

The situation was compounded because when young people left home in their early teens to work as servants or apprentices, the law forbade them to flee the homes of their masters and mistresses. This only encouraged many such masters to mistreat them and abuse them in a miserable way. Only the most flagrant brutality was regarded as sufficient grounds for leaving a master. Neither could those boys or girls who ran away expect much sympathy from their parents if they returned home: a 12-year-old lad called Daniel Rose who was unhappy after having been apprenticed to a weaver returned home and was sent back to his master with a warning; he left the house that evening and was found dead the next morning. He had hanged himself in his master's garden.

Girls who found themselves pregnant would also be likely to kill themselves. In some cases girls made pregnant by their masters found themselves abandoned by those masters, as well as by their parents. Since there was no way out, suicide was common.

Running through all these stories are the elements of helplessness and the impossibility of escape and, particularly, fear of punishment. We see the same in contemporary society with its fear-based school system that prioritises examination grades as the central criterion of success, then wonders why many children and young people disengage. Similarly, we see it with the bullying which is often the origin of suicidal thoughts in young people trapped in the school yard or by internet bullies, as well as in people serving in the army, navy or air force. Finally, we see it dramatically illustrated in the suicides of those in prison, especially young people on remand, who can escape neither the prison nor the terrible fear that they will be bullied there.

SELF-HARM AND SUICIDE: CONNECTIONS

High suicide-intent self-harm and completed suicide do not require a different theory from that needed to explain less serious suicidal behaviour. The less serious behaviour represents the early active 'protest' stage of response to threatened loss of rank or to threatened entrapment. After repeated exposure to social comparison, resulting in feeling a 'loser' or 'non-belonging/abandoned', the more severe manifestation of conservation-withdrawal emerges: self-denigration, worthlessness and despair and, with them, the high suicide intent. Low-intent suicide attempts can thus be seen as the 'reactance' (the increased activity in response to threatened loss) which precedes the 'helplessness' (the decreased activity in response to actual loss) associated with high-intent-to-die suicidal behaviour.

The recent rise in younger and middle-aged males attempting and committing suicide can be related to reduced role both through loss of employment opportunities and loss of opportunities of long-term relationships. This latter effect arises from the increases in divorce and family breakdown. In later life, separation or divorce or living alone can reactivate such feelings of being a 'loser' and that one doesn't belong.[15] Such are the components of Durkheim's 'anomie' that he saw as closely associated with suicide. We can now see how such anomie, a sociological concept, relates to the psychological concept of social comparison, which itself relates directly to evolutionary old biological sub-systems, each having a generally adaptive function, but sometimes producing a maladaptive outcome. Social comparison has two important elements: ranking (upwards v. downwards) and similarity to others (like v. unlike). Those who are depressed and 'anomic' feel both *inferior to* and also *different from* others.

Thus low self-esteem is the manifestation of a biologically old tendency that may be activated relatively early in life, and reactivated at times when individuals are, or imagine themselves to be, defeated, powerless and failing to meet the challenges of the world of work or of interpersonal relationships. Each time these feelings are reactivated, the pattern of thinking (defeat, anguish and hopelessness) becomes more ingrained, and increasingly linked to whatever mood occurred when the pattern was first established. When that mood occurs again in the future, it 'calls up' the old thinking pattern, and the cycle starts again. It is the reactivation of these 'well-worn grooves' in the mind that causes such devastating effects.

How is the gender effect to be explained within the 'entrapment' model? Historically, women have been given roles in society in which they have less control, e.g. in earning power, influence over resources, in jobs even when working. In Western society, women are likely to attribute their failures to themselves and their successes to luck or to other people or circumstances. Women have thus explored the boundaries of 'no control' more than have men. When the trap begins to close, they are more likely to see it closing. The result is that they take action earlier than men. The cry of pain comes earlier in the entrapment process. At this early stage, people are more ambivalent about dying, and use less lethal methods. The historic tendency for women to be more likely to *attempt* suicide, but less likely to *commit* suicide, is explained by this 'time course' model. In the past, men did not show self-punitive behaviour at this stage. However, having not reacted to threatened loss and entrapment early on in the sequence, they miss out on the important benefits that earlier cries of pain may bring, and are more likely to move, in the extreme cases, to helplessness and social isolation. When the trap closes, the effect is more catastrophic.

For men, with less opportunity for receiving care (fewer social support networks) and less opportunity for caregiving (fewer caring roles), the expectation of no escape feeds directly into a sense of hopelessness and the possibility of suicidal behaviour as the escape route. As men become more marginalised in the job market, they may experience, as women have always done, more uncontrollable aspects of life at a younger age. The effect will be that they too show suicidal behaviour at an earlier stage in the entrapment. This may be why the numbers of young men are beginning to match the numbers of young women in the *attempted* suicide statistics.

CONCLUDING REMARKS

If social signals switch on old biological scripts of defeat and submission, then antidepressants may switch off these processes to give the person more energy to explore other response options, with reduced sensitivity to signals of social loss and failure. Equally, psychotherapy may help the person recognise their patterns of thinking that see every situation as potentially threatening, every encounter as win-or-lose. In this way, the person may learn to let go of goals more easily, to accept things as they are for the time being, so they can see more clearly how they may change. The limits of such interventions are set by the persistence of a real state of powerlessness arising from, say, bullying by other students or domination by a violent partner. However, psychotherapy has often been able to empower people to change relationships, to move away from non-supportive or threatening individuals and to change the external factors that normally conspire to keep them trapped.

How far a person has the capacity to find alternative escape routes may depend on an important psychological factor: their memory of their own past history. There is evidence that autobiographical memory may be so affected that it reduces the ability to solve current problems and restricts any view of the future. The next chapter will consider this aspect in depth, for it promises to provide a way in to break the vicious circle of biological and social influences on suicidal feelings and behaviour.

CHAPTER NINE

Mind-lock: Why the Past Obstructs the Future

I have suggested that a major factor in suicide and attempted suicide is the feeling of being trapped – both by circumstances and one's own thoughts and feelings. The psychological aspect – the thoughts and feelings – were seen as important in worsening the effects of the external realities. Though people rarely think themselves into a hole, once there, thoughts about their own helplessness often maintain the depression and prevent them from climbing out. One response to these negative thoughts is to view them as the symptoms of underlying depression. When the depression clears up, or is treated, they will stop.

In one sense this is true. We know that such negative and hopeless thoughts go up and down with depressed mood. We know that when a person takes antidepressants the thoughts may lose their grip, given time. However, if the antidepressants are stopped, the risk of becoming depressed returns. Once a person has been clinically depressed, they remain at an increased risk of becoming depressed again. In 50 per cent of cases, the depression returns within two years. For those who have been depressed more than once in the past, the risk of recurrence is 70 per cent. The thoughts return, the helplessness returns; the pills have clearly not dealt with the underlying vulnerability to becoming depressed and suicidal, much of which may stem from a person's memory of the past.

The importance of memory is hard to overstate. Memory provides us with all our knowledge about who we are, what we have been through in the past: happy times and sad times. It is on the basis of our memory that we make predictions about the future. If our memory is biased or faulty, then our predictions are also likely to be biased or faulty. Our self-esteem also depends on memory; it is based upon our past successes and failures, and how successfully we have navigated a path through the world so far.

Depression is one of the major vulnerability factors for suicidal behaviour and does not only affect mood, but memory as well. Memory provides the key to understanding how, when someone feels under pressure from their life circumstances, they begin to feel trapped in a mental cage from which they appear unable to escape. First, memory can be biased, so that it tends to retrieve only negative events. Second, memory can be over-general. Instead of recording specific events, a person tends to lump together events of the same type or category without distinguishing between them. The story of how this memory problem was discovered is interesting in its own right.

MEMORY BIAS

I originally wrote this paragraph on a train from Bangor in north-west Wales, on the way to a meeting of the British Association for the Advancement of Science. As I gazed out of the window at the mountains on my right and the sea on my left, my mind wandered. I saw a sandy beach, empty but for a lone figure and his dog. It triggered a memory of me walking along a similar beach many years ago with my own collie dog. Such triggering of memories happens constantly, whether we are day-dreaming or engaged in conversation. Many of the triggers are fairly neutral and ambiguous. A man, out with his dog, might be 'peaceful' or 'lonely'. In other words, seeing something like that might trigger memories of positive or negative events from our past.

When something triggers or 'cues' memory, the event seems to come to mind immediately. This is not the case. There is a small time lag between the cue and the event coming to mind. During this brief interval there is a race between a number of events which the same cue could trigger. A single cue can activate a range of memory fragments, each of which could be completed by a number of different memories. Some psychologists have likened memory retrieval to a horse race. Whichever event gets to the line first wins, and when it wins, that is the event that comes to mind.

It is now known that such a 'horse race' occurs between positive events and negative events from the past. One can imagine positive memories as a white horse, and negative memories as a black horse. My seeing the man and his dog activated a pleasant memory of long ago; the white horse won. But one effect of depressed mood is to bias memory, so that the black horse wins much of the time. Had I been depressed, the sight of the man and the dog might have brought to mind the day I took my dog to the vet to be put down, when he was very old and grey and ailing. Further, the depression would have suppressed any happy memories of subsequent dogs, thus allowing me to conclude, unhappily, that I have never had a dog as wonderful again.

Some of the first experiments on depressed-mood memory-bias phenomena were performed by Professor Alwyn Lishman at the Institute of Psychiatry in London and by John Teasdale and colleagues at the Warneford Hospital in Oxford. Lishman concluded that patients who were more depressed in mood found it easier to recall negative events, but a problem with this early study was that the apparent mood memory 'bias' might have arisen because the people who were more depressed had experienced fewer actual positive events in their lives.

To avoid this problem, John Teasdale took student volunteers who were not depressed and experimentally manipulated their mood using a 'mood induction procedure'. All students started by being randomly allocated to different mood groups, so that results could not be explained by differences in the number of positive and negative events in their lives. The earlier effect was replicated, with the additional finding that negative mood did not so much speed negative events as slow down the recall of positive ones.[1]

Taking the analogy of the horse race, the finding that depression does not seem to work by speeding up the 'black horse' (negative memories) is important. In psychotherapy for depression, it will not be sufficient for a client to work to make negative events less accessible. The therapy will also need to increase the availability of more positive aspects of the past. There is abundant evidence that depressed people have suffered a great deal of genuinely negative life events and chronic difficulties. Given the real difficulties of these people's actual experience, the effect of their mood on memory is to place an additional burden on them by making it difficult for them to remember any positive events, the recall of which might alleviate some of the distress.

When I and my colleagues began our research on suicidal behaviour in the early 1980s in Cambridge, we wanted to find out what turns a crisis into a suicidal crisis and we reasoned that bias in memory could be an important part of the answer. Perhaps some people, at certain points, became so dominated by negative memories that their past seemed nothing but a string of failures, disappointments and arguments. We set out to see if this bias operates in people who are feeling suicidal, even if they are not clinically depressed. We were to find something about their memories more significant than the memory bias we expected.

MEMORY IN SUICIDAL PEOPLE

In research of this sort, it is important to obtain as accurate a measure as possible of how fast people are in recalling events from their past, so we followed previous research in giving patients words one at a time, a task reminiscent of the word-association test pioneered by Carl Jung. But instead of responding with the first word that came to mind, participants were asked to respond with the first *memory* that came to mind. By giving some positive and some negative words as 'cues', it is possible to examine how long people take to recall positive and negative events.

The first patient I gave the task to was a young woman in her early twenties who had been kept in hospital following an overdose. She was still quite sad and hopeless, but had no hesitation in volunteering, saying she was glad of someone to talk to. I had carefully prepared my questionnaires and memory tasks, choosing five positive and five negative words to use as memory cues. The words – *happy*, *safe*, *interested*, *successful* and *surprised*; and *sorry*, *hurt*, *clumsy*, *angry* and *lonely* – were chosen because a colleague at Cambridge had used them in a memory experiment on a large number of non-depressed people who had found no difficulty in responding to the words with events from their lives.

I had typed each word on the top of a piece of paper, and printed the instructions on the top of the first page, asking the participant to look at each word in turn and to write down an event from their past which the word reminded them of. It could be recent or something that happened a long time ago; it might be important or trivial.

I timed how long it took this first participant to start writing in each case. She responded to each word. Later I found that to the cue word 'happy' she had written 'my father'; to the cue word 'sorry' she had written 'when I do things wrong'; to 'surprised' she had written 'when my brother plays tricks on me'. This was not what was supposed to have happened. She was meant to be recalling specific events, but one response was a person (her father) and the rest were summaries of many events.

We tried the task with one or two other patients (who, like all the others, had recently taken an overdose) and seemed to get similar results. We thought that perhaps asking them to write down their memories was the problem, so we changed to reading out the words and asking for a verbal response, which we then wrote down. Then we could prompt them if they started to produce such general responses. Things did not improve. Perhaps the instructions were not being understood. We started to give more detailed directions and asked people to recall specific events, defining them clearly as events (important or trivial) that had happened at a particular place and time and lasted less than a day. We gave some practice words until the participants were able to produce a specific memory and repeat the instructions back.

The first consistent result to appear was that the suicidal individuals do indeed take much longer to retrieve positive events from their lives, though they are not much quicker than non-depressed controls at retrieving negative events.[2] In this respect they behaved like the depressed participants in the studies mentioned earlier. This is an important issue. The difficulty in being able to recall good memories from the past is likely to become more and more extreme as the suicidal depression deepens, until the person remembers only bad things that have happened. The result is that anything bad that happens now is immediately seen as part of this overall pattern, reinforcing a sense of unremitting darkness – that things have always been this way and will always be.

But there was another feature of our patients' memory that particularly interested us. In many cases, the cause of the delay in retrieving a specific positive memory was because they persisted, despite all our prompting, in retrieving an inappropriately *general* memory when the cue word was first given. Let us look in more detail at the psychology of memory to understand what was going on here.

SEARCHING OUR OWN PAST

Memory of events in our lives is hierarchically organised, with the 'upper' layers containing general memory information that can act as pointers to the more specific and detailed 'lower' layers. Thus, these upper layers act as intermediate stages in the laying down and later recollection of events. When we try to recollect an event, we first find an 'upper-layer' general description. This is then used to search the 'lower-layer' memory database for an appropriate candidate memory. For example, in response to the cue 'happy', people generate an intermediate description based on the implicit question, 'What sort of people, activities, places make me happy?' This 'upper-layer' description may be such things as 'gardening' or 'my girlfriend' or 'drinking in pubs with friends'. It appears that suicidal and depressed patients get stuck at this intermediate stage, and cannot use the general descriptions they generate to help them retrieve specific examples.

Why do they stop the search for a specific memory at this intermediate stage? Further research suggests that this difficulty may arise for two reasons.[3] First, it may come about because of some traumatic past event or events, so that the search is stopped as a way of defending against the pain of remembering.[4] Second, in some cases, the depressed mood itself activates rumination, a tendency to ask questions such as, 'Why am I feeling like this?', 'What is the matter with me?', 'Why can't I be as happy as others seem to be?' These questions feel as if they could produce answers, but they simply go round and round in the mind, maintaining or worsening the very mood that had set them off in the first place. Rumination and depressed mood block access to specific memories, partly because they tie up 'space' in the mind that is required to keep retrieval of memories on track, partly because the process of retrieving personal memories gets 'hijacked' by the 'Why?' questions, and people simply do not have the mental capacity to keep memory retrieval going. This can affect anyone, whether they have had a traumatic past or not.

Patients seem to become caught up at the intermediate description level – a phenomenon called 'mnemonic interlock' – *mind-lock* for short. Evidence suggests that whenever the memory system attempts to retrieve an event using a personal description, the description itself simply tends to activate other general memories (see Figures 9.1 and 9.2). So the word 'sorry' may elicit the over-general memory 'When I've hurt someone.' Instead of proceeding to generate possible specific memories which fit the general description (e.g. the time someone received a letter telling him their partner was leaving because they felt hurt), the general memory activates further self-descriptive summaries such as 'arguments' and 'I always hurt people I love'.

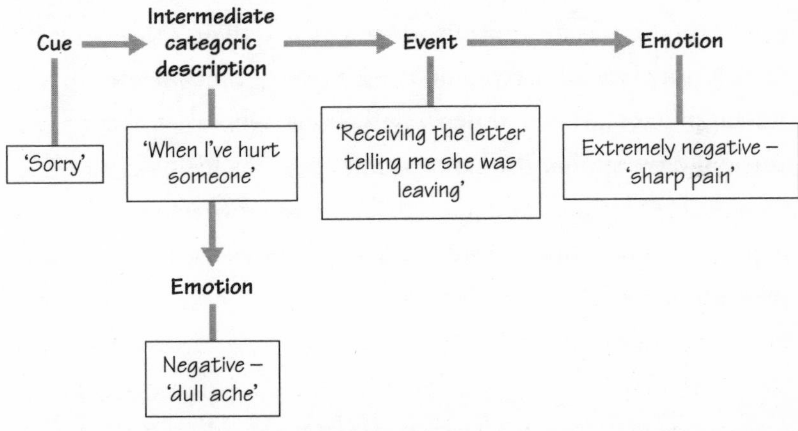

Figure 9.1 The usual sequence of recalling an emotional event, starting at the general level and becoming more specific.

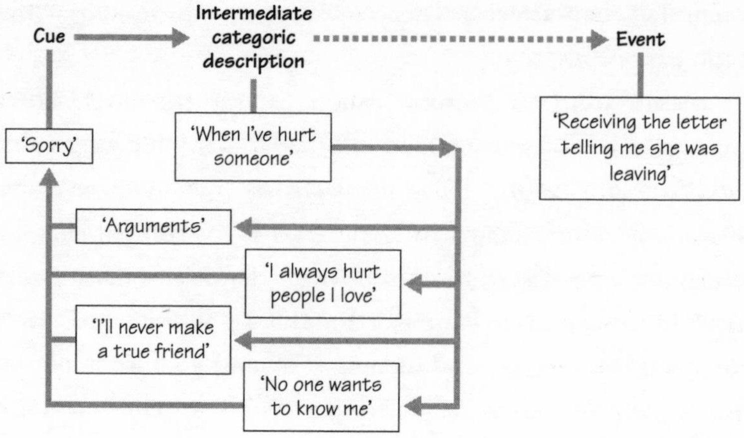

Figure 9.2: Mind-lock: the repeated circling around of over-general memories either as an attempt to avoid the distress of a specific memory or due to lack of top-down control of the memory process due to 'capture' by rumination.

We begin to see how an event can become a 'final straw' for suicidal behaviour. The final straw is not simply one extra source of stress; rather, it is any extra source which activates this network of intermediate, self-referent descriptions, causing mind-lock. Research has shown that depressed people who are not currently suicidal have similar difficulties. They are much slower to recall positive events (confirming the earlier researches on memory and depression) and much more likely to respond with over-general memories.

THE CONSEQUENCES OF OVER-GENERAL MEMORY

Therefore, what sorts of things are likely to make a person who is suffering from real adversity or whose mood has convinced them that they are worthless decide to make an attempt on their own life? Why this person? Why now? Mind-lock means that any one small event (the final straw) can activate a sort of blockage in the mind: summaries of the past that don't have enough specific information to help navigate through a crisis. Whether these are positive or negative, they are still likely to have damaging consequences. In the case of negative memories, the person's mind is quickly dominated by global self-referent descriptions such as 'I've always been a failure', 'Nobody's ever really liked me'. But even mind-lock about positive events may have damaging effects: where the person has no speedy access to specific positive events which would allow him or her to generate specific ideas for how to bring about similar positive events in the future this is likely to undermine attempts to solve current problems, to increase hopelessness and thereby, finally, to deepen mood and lengthen any episode of depression.

Mind-lock and problem-solving

If the word 'happy' simply brings back a summary memory – 'There were lots of happy times when I lived at home' – the summary memory does not deliver especially good hints for what to do about current unhappiness. The much-loved home may have broken up, and the resulting conclusion may be 'I cannot be happy'. By contrast, those able to retrieve specific events, positive or negative, are more likely to be able to generate alternative problem-solving strategies for current problems. So those who, when given the cue word 'happy', are able to remember a specific event when they lived at home, such as 'Going out with a friend to the cinema, where we met Jan and Pete and went back to their house for a coffee', are more likely to find in this some hints for what to do about their current unhappiness: the event, the cinema, the friends, the coffee, etc.

The hypothesis that over-general memory impairs problem-solving ability was first tested in a study at Kidderminster General Hospital in England.[5] It contrasted the memory performance of people who had recently taken an overdose with carefully matched control patients who were in hospital for surgery. Not only were depressed patients unable to produce as many alternative means of solving the problems as the non-depressed controls, but when they did generate a possible solution it was less effective, i.e. less likely to produce the desired outcome. Were these difficulties associated with problems in retrieving specific memories? The results confirmed, as predicted, a significant correlation between low effectiveness of solutions and greater generality of autobiographical memories. Further studies have shown that the link between over-general memory and problem-solving difficulties is causal, rather than just correlational: inducing people to be more over-general in their retrieval from the past reduces their ability to see solutions to current problems.[6]

Over-general memory and hopelessness

Hopelessness has been seen as the critical factor mediating between depression and suicidality. Hopelessness about the future appears to combine so lethally with depression as to produce suicidal ideas and behaviour. Hopelessness has been found to predict repetition of attempted suicide six months later and completed suicides up to ten years later. If over-general memory is seen as a significant influence on future suicidal behaviour, then we need to examine its effect on people's attitude to the future.

With my colleague Andrew MacLeod, I began to investigate the components of hopelessness. We were particularly interested in looking at the effect of over-general memories on how specifically or vaguely a person imagined the future. We reasoned that an important element in hopelessness was that people cannot imagine any future with certainty, either positive or negative.

One experiment asked people to remember times in their lives when they had been either unhappy or happy. We cued them with sentences such as 'Try to remember an event in your life when you were in tears', or, 'Try to remember an event in your life when you were laughing'. Similarly, we asked the participants on another occasion, 'Try to think of a time in the future when you might be in tears', or, 'Try to envisage a time in the future when you will laugh'.

Patients admitted to hospital following an overdose were compared with matched medical patients and matched non-hospitalised volunteers. The results were as predicted: overdose patients were more vague than the controls in descriptions of future and past. Furthermore, subjects who were less specific about past and future were more hopeless about the future. General memory can undermine the very process by which a person constructs a specific future for themselves, and thereby allows hopelessness to become more and more severe.[7]

Over-general memory, mind-lock and persistence of depression

Finally, if these memory deficits affect both problem-solving and levels of hopelessness in this way, then one might expect that people who have such a problem will have unusually prolonged episodes of depression, since they will not have the resources to take advantage of any breaks in mood that other treatments (e.g. antidepressants) might bring about. Can we therefore improve our prediction of how long depression lasts by taking account of how over-general patients are when asked about their autobiographical memory? Is it the case that two equally depressed people will have different prognoses, depending on the level of specificity in their memories? This is an important question. We know it is the longer-lasting depressions which are most likely to lead to suicide.

We examined this question in some seriously depressed patients admitted to a psychiatric unit in Newcastle upon Tyne.[8] When patients were admitted, we assessed the severity of their depression and gave them the autobiographical memory test. Each patient was followed up after three and seven months. The more over-general in memory the patients were at admission, the worse their depression scores at both three and seven months. Other studies have shown that over-general memory in adolescents predicts episodes of depression if a person suffers adverse events.[9]

These results show the importance of memory in contributing to the 'cage' in which the suicidal person gets caught, producing 'arrested flight' (see page 152). The past is dominated by generalities, which undermine the ability to see an effective way to solve current problems. If this were not bad enough, the memory problem has an additional effect on how the future is viewed, contributing to the feeling of vagueness about what lies ahead. Non-specificity about past and future is significantly associated with hopelessness, that aspect of depression which most points towards suicidal behaviour as an option – it seems like the only way out of the cage in which a person is trapped.

CONCLUDING REMARKS

Mind-lock provides the understanding we need to see clearly how a person can become trapped not only by their objective circumstances but also by the way the mind exacerbates these circumstances that are already difficult to cope with. It gives us a theory that can connect together sociological, psychiatric and biological perspectives, and that specifies more clearly the nature of the final common pathway leading from depression to hopelessness, then to suicide. It gives us a better appreciation of why some people are more vulnerable to suicidal behaviour than others.

An inability to be specific in retrieval of personal memories is due either to a history of negative events or to current unhappiness which is made worse by ruminating. The result is that a person's mind is constantly interrupted, and all their attempts to push away their unwanted thoughts and feelings seem in vain. Such general memories also lead to a situation in which people are vague about the future and fail to produce good, effective problem-solving alternatives. It sets the context against which the final straw – that event which produces a global summary of the emptiness of one's life – may have its devastating consequences. If life circumstances are the factors that put a person in a cage, it is memory that closes the door. Under these circumstances, suicide can seem to be the only option. Yet such self-destructive behaviour may still not occur without catalysts that translate thinking into behaviour, and the next chapter will look at some of these.

CHAPTER TEN

The Media as a Catalyst for Suicidal Behaviour

Some years ago, my teenage son and I were tidying up the back garden. I was clearing parts of a tree which had been trimmed some time before, and he was sawing them into logs. He remarked that it was exactly a year since he had last been sawing logs. When I expressed surprise at his accurate memory, he said he remembered the date clearly because it was the anniversary of Kurt Cobain's death by suicide. (Kurt Cobain was the lead singer of the band Nirvana.) Cobain had harmed himself in the past and finally shot himself, having left a long suicide note.

When such a high-profile suicide occurs, people want to know what effects the death has on all the fans. The debate about whether accounts of suicides (whether fictional stories or actual suicide) act as a catalyst by causing people to imitate them has a long history.

In the eighteenth century Goethe was accused of encouraging

suicidal behaviour by the publication of his novel *The Sorrows of Young Werther* (1774), in which a young man ends his life by shooting himself. The book had a huge influence on attitudes to romantic suicide. Coroners all over Europe began to believe that the 'Werther effect' was influential in bringing about suicides by lovelorn young people. The book was said to have sentimentalised self-destruction, but whether or not it produced imitative suicides, it certainly produced imitative poetry and literature. The sentimentalisation of death which followed such literature inspired pity for those who committed suicide and helped to erode the revulsion that suicide had formerly inspired. The result was that many became concerned that suicide would spread by imitation.

Émile Durkheim agreed that 'no other phenomenon is more readily contagious', but he did not agree that imitative behaviour would affect suicide rates when they were calculated over a longer-term period.[1] However, evidence from several studies suggests that imitative suicidal behaviour can and does take place.

EVIDENCE FOR IMITATIVE EFFECTS

David Phillips of San Diego University, California, examined the monthly suicide rates in the United States for the period 1947–68.[2] After correcting for the effects of seasonal fluctuations and linear trends, he found that suicide rates were higher just after a heavily publicised suicide story.[3] The more publicity devoted to the story, the greater the increase in suicides; the increase occurring mainly in the geographical areas where the story was publicised.

Similar work in the United Kingdom examined seventy-six deaths by suicide or undetermined in the Portsmouth area over the three-year period 1970–2.[4] It also looked at newspaper reports about suicide inquests recorded in a local newspaper which reported 80 per cent of inquests on suicides and was read by 70 per cent of the local adult population. Over the few days following the newspaper report of a suicide verdict, the researchers found an excess of observed suicides which was statistically significant for males under 45 years of age.

Do television reports of suicides have a similar effect? Phillips and colleagues examined the US daily mortality figures for the period 1972–6 in relation to national TV news coverage of suicides.[5] They identified seven suicide stories which had been featured on national TV news. Following five out of the seven, there was an increase in the daily mortality figures for deaths by suicide.

A spate of suicides occurred on the Viennese underground system in the 1980s. Between 1980 and 1984 there had only been nine suicides in total on the underground system. However, in 1986 one or two suicides were followed by dramatic reporting of the events, and several other (apparently copycat) suicides followed, so that in 1986 alone thirteen suicides occurred. A further nine followed in the first few months of 1987. Reporting restrictions were introduced and the number of suicides on the underground reverted to more normal levels (three in 1989 and four in 1990). Such events appear to show that reporting of real suicides can have a contagious effect[6] and other recent studies confirm this conclusion.[7]

Fictional portrayals

Does this effect generalise to suicides or attempted suicides shown in fictional stories on television? To examine this question,

Phillips turned to soap operas shown during 1977 on US television. Since these attract a larger audience than any other sort of television programme (40 per cent of all US homes with televisions are turned to at least one soap opera in any week), he assumed they were likely to provide a large potential source of behaviour which people might attempt to model.

Phillips identified nine separate weeks in which one or more soap operas carried a story in which a character committed or attempted suicide. From the US daily mortality statistics, he then examined whether there had been a rise in suicides in those particular weeks. As control periods, he took the weeks before, correcting for trends and eliminating public holiday periods and any in which there had been an actual suicide publicised in the media. The results showed that in eight out of the nine periods there was a rise in suicides in the latter part of the weeks in which suicidal behaviour was depicted in a major soap opera.[8]

The 'Angie' phenomenon

An estimated 14 million people watched the episode of the soap opera *EastEnders* on British TV on the evening of Thursday, 27 February 1986, and 9 million watched the repeat showing during an omnibus edition the following Sunday. The Thursday episode included one of the main characters (Angie) taking an overdose together with alcohol (neat gin). Although the overdose involved several bottles of pills, the programme had also shown this character buying one of the bottles – a bottle of aspirin – from a newsagent. The supposition was that this was an overdose with analgesics and that, like many overdoses in real life, it arose out of a difficult interpersonal situation in which the character's husband had been unfaithful. Following that programme and the omnibus edition on the Sunday (in which the actual overdose was not shown, though all the other elements were present), a large number of attendances for deliberate overdose at Hackney Hospital and St Bartholomew's Hospital in London were claimed. A letter to the *Lancet* reported that the number of patients admitted to Hackney Hospital during that week was far in excess of the average for the previous ten weeks, and of the average for the same week in six out of the previous ten years.[9]

Together with some colleagues, I investigated the Angie phenomenon. We examined in detail the numbers attending the departments that had made the original claim at Hackney and St Bartholomew's Hospitals. We studied data for the period up to and including the dates of the broadcasts and for the same periods for two control years.[10] We also not only compared the number of 'imitative' cases with the numbers of people attending in control years, but looked for any trends which might have contributed to an apparently large number in the target period. For both hospitals, overdose attenders in the fourteen days after the broadcast were higher than those in the corresponding period for the two control years, but the rise in numbers began well before the programme was shown – in December in one hospital and in January in the other. Analysis of daily data showed no evidence of unusual short-term changes within the fortnight after the programme. We concluded there had been no copycat effect. It was one of those periodic fluctuations that appear in hospital statistics from time to time and it just happened to coincide with the television programme.

Does this mean that no imitation ever takes place? Clearly, that cannot be concluded on the basis of this study. There remains enough *prima facie* evidence to suggest caution when editors decide what to print or to show. Other studies, which have provided a more rigorous 'natural experiment', indicate that fiction can be powerful. Arnold Schmidtke showed how a fictional portrayal of a young man's suicide on a railway line could have an imitation effect on viewers.[11] He studied the number of railway suicides in the seventy days after the fictional suicide was broadcast and found an increase. The suggestion that this was indeed imitation was reinforced by the finding that the suicides most often occurred in people of the same age and sex as the fictional character. Furthermore, the numbers of suicides correlated with the viewing figures. The broadcast was repeated by the television company and Schmidtke found, once again, an increase in suicides. In total, his report estimated that an extra sixty suicide deaths occurred as a result of this fictional one.

Similarly, in 1999 Keith Hawton and colleagues found a marked increase in self-poisoning cases following a television programme featuring a paracetamol overdose. Forty-nine accident departments around the United Kingdom were put on alert and monitored their attendances before and after a fictional account of an overdose was aired on the BBC's *Casualty* drama. Total overdoses increased by 17 per cent in the week following the broadcast. Among those who saw the programme and went on to take an overdose, there was a twofold increase in the use of paracetamol.[12]

Criticisms of imitative research

Research on imitative suicidal behaviour has, however, been surrounded with controversy. There are three sorts of criticism.

First, that there is very little theory which can explain some of the anomalies in the data. For example, some of Phillips's work found a lag of three days before 'imitative' behaviour became apparent, but no theoretical account has been given for this. Furthermore, in the sort of 'macro' research that looks only at the gross numbers of suicides and only at whether a suicide story has occurred or not, there has been no attempt to match the properties of the media stimuli with the set of behaviours that qualify as an imitative response. Perhaps more serious than a lack of good theory is the possibility that at least part of the phenomenon is a mere statistical artefact: when one group of researchers re-analysed data from Phillips's 1982 soap-opera study, corrected some dating errors, increased the sample size and used a more reliable regression analysis, they failed to replicate his results.[13]

However, in a subsequent study Phillips and Carstensen[14] examined the daily fluctuation of a large number of teenage suicides during 1973–9 in relation to news or feature stories on the major TV networks. Using statistical analyses that corrected for the day of the week, month of the year, yearly trends and holidays, they found a mean increase per story or feature of 2.91 in the number of suicides. They also found a significant correlation between the number of news bulletins that featured a story and the increase in suicides in the subsequent seven-day period. Taking into account all previous criticisms, they also looked at similar time periods for the year before and the year after, and found there were no effects when there had not been a suicide story or feature article. Taken together with data from other researchers in very different contexts (such as the railway suicides reported by Schmidtke), there can be little doubt that imitation does occur.

Media guidelines

1. Detailed descriptions of methods of committing suicide or deliberate self-harm should not be given, nor shown in fictional portrayals, since these will demonstrate possible means for those who are suicidal.

2. Physical consequences of suicide attempts, where these have occurred (e.g. paralysis, brain damage), should not be minimised, but neither should such harmful consequences be dwelled upon, as this might attract those who seek victim status.

3. If the victim had prior mental-health problems, these should not be ignored. Many stories refer to life circumstances or philosophies as if these were sufficient precipitants. (See Chapter Six, where Arthur Koestler's suicide is discussed, and it is pointed out how reports of his death failed to focus on his long-standing psychological problems.)

4. Simplistic psychological notions, such as 'pressure', should not be used. Many people have such pressure, but few commit suicide, and such references belittle the complexity of the situation. Similarly, simple motives such as 'getting even' or 'becoming famous' should be avoided.

5. Where possible, stories should avoid emphasising the attractive qualities of the deceased in such a way as to make the suicide a part of this attractiveness.

6. Such stories should be accompanied by details of what help is available, together with hotline numbers (such as the Samaritans or other befriending agencies).

7. Extensive or unnecessary repeated coverage of such episodes should be avoided.

8. There should be ongoing discussion between those working in the media and mental-health experts in which the evidence for such imitative effects is kept under review.

Mechanisms of imitation

Much of our behaviour is learned by copying that of others. This is especially true when we are in situations where we do not know the right thing to do. Such processes determine children's behaviour much of the time, but are found later in life too. Uncertainty may be the key to when modelling is most likely to occur in suicidal behaviour. It is when prior suicidal feelings are accompanied by feelings of uncertainty about what to do that imitation will be most likely to increase the probability of suicidal behaviour. If the model is attractive or famous, the imitative effect will be stronger because their behaviour will resolve more of the uncertainty about suicide as the right course of action. Indeed, Phillips has found that the increase in copycat suicide is greater if more prominence is given to it. Other researchers have found that celebrity suicides in the United States produced imitative behaviour only if the celebrity was famous enough to merit the front page of the *New York Times*. Do any recommendations follow from this for media presentation of suicide?[15] The suggestions in the box above are based on those of Gould and Pirkis.[16]

INCITEMENT TO SUICIDE THROUGH THE INTERNET

One of the major concerns over recent years has been the easy access to models of suicide and graphic (often visual) information about methods. The problem is that the web may be a great source of finding help in a time of crisis. However, even searching for such information for help to reduce distress will undoubtedly lead internet users to sites that give technical information about methods of suicide. This information, that used to be on dedicated sites, may now be found on more accessible ones, and support groups that share information on how to kill oneself are common.[17] It is clear that this may potentially have a major role in exerting peer pressure.

Suicide researchers Jane Pirkis and Warwick Blood[18] reviewed evidence from eighteen studies on exposure to suicide-related material and subsequent suicides and drew the following conclusion: 'The Internet studies reviewed provide cautious support for a causal association between exposure to suicide-related material on the Internet and actual suicidal behaviour, although further analytical studies are required to confirm this relationship.' They also point out that legal control of pro-suicide websites has generally been regarded as too difficult, with the result that Australia is the only country to have introduced legislation that uses criminal sanctions to restrict the operation of such sites.[19]

CONCLUDING REMARKS

There is compelling evidence that imitation is a factor in adding to the risk of suicide. We've seen that the risk of both suicide and attempted suicide can be increased through exposure to seeing these portrayed in the media, and it does not matter if the portrayal is of a real or fictional event. Seeing others commit suicide, especially someone with whom there is a strong identification, may lower the barrier to suicide. However, there is little evidence that imitation effects have a large impact if there are no other risk factors present, and the overall impact on the suicide rate is relatively small. We need, therefore, to ask why imitation is not more common.

The first, most obvious reason is that most people are not in the 'vulnerability window' that gives them a strong motive to die. Decreasing barriers to suicide are simply irrelevant for the majority. But the second reason takes us back to the example of Kurt Cobain. Although some of his fans have apparently imitated his suicide, many of these deaths occurred a considerable time afterwards, so the role of direct imitation is questionable. The puzzle is why there have not been more. I believe the answer lies in the fact that the death of such an idol, though it upsets many fans, can unite them in mourning. At the very least, many followers of his music have a major topic of conversation, which acts as a source of bonding. The increased social support countermands the tendency to imitate. It follows that imitative suicide is more likely to happen in those individuals who are loners, or who are temporarily outside their social group. Obsessing about the death in isolation, without the social support of others, is most likely to result in imitative suicidal behaviour.

CHAPTER ELEVEN

Can We Prevent Suicide?

In assessing what means exist for preventing suicide, one of the most obvious measures would seem to be the more sensitive assessment of suicide risk by health professionals. Depression is a frequently occurring psychiatric disorder and most depressed patients are treated in general practice. Training primary-care professionals to identify depressive symptoms and treat them appropriately is a potentially important prevention strategy. Evidence suggests that 50 per cent of sufferers are not recognised by their general practitioner as suffering from major depression. A further 10 per cent are subsequently recognised, and of the 40 per cent who are not half will remain depressed. Twenty per cent of the original sample, therefore, are still depressed and not recognised six months later.

There are a number of reasons why depression is missed in the context of a GP's clinic. The patient may present somatic symptoms and physical problems; they may feel there is a stigma about presenting psychological problems, compounded by a belief that the doctor does not have time to listen to their psychological problems. There is also some evidence that depression is more likely to be missed if it is of recent origin, where the symptoms are atypical, the depressed mood is less severe or the person has less insight into their own symptoms. A picture emerges of a complex interplay of factors which results in the primary-care physician not spotting symptoms of depression.

Depression and hopelessness are clearly associated with suicidal ideation and behaviour. If depression is going unrecognised, then suicidal ideation is also likely to go unrecognised. Implicit blame is often put on the physician or mental-health professional who has failed to pick up the signs, yet it is never quite so simple. Data from twenty years ago seemed to suggest that between 50 and 80 per cent of people who commit suicide had seen a doctor up to one month prior to death. More recent reviews suggest that only 20 to 25 per cent of those committing suicide have seen their GP or other healthcare professional in the week before death, and 40 per cent in the month before. It is likely that the decrease in suicide among the older population and the increase in younger men account for this change. Young men are much less likely to visit their doctors than young women or older men.

Identifying scope for improvement in the recognition of depressive symptoms in general, and suicidal symptoms in particular, need not be associated with blaming the primary-care physicians for not spotting them in the first place. We need to understand more about the interpersonal processes that govern the interaction between doctor and patient. Studies examining the consultations between care-givers (physicians, psychiatrists, psychologists and mental-health counsellors) and patients who subsequently attempted suicide up to three months later found that 36 of the 50 patients studied (72 per cent) had, by their own accounts, sought professional help for depression or suicidal thinking in the three months prior to the episode.[1] However, according to the patients' own reports, they made direct reference to suicidal thinking in only 23 per cent of all consultations. How much this was because of reluctance to talk about these feelings and how much a result of the professional failing to ask the right questions is open to debate. According to the professionals' reports, they said they asked about suicidal feelings in 48 per cent of cases.

The study also found that people were much less likely to disclose symptoms to the physicians than to mental-health professionals. This confirms that a major determinant of what is talked about is the context of the visit. Even when a person *intends* to communicate emotional and psychological distress, once they enter the context of the physician's surgery, the evidence of physical medicine all around them elicits talk about their physical symptoms, rather than their psychological difficulties.

Another indication of how the interpersonal context determines what takes place between health professional and patient emerges from a study of how doctors ask different questions when talking to patients of different ages. Patients of fifty-five or older were not asked at all about suicidal thinking. Given that these patients were the most vulnerable for completed suicide, it seemed a surprising result. One possible explanation is that older people are more likely to express problems through physical symptoms. Another is that care-givers feel more reluctant to ask about the psychological symptoms of people older than themselves. Social mores that dictate respect for older people and their privacy may be a more powerful determinant of professionals' behaviour than previously thought.

Of course, even where suicidal ideas are picked up, there is a challenge for all clinicians about how best to react. If suicidal symptoms are reported, clinicians may still not enquire about patients' *reactions* to them (which may be the main determinant of whether they persist) or about accompanying, intrusive suicidal imagery. In the case of patients who are known to have deliberately self-harmed in the past, there is a well-documented tendency to be biased against any who have engaged in behaviour that is considered medically 'non-serious'.[2]

SUICIDE PREVENTION THROUGH KEEPING IN TOUCH

Can simply keeping in contact with vulnerable people prevent suicide? A study was conducted in San Francisco, concerning people who had attempted suicide,[3] whereby they were contacted one month after the event and asked if they had taken up offers of help. Those who had not done so were randomly allocated to one of two groups: a contact group and a no-contact group. The contact group received a note every month (for four months), every two months for the next eight months, and every three months thereafter for the next four years (a total follow-up of five years). Over this five-year period there was a significantly lower number of suicides in the contacted group. A subsequent report stated that these differences later disappeared, so that after four years there was no difference in the groups. This seems at first sight to indicate that the contact had not worked in the long term. On the other hand, since the study was stopped after five years, if it had been the regular contact that had made the difference, one might expect a rise in risk when that contact came to an end.

PRIMARY CARE AND PRIMARY PREVENTION: SOME CAUTIONS

We have seen that physicians sometimes miss the seriousness of depression, treating the single symptom of insomnia or agitation without checking for others. However, it remains painfully true that the chances of a GP successfully spotting a suicidal patient are relatively low, given that there is likely to be a suicide only once every four to five years among his or her patients. Because of the 40 per cent rate of contact of suicide victims with their doctors in the month prior to suicide, this means that a GP is likely to receive a consultation from somebody in the month before they commit suicide only once every eight to ten years. This makes it an extremely rare event compared with the large proportion of people who consult their doctors with emotional problems.[4]

Some have suggested that just because suicide is rare, that does not mean the doctor should not test for it. If a GP sees a child with a fever, he or she will test for meningitis, although this is also very rare. By analogy, it is suggested that the GP should spend some time testing for suicide risk. However, physical tests for rare diseases are not a fair analogy, as they often produce a greater certainty of diagnosis, and even if they do not, an 'at-risk' result may warrant further, more specialist testing. Yet even if a health professional used every available measuring instrument to assess suicide risk, the evidence suggests that he or she would successfully detect only half the people who would go on to commit suicide. Moreover, an enormous number of false positives would be 'detected'. The clinic would be full of people whom the GP suspected might kill themselves, but who, the statistics show, will not actually harm themselves.

THE GENERAL PROBLEM OF PREDICTION

In every branch of medicine, clinical psychology or social policy the search is always on for tests that will tell us who is at risk of a particular condition, so we can take steps to intervene earlier. It is rare, however, to find the perfect test that helps us to be sure who will develop an illness. Even when someone is at high genetic risk, it does not mean it is certain that they will have the condition. Why is prediction so difficult?

Sensitivity and specificity

There are two problems in predicting suicidal behaviour: sensitivity (not having many 'misses') and specificity (not having 'false positives'). Any method of assessment needs to have adequate sensitivity (i.e. a high hit rate for 'true positives', predicting suicide and getting suicide). It must also have adequate specificity, predicting the true negatives (predicting no suicide and getting no suicide).[5] The issue of specificity is particularly significant because of the low base rate of suicidal behaviour. Thus, even in a highly selected group, there will be more people falsely identified as at risk (false positives) than correctly identified as at risk (hits). When trying to predict suicide the problem is even greater.

One study followed up almost 5000 in-patients.[6] The predictive model identified 35 out of the 67 subsequent suicides but at the cost of over 1000 false positives. Whichever analysis was used, the result was a false positive rate of 25–30 per cent. Over 1000 people would have been put on the vulnerable list, but would *not* have committed suicide. Perhaps more worrying was the 44 per cent false negative rate. This meant that of the people who did commit suicide, 44 per cent would have been allocated to the 'low-risk' category.

This pessimistic message is reinforced by other studies.[7] So-called 'high-risk' groups are not, after all, at that high a risk of suicide. Take the statistic that 15 per cent of those who have been in-patients in psychiatric units with a diagnosis of major depression will commit suicide. They are at a greatly increased risk compared with the general population. Yet even they will commit suicide at a rate of some 1 per cent per year over a period of about 30–35 years. For every 100 patients in the 'suicide high-risk' category, only one will actually commit suicide in any one year, and we cannot be sure which one, or when. The question of 'when' is one of the most difficult to answer.

Timing

It is clear that assessment of suicidal risk cannot merely be done at a single point in time, on the basis only of predisposing (and pre-existing) vulnerability factors. Changes over time also need to be taken into account. Are there any indications about what the vulnerable times might be?

Perhaps the greatest indication that change in circumstances puts people at greater risk is the finding that the period following discharge from psychiatric hospital is the time of most suicide risk. This is one of the major conclusions of British psychiatrist and mental-health policy expert Professor Louis Appleby and his colleagues who conducted the UK's National Confidential Inquiry into Suicide and Homicide by People with Mental Illness, first reported in 1999.[8] The inquiry found that, of around 10,000 cases of suicide (or cases where open verdicts had been returned) over two years, some 2400 had been in contact with mental-health services in the year before their death, and details were available for 2177 of them. Of this sub-sample, 358 (16 per cent) suicides had occurred while the person was an in-patient (this represents 3.6 per cent of all the suicides over that period) and 519 (24 per cent) within three months of discharge from hospital. The statistics confirmed that the risk of suicide is highest immediately after discharge, and falls day by day during the first week, and week by week thereafter. In terms of prevention, it seems that better aftercare immediately following discharge is a major priority.

On the other hand, we need to bear in mind that over the two-year period of the study, there would have been around 300,000 admissions to psychiatric units and wards. Knowing who is most at risk might seem to be the best way of planning aftercare, but this study found, as others have done, that the usual characteristics that indicate higher risk of suicide in a community sample (being male, single, living alone, unemployed, having a history of alcohol or drug abuse) do not identify a high-risk group in a sample of people who have been admitted to a psychiatric unit. Further analysis of the data showed that 45 per cent of suicides by people who have been in touch with a psychiatric service in the year before their death will be by those who have harmed themselves before *and* either have a history of alcohol and drug abuse or a previous admission to a psychiatric unit. The inquiry also raised concerns about the fact that many of the patients had not been taking the medication that had been prescribed for them.

A further study investigated whether there are any aspects of a person's behaviour while they are in hospital that might indicate a special risk of suicide later.[9] Perhaps unsurprisingly, the researchers found that previous compulsory admission together with actually expressing suicidal ideas while in hospital predicted suicides within three months of discharge. More seriously, another study found suicide often took place following a reduction in care.[10] This reduction of care had been decided at the final appointment with the health professional responsible for the patient. It seems that only in retrospect is one able to determine who was at risk.

These studies all confirm that patients are most vulnerable following discharge. But other studies show that *any* time of change can increase risk. For example, in prison populations the first twenty-four hours are the most risky time: over 50 per cent of prison suicides occur in the period immediately following incarceration. The vulnerable times for psychiatric patients are also those of change: a move out of hospital, whether on a weekend pass or at discharge, or even a move within the hospital to another unit; or change in symptoms, such as in activity, sleep and appetite that may precede a change in mood and hopelessness; or in social, family or living arrangements.[11]

This is an under-researched topic, so any theory must be speculative. Nevertheless, we can narrow the possibilities. I suggest that any disruption to a settled routine triggers a state in which a person reviews his or her goals and plans. They start to compare current circumstances to goals – what they would *like* to be the case or what they feel *ought* to be the case. The review includes an assessment of their own energy and the ability levels needed to achieve these goals. If the individual feels that they do not have the energy or resources to reduce the gap between current reality and future goals, they are in danger of feeling even more hopeless.

The change in circumstances that can trigger such a life review may be subtle. It may be a change in the external or 'internal' environment (i.e. a person's mood state). But however it has been triggered, once the life review has started the individual may find it very difficult to switch it off. The ruminative habits of thought in such circumstances can produce, for the individual, extremely pessimistic self-assessment and further catastrophic downward spirals in mood.[12] These are the critical periods for suicidal thoughts and behaviour, and this is when the availability of the means of suicide becomes an important factor.

Availability of means

The devastating effect of the availability of lethal substances is illustrated by the case of a brilliant Cambridge postgraduate student who killed himself with a lethal injection some years ago. He had been the best biology student at his school, and at Cambridge he performed as well as his early school career had promised, coming top in all subjects in the university examinations in his first and second years. At 24 years old he was thought by his tutors to be one of the brightest students of the past decade. It was clear he was heading for a brilliant academic career, and he started on a course that would eventually give him not only a medical qualification but a Ph.D as well. But his private life was not going so well.

According to friends and tutors, he loved a woman who did not love him, and his academic work and achievements seemed no compensation for such unrequited love. He was quite a private person, but nobody expected the devastating effect this relationship would have. At a party in Cambridge one Saturday night he appeared cheerful, and may have gone home briefly before going to the laboratory. It was there that the availability of lethal substances had its effect, for none of his friends or tutors doubted that, had he been able to get over his acute feeling of desperation, the weekend would have passed and he could have recovered his composure. But the laboratory held chemicals used on animals in research – substances lethal if used in an unsafe manner. They were at hand when he felt at his worst, and suicide was the result.

Clinicians and researchers have had little doubt for some time that if help and protection are available during a period of suicidal crisis, and lethal methods are not to hand, the crisis may pass and the person may not commit suicide. It may not even be help that is needed, but simply distraction at a critical moment. One person who put the muzzle of a revolver into his mouth and was feeling for the trigger suddenly heard his children laughing and running through the hall. 'That snapped me out of it. The suicide impulse lasted only a moment – but that's all it takes,' he reported later.

The basis for expecting that availability of lethal methods makes a difference is this: if the preferred method is not there, the motivation to seek out an alternative may not be high enough to prompt such a search. The suicidal feelings may pass without being acted upon. If this seems difficult to understand, we only need recall that suicide occurs in the context of hopelessness and despair. If a single opportunity appears to present an escape, yet that escape route is blocked, the despair may turn into hopelessness about suicide as an effective solution. The 'Russian roulette' aspect of suicidal motivation produces a sense of not caring 'whether I live or die'. If a person has effectively 'allowed the Fates to decide', then their verdict in favour of staying alive may be passively accepted. But if, at that moment, the person has access to lethal methods, the outcome will be suicide.

Of course, a person who is determined to kill him- or herself may take many steps to ensure success, including taking themselves away to a place where they will not be interrupted. Even where this does not occur, the family or friends of a suicidal person cannot be on hand twenty-four hours a day. To try to be constantly present in this way would put so much pressure on a relationship it would be unsustainable. Nevertheless, many family members have tortured themselves with the thought that it should have been possible to ensure that lethal means of suicide were unavailable. The problem here is knowing which threats to remove.

In *Savage God*, Al Alvarez quotes the views of Seneca, who said that the means of committing suicide are everywhere: each precipice and river, each branch of each tree, every vein in the body will set a person free. Alvarez disagreed: 'No one is promiscuous in his way of dying. A man who has decided to hang himself will never jump in front of a train. And the more sophisticated and painless the method, the greater the chance of failure: I can vouch, at least, for that.' If true, this means that a health professional may ask someone who is suicidal what they have thought of doing, and try to ensure that these means are removed. While this may be difficult or impossible in the private realm of family life, it may yet be possible in public spaces.

The preventative effect of removing lethal means has indeed been demonstrated many times. The most commonly cited example is the fall in suicide rates during the 1960s and 1970s in the United Kingdom as domestic gas was detoxified. In 1948–50 poisoning by domestic gas accounted for 41 per cent of male suicides and 60 per cent of female ones. By 1970, only 16 per cent of males and 9 per cent of females used domestic gas in suicide. Death by this method had completely disappeared by

1990. It has been estimated that the detoxification of domestic gas has prevented approximately 6700 deaths by suicide. Detoxification of domestic gas in Japan and USA has been shown to have had a similar effect.[13] Similarly, the introduction of catalytic converters in cars in the US in 1975 and in the UK from 1993 onwards, involving drastic reduction of exhaust toxicity, was followed by a reduction in the use of vehicle exhaust for suicide.[14]

However, the reduction in overall rate from the unavailability of one method may gradually bottom out as alternative methods become more common. In England and Wales, prior to the introduction of catalytic converters, car exhaust had replaced domestic gas as a major means of suicide. The increase in vehicle-exhaust deaths paralleled the increase in motor-vehicle use over that period. In fact it slightly *exceeded* the rate of increase in car usage, but this might have been due to the fact that within the car market there had been an increase in the proportion of hatchback models, which made suicide by this method easier. As emission controls on car exhausts were adopted by more and more countries, a reduction in suicide using car exhaust occurred. A worrying trend in the UK is that, as such emission controls on car exhaust has reduced the number of suicides by this method, there has been a corresponding increase in the use of hanging.[15]

Dangerous weapons

Suicide rates using firearms are, of course, another indicator that availability of means is important. Guns are used in over 50 per cent of suicide cases in the United States compared to only 3 per cent in Great Britain. In the United States the impact of availability has focused on the strictness of gun legislation from state to state. There are significant correlations between 'gun-control statute strictness' and rates of suicide over the forty-eight continental states.

Legislative efforts to restrict firearm ownership have been associated with a reduction in firearm suicide rates in many countries, including the UK,[16] New Zealand,[17] Australia,[18] Canada,[19] Austria[20] and the US.[21] In the US, suicide rates are consistently lower in states operating a restrictive firearm policy (e.g. safe storage of guns and waiting periods before gaining access to bought guns). In the UK, legislation introduced in 1989 to restrict access to guns (e.g. safe storage, registration) led to a substantial reduction in suicide by firearms overall, as well as in the subgroup of farmers who most frequently used this method in suicide.[22] This, and similar studies from countries where firearms are not widely accessible, shows that even in these contexts restriction to access can affect fatality rates considerably.

Although stricter gun laws correlate with fewer suicides by firearms (suggesting that making the method less available will reduce fatalities), there is also a slight association between lower firearm availability and the more frequent use of alternative methods (though not poisons or hanging). Despite this, there are reasons to think that availability *is* important. The positive correlation between strict gun laws and alternative methods does not tell us the overall *level* of suicide by these other methods. Indeed, it has been found in the US that the *total* suicide rate is *lower* in states with strict gun control laws.[23] It appears Alvarez may have been at least partly right: only a few suicidal people switch to an alternative method for suicide; it seems that people do have a preferred method they would use to kill themselves, and are unlikely to deviate from this when actually suicidal. This is important clinically, because depressed patients who are at risk but not currently suicidal may agree to get rid of the means of killing themselves that they know they might use later, when feeling worse.

Dangerous medication

Other evidence of a link between suicide and availability of method is shown by the marked correlation between the number of prescriptions given out for sedatives, sleeping pills and tranquillisers and the rate of suicide by self-poisoning.

One aspect is the danger of specific drugs. Prescribed mood-altering drugs, such as tricyclic antidepressants, used to account for 15 per cent of all suicides. Some suicides have, therefore, undoubtedly been prevented by the prescribing of relatively non-toxic antidepressants.

Another aspect is the question of the total availability of medication to patients. Polypharmacy (the prescribing of many different medications to the same person) may in itself not be a problem; indeed, it has indisputable benefits for many patients. However, if an individual has many health problems and one of them (e.g. depression) results in their becoming recurrently suicidal, easy physical access to large amounts of different drugs is likely to increase risk of suicidal behaviour and a fatal outcome. The exponential rise in prescribing of medication seen over the last few decades, particularly in response to psychological difficulties, is likely to have made this problem more acute.

What is physically available tends to be used in self-harm and, consequently, changes in availability influence both occurrence and lethality of episodes of deliberate self-harm (and the likelihood of dying from the episode had it not been medically treated). However, with co-proxamol as a notable exception (see

p. 204), research into the availability of drugs has, to date, focused on medication bought over the counter. Yet, data from monitoring systems and systematic studies internationally suggest that the current level of access to prescribed medication is historically unprecedented: in the US, spending on prescribed medication increased sixfold between 1990 and 2008, with an average annual growth of 9.9 per cent estimated from 1997 to 2007.[24] A comprehensive US study of opioids in musculoskeletal pain showed that despite a stable number of visits to a general physician related to musculoskeletal pain, prescription of opioid drugs increased dramatically, suggesting that the threshold to prescribe these drugs has dropped.[25] Prescribing of psychotropic medication has also increased dramatically over the last twenty years both in the US and in continental Europe.[26] In the US, psychotropic medication is the most commonly used type of medication overall, and in 2010 sales of antidepressant, antipsychotic and stimulant medications accounted for 11.4 per cent of total US spending on pharmaceuticals.[27] In France, an estimated one in ten people uses at least one antidepressant,[28] while in Norway the sale of antidepressants has increased dramatically over the two last decades, from 12 defined daily dosages (DDD) of antidepressants per 1000 inhabitants per day in 1990 to 58 DDD/1000/day in 2012.[29]

Research into the association between access to medication and medication-related self-harm is premised on the assumption that substances used in overdoses reflect ease of access, i.e. that patients will use in their suicidal episodes whatever is available to them. While it may be reasonable to deduce this from the above studies, this assumption has not been empirically verified. The data are correlational, not causal.

Research clinical psychologist Bergljot Gjelsvik found in a

large sample in Norway that patients engaging in deliberate self-poisoning had been prescribed much more medication compared to the general population.[30] Hyper-prescribing may be medically warranted, but it has obvious dangers. In Gjelsvik's study, the majority of patients who took an overdose ingested medication prescribed to them. She has also found that physicians did not curb prescribing to patients following an episode of self-poisoning.[31]

Consistent with these results, a clear relationship between prescribing patterns and the deaths by these drugs can be found. The clear implication is the need to give at-risk patients medication for a few days only wherever possible, and/or give the medication to another family member for safekeeping. Neither of these preventative strategies has been systematically studied.

There are even more deaths attributable to analgesics, anti-fever and anti-rheumatic medications, many of which are available without prescription. Ten per cent of all suicide deaths by overdose involve paracetamol, while 5 per cent involve aspirin. However, nearly all patients (94 per cent) who take an overdose use the first drug they can obtain. Few (only 20 per cent) are found to know about the toxicity of a drug or what quantity would be lethal, though this varies considerably depending on whether it is a first-ever or repeat episode. Many wrongly believe that because aspirin and paracetamol are freely available from the pharmacist they are relatively non-toxic. In France, it was known for a long time that the fact that paracetamol was not allowed to be sold in quantities greater than 8g (16 × 500mg tablets) meant that there were very few fatal paracetamol overdoses. Similar limits were introduced in the United Kingdom in 1998 and immediately resulted in a reduction of a quarter in suicide deaths by this method.[32] A recent follow-up study has shown a long-term effect of the legislation, estimated as a 43 per cent reduction in deaths by paracetamol overdose between 1998 and 2009.

Due to the very high relative toxicity of co-proxamol (around thirty times higher than paracetamol),[33] this drug was withdrawn in the UK in 2005. The withdrawal has shown a similarly beneficial effect – a significant reduction in suicide by co-proxamol, without a pronounced increase in deaths caused by overdoses from other drugs.[34]

Note, however, that reducing access to means, although it may hinder specific episodes from occurring, may not affect a person's underlying risk of trying to harm themselves in the longer-term future, if circumstances do not change. Even in environments with severely limited access to suicidal means, such as prisons, suicide rates are high. There are clearly, therefore, limits to what can be done to prevent someone from harming themselves if they are of firm intent.

Dangerous jobs

It used to be thought that the link between availability of means and suicide was underscored by the high rate of suicide in those professions that had easy access to lethal means (veterinary surgeons, dental practitioners, pharmacists, farmers and medical practitioners). Indeed, until the mid-1980s there was strong evidence to suggest that this was the case. However, a UK study showed that by 2005 the situation had changed, and that the rate of suicide in these professions had dropped dramatically, leaving the highest risk among manual workers (such as labourers, refuse collectors and dockers).[35] There are no good explanations for this change, nor yet data from other countries that could tell us whether the shift is cross-national. The only explanation of such a reduction is that the amendment in legislation about safe storage has gradually affected a new generation of professionals, giving them a general 'aversion' to handling these lethal objects and substances, so that they have gradually lost their ability to represent an 'opportunity'.

SAMARITANS AND SUICIDE PREVENTION CENTRES

Between 4 and 7 per cent of people who commit suicide in the United Kingdom have had past contact with the Samaritans, but how recent these contacts are is not clear. For many years there has been a debate about whether suicide prevention centres and organisations significantly affect the suicide rate. What is not in dispute is that there is a great need for such centres and organisations, as shown by the extensive use made of them. However, even though people know where to turn for help, when they are very suicidal they may not act on this knowledge. One study found that of those patients who attempted suicide, 72 per cent had sufficient knowledge of the Samaritans to be able to have contacted them, yet less than 2 per cent had actually sought their help on that occasion.[36] Another found that those towns which had established a Samaritans branch did not differ in suicide rate from those which had not.[37]

A more encouraging report came from an analysis of the changes in the suicide rates in 226 cities in the United States between 1968 and 1973. Some had developed suicide prevention centres over the period, others had not. There was a reduction in suicide rates among white females below the age of 25 in those cities that had introduced such centres. Given that this was just the sort of client who most frequently used those centres, here indeed was a promising finding.

SCHOOL-BASED INTERVENTION

Following the rapid increase in youth suicide in the United States in the 1980s, many school-based suicide-intervention programmes were introduced. Their aims were to increase awareness of the problem of suicide, to provide information about the help available and to encourage suicidal teenagers to come forward and seek it. Wherever such programmes were evaluated, however, they had little or no effect.[38]

Such education programmes target a relatively low-risk audience. The suicide rate among teenagers in school, though increasing, is still low compared with the general population. Indeed, such programmes might not reach those adolescents who are most at risk, such as regular truants. More seriously, the risk profile of a potential teenage suicide patient is still not fully known. This means that the warning signs as taught may not be representative or accurate.

A further study has assessed the impact of suicide-prevention programmes on teenagers' attitudes and knowledge about suicide, with evaluation based on a questionnaire completed before and after exposure to the programme.[39] Even before, most students had a sound knowledge of the issues relating to suicide: the warning signs; the fact that suicide threat should be taken seriously; and that vulnerable individuals should be helped in consultation with responsible adults. But where the research found attitudes that would be considered inappropriate (e.g. that suicide could be a reasonable solution to problems), the education programmes did not change them.

Chapter Ten reviewed the evidence suggesting an increased risk of copycat suicidal behaviour if vulnerable people were exposed to examples of people who harmed themselves. Given this risk, school-based suicide-awareness programmes would need to be shown to be clearly effective in reducing the risk of suicidal behaviour for them to be justified. Such effects have not been shown. It is possible that any benefits of such programmes are offset by the fact that they destigmatise suicide. By portraying it as an understandable response to stress, the intervention may actually backfire by encouraging an unrealistic, romantic view of suicide, increasing the chances of imitation. The UK government's NICE committee is also wary of such programmes and calls for further evidence.[40]

CONCLUDING REMARKS

Given all this information about who is most vulnerable and what are the most dangerous circumstances, can we estimate the possible effects of different prevention methods? The evidence strongly suggests that, for any individual, suicidal impulses come in waves. This implies that if such impulses can find no ready expression, they may pass without the person having harmed him- or herself. The precise timing of such compelling suicidal urges remains unpredictable, but further research should focus on times of change and how such changes can be prepared for, so they do not bring about a life-review process that sends the person's mood spiralling out of control. Meanwhile, if suicide occurs, there will always be some who feel they should have seen it coming: family, friends, health professionals. Hindsight is hugely painful and, as those bereaved by suicide know all too well, it adds a dimension to grief that feels impossible to resolve. Primary prevention needs urgently to focus on measures to reduce the number of 'invitations to suicide' in the environment, and public policy should always try to make our environment safer, but families and friends should also know that a person who is determined will often find a way, no matter what any of us do as individuals.

CHAPTER TWELVE

Healing the Pain: Therapy for the Suicidal Mind

When inconsolable sorrow threatens to overwhelm any of us, it is the most natural thing in the world for us to want to get rid of it. We'd do anything to stop it from hurting so much. Over the years, there have been many attempts to find a therapy that might help those who are at risk of reacting to mental pain by harming themselves. At the time I wrote the first and second editions of this book, I was very hopeful that one or more of these therapies would prove effective – that by now we could give clear recommendations to sufferers about where they should go for help. There are one or two approaches that have shown promise, but these tend to be limited to self-harm that is linked to specific types of psychological problem, rather than being applicable to the majority of those who harm themselves. Clinicians and scientists are therefore taking stock and considering a radically different perspective.[1]

REVIEWING THE EXISTING EVIDENCE

The most commonly accepted way to answer the question of what type of treatment may be most helpful is to combine all the research studies that have used randomised controlled trials (in which an intervention is compared to a control condition) in what is called a 'meta-analysis'. This ensures that we can see if the treatments are really having an effect over and above any of the natural healing processes, such as simply the time elapsed since a suicidal crisis.

A comprehensive meta-analysis in 2011 looked at all such studies of psychotherapies that aimed to reduce suicidal behaviour.[2] Its conclusions were very pessimistic. It said that there was still considerable uncertainty about which, if any, treatments could alleviate suicidal mind-states and reduce repetition rates. The review included trials of a wide range of therapies, including problem-solving therapy, Cognitive Therapy, psychodynamic therapy and interpersonal problem-solving skills training, as well as psychosocial interventions, such as emergency card interventions, telephone contact and postcard interventions. The main thing that the review looked at was whether these therapies and interventions could reduce the risk of repetition of suicidal behaviour, although change in level of suicidal thinking, degree of hopelessness and depression were included when feasible.

Although there was some (very limited) evidence to suggest that psychological interventions *may* be helpful in reducing rates compared to usual care, the overall conclusion was that the evidence was weak. (In randomised trials 'usual care' refers to 'the control group' who continue to receive the care they'd usually get from their GP or psychiatrist, so the researcher can see if the new treatment is better than this.) They did not feel that they could recommend any specific therapy, confining their suggestions to the very generic recommendation of three to twelve therapy sessions, aimed at identifying the stressors found to be most difficult and seemingly intractable, with a qualified therapist.

The situation was more optimistic when reviewing evidence for therapies for specific disorders in which suicidal behaviour frequently occurs. For instance, American psychologist and expert on suicidal behaviour Professor Marsha Linehan developed Dialectical Behaviour Therapy (DBT) for people diagnosed with borderline personality disorder and it has been shown to have reliable benefit in reducing repetition rates (see box below).[3] Overall, the reviewers pointed out that considerable caution is warranted when implementing a psychological intervention for suicidal patients.

Dialectical Behaviour Therapy (DBT)

Professor Linehan's Dialectical Behaviour Therapy (DBT) combines weekly individual and group therapy over a one-year period. It uses treatment strategies from behavioural, cognitive and supportive psychotherapies. A behavioural/problem-solving component focuses on enhancing capability, generating alternative ways of coping, clarifying and managing contingencies, all with the emphasis on the 'here and now'. The 'dialectical' aspect lies in its emphasis on balancing *acceptance* of (seeing clearly) the stresses that exist in the environment on the one hand with the need to *change* them on the other. The theme is encouraging clients to really grasp things, to understand them deeply as they are and to step back from them temporarily in order to see what might be changed.

The individual therapy (lasting one hour each week) stays within a strict agenda and prioritises themes related to suicidal behavior. Linehan believes this is a critical part of the therapy; she asserts that newly trained therapists too easily avoid explicit discussion of suicidal thoughts, threats and behaviour. The client needs to learn that help for other problems can only be discussed when the self-harm behaviour has been faced directly and then brought under control.

Individual therapy sessions are supplemented by weekly group skills training, which lasts for two and a half hours a session, focusing on four modules:

- interpersonal problem-solving
- distress tolerance
- mindfulness
- emotional regulation.

Studies to assess the effectiveness of DBT have been very encouraging. Altogether, they constitute impressive evidence that this approach provides a major source of hope for many people with some of the most intractable social and emotional problems.

This leaves a puzzle: if the processes leading to suicidal behaviour are predominantly psychological, why are there not more psychological treatments that can affect it? Partly, the weak evidence may reflect the fact that self-harm is a group of vastly heterogeneous behaviours with many different causes, rather than a distinct psychiatric 'disorder'. This means that studies include patients that differ hugely in their needs, so that the constraint of any randomised trial – each examining a single therapy approach – is simply inadequate to cope with the diversity of the problems brought to the clinic. Sociologists would not be surprised by the lack of evidence for therapy: they would say that suicidal behaviour arises from societal conditions, so psychological therapy for individuals will never make a substantial difference. Of course, social conditions are hugely important; yet when it comes down to it, the task for all of us is to learn to navigate in our social world, dealing as best we can with the setbacks that come when we fail to achieve a goal we've been longing for, or when we feel estranged from others at work, in the community or in our personal relationships – so psychological factors still come into play. Emotional, physical and sexual abuse is a societal problem, but it does its damage to men and women as individuals, who feel alone with their suffering.

Another possibility for the weak evidence base is that we may not yet understand how risk factors translate into key mechanisms involved in ongoing suicidal risk, and how these can be rendered amenable to psychological intervention. I shall return to this possibility later.

GENERAL CONSIDERATIONS: EXPLORING SUICIDAL SIGNS AND SYMPTOMS

Although, as we have said, depression is often associated with suicidal thoughts, not all depressed people are suicidal: it is when depressed people also become defeated, hopeless and trapped that they are most likely to feel suicidal. Therefore, a primary goal of therapy with suicidal people must be accurate assessment of: their state of hopelessness and entrapment (now and at their worst time in the past); getting a sense of how stable their current life situation is (both objectively and subjectively to the person themselves), especially their interpersonal relationships (by far the most common precipitant); how impulsive they are/have been at their worst time and whether they tend to use alcohol and drugs that might lower the threshold for dangerous behaviour. Given that two-thirds of episodes of self-harm are contemplated for less than an hour beforehand, impulsiveness may be considered an important vulnerability factor.

Virtually all structured approaches to helping those who feel suicidal have certain key characteristics. First, they have a well-planned rationale. This provides an initial structure that guides patients to the belief that they can control things in their lives and thereby their own emotional problems. Second, they give people the motivation and the training in skills to feel more effective in solving problems in their lives. Third, they emphasise the independent practice of these skills by the person outside the therapy context, and provide sufficient structure to help this to happen. Finally, they allow patients to attribute improvement in their mood to their own increased skilfulness and not that of the therapist.

Insights from Cognitive Therapy (see box, page 215) provide a useful 'roadmap' for exploration for both patient and therapist. The patient may arrive at the conclusion that life is intolerable through combinations of the errors in reasoning that are characteristic in depression. In *dichotomous thinking* (black/white, all-or-nothing thinking) there is no perceived middle path – just the extremes. *Selective abstraction* consists of the selecting out of only a part of a situation and ignoring others. So, for example, in a supervisor's report on a piece of work that gives praise, but mentions at one point that some aspects need more work, 'He doesn't like my work at all' would be selective abstraction. In *arbitrary inference* a conclusion is inferred from irrelevant evidence – for example, a person phones a boy/girlfriend and no one answers: 'S/he's probably out with another partner' would be an arbitrary inference (if inferred on those grounds alone). *Over-generalisation* is concluding from one specific negative event that other negative events are therefore more likely, for example, failure at maths means failure at everything. Finally, *catastrophising* is to think the very worst of a situation.

Cognitive Therapy (CT)

Professors Greg Brown, A. T. Beck and colleagues in Philadelphia conducted an important study of CT for people who had attempted suicide (participants in their study were highly socially vulnerable, with over 40 per cent with an income of $8000 or less and 66 per cent unemployed or disabled). They found that many people failed to turn up for appointments or arrived at the wrong time and could not be seen in the usual clinic where the therapists were engaged in other clinical duties. So the authors radically changed what they were doing, introducing case managers for every patient in the study who were responsible for keeping in touch with everyone, giving out bus tokens, making home visits, picking up some patients in cars, arranging community voicemail facilities, using the Philadelphia Homeless Database to track patients, agreeing at the outset some contact people who would be likely to know where the patient was at any time. The authors found a drop from 38 per cent to 20 per cent in repeated suicidal behaviour in the period following the active intervention.

Many of the errors of logic which underlie such beliefs and assumptions are exactly those found in depression. The danger with suicidal people is that they act so decisively and violently on their beliefs, and often this process takes place in only a few minutes. First, their thinking about their problems is dominated by the distortions described; then they react to these thoughts as inescapable facts and take proportionately drastic action. Because this is a process – however swift – intervention to prevent acts of extreme hopelessness about the possibility of ever ending the mental pain (which is felt to be intolerable) is the factor that turns depression into suicidal depression. Sudden changes in emotion in either direction may also signal impending suicidal behaviour.

PSYCHOLOGICAL BARRIERS IN CLINICIANS SEEKING TO HELP THE SUICIDAL

If clinicians are to offer help to those at risk of suicide they need to feel that there is something useful that they can do to reduce the risk. But there are problems. Many clinicians believe that it is just too hard to say who is at risk, but this is not the only barrier. Some believe they are hampered in contacting wider family or friends by confidentiality issues, or they may feel that if a person has real-life problems, psychotherapy of any sort is inappropriate. Others feel that talking about suicide might 'put the idea into their heads'. Let us look briefly at each of these issues.

Assessing risk of repetition in those who have harmed themselves

As we have seen in the discussion of specificity and sensitivity issues in predicting suicide (see pages 192–3), this is not straightforward, and it is easy to feel that it is not worth doing at all. Despite robust evidence showing that previous attempted suicide, previous out-patient and in-patient psychiatric treatment, not living with relatives, previous diagnosis of personality disorder and problems in the use of alcohol are associated with increased risk of repeated suicide attempts, it is still difficult to identify who will be at future risk. Apart from 'historical' risk factors (e.g. previous attempted suicide), assessment of future risk typically relies on assessment of the seriousness of the most recent/current self-harm episode.

So what constitutes a serious suicidal episode? As we have seen (see page 68), 'seriousness' is not simply a case of *medical* seriousness. However, most health systems continue to demand that some risk assessment, however crude, is done; and so long as the lack of sensitivity and specificity are noted, it can be used as a therapeutic procedure in its own right.[5]

Confidentiality barriers

Wherever possible, it is important to draw in family or friends, if it is felt this will be supportive. One of the most difficult things for the families of those who have harmed or killed themselves is the later disclosure that their loved one had talked to a physician or therapist, but that the seriousness of their suicidal thinking had stayed within the consultation room because the therapist imagined that it would be breaking client confidentiality to communicate the suicidality to anyone else. It might indeed pose ethical problems *if the clinician did not ask permission to do so*, but many do not realise that it is permissible simply to ask the patient if there is anyone who it might be helpful to tell, and to check if they mind if they (the clinician or a colleague) got in touch with the person, if the patient did not feel able to do so themselves.

Is therapy appropriate for those with real-life problems?

Many people have overwhelming problems in living, so a therapist may feel it is unethical to 'do therapy'. Is not the patient's hopelessness understandable? Reality-based hopelessness is indeed often found. Many suicidal people have real problems that must not be minimised by the therapist. On the other hand, some people appear able to cope with apparently unbearable problems without becoming suicidal. Why? Possibly because depressive hopelessness is not the same as normal sadness. Financial hardship and interpersonal chaos may reasonably cause a great deal of anger, frustration and sadness. However, a person becomes depressed and suicidal when their sadness changes to a situation in which the person tells themselves, 'I'm to blame', 'I've never succeeded at anything in my life', 'If my love leaves, I am nothing'. People under great stress – stress which has understandable consequences on mood – need all the coping resources they can muster. What suicidal depression adds is a constant stream of negative thoughts and images to convince them they are a bad or worthless person who does not deserve to live. Therapy may be conceived as enabling the person to discriminate between realistic and depressive hopelessness, so that the real problems can be faced realistically.

Might discussion of suicidal feelings precipitate a suicide attempt?

If the client believes there are overwhelming reasons for dying, as Linehan has pointed out, it is not useful to proceed with therapy as if these reasons did not exist. The feelings of wanting to self-harm need to be faced with courage and patience. Seeing clearly that there are reasons for wanting to escape into oblivion or death is only the first step to deciding whether any of the problems that seem so overwhelming can be endured and met in a different, more compassionate way. There is no evidence that explicit discussion of such issues increases suicidal intent. Indeed, clinical experience suggests the opposite. A research study headed by Madelyn Gould at Columbia University that looked specifically at the issue came to the same conclusion.[6]

TOWARDS A NEW UNDERSTANDING AND THERAPEUTIC APPROACH

Research on the psychological processes underlying hopelessness and suicidal behaviour would suggest that any successful therapy needs to affect the global and undifferentiated cognitive style in suicidal patients, which is likely to to be activated whenever any change triggers a ruminative review of their lives. The tendency of clients to recall events in their lives in a generalised, undifferentiated way is associated with an inability to problem-solve, both in terms of the number of alternatives people can generate and the effectiveness of those alternatives.

We have seen that research suggests that non-specificity of memory and difficulties in emotional regulation are closely related in exacerbating suicidal crises. The therapies that appear most promising are those that make the links between thoughts, feelings and behaviour more explicit. Might these therapies be helping the person become more specific in their encoding and retrieval of events in their lives? According to Linehan, this appears likely. She points out that DBT, for example, involves 'an exhaustive description of the moment-to-moment chain of environmental and behavioural events that preceded the suicidal behaviour … Alternative solutions that the individual could have used are explored, behavioural deficits as well as factors that interfere with more adaptive solutions are examined, and remedial procedures are applied if necessary.' All this, Linehan asserts, is helped by training in mindfulness skills (see pages 223–5) that helps people to sustain their attentional focus when it is under threat, to stand back and see that their thoughts are mental events and to *turn towards* their suffering instead of trying to fix, suppress or over-analyse it.

Notice what has happened here: it is not just the *occurrence* of suicidal thoughts or images that is seen as important. It is how people relate to them that matters. The case of flash-forwards (strong images of future situations) is a good illustration of this. Flash-forwards imitate the situation with flash-*backs* in post-traumatic stress disorder (PTSD). In PTSD, whereas flash-backs are the most prominent clinical feature, it is what happens *after* such intrusive imagery that is critical in determining whether the symptoms persist. That is, it is *negative ruminations about* the intrusion, motivated by the wish to get rid of them (e.g. 'I should be over this by now'; 'I'm weak to be thinking like this'; 'These feelings mean I must be going crazy'), that cause symptoms in PTSD to persist and escalate.[7] What if it was exactly the same situation for suicidal thoughts and imagery? It would imply that we need to change the focus of our therapy away from the content of the thoughts and images, however horrible and compelling they are, towards the processes that arise immediately after any such thought has occurred.

Let us summarise the situation: defeat and entrapment begin to create suicidal feelings when a person's attention is constantly hijacked by thoughts and feelings of defeat, humiliation, failure and despair. But this sense of entrapment is then amplified by what happens next: global self-denigrating conclusions, rumination and attempts to reduce the impact of these thoughts by suppressing them in ways that simply backfire. When suicidal thoughts and images arise, a person may redouble their attempts to suppress or avoid them, or to analyse them through ruminating. In reacting to suicidal intrusions in this way, suicidal vulnerability that might have been momentary, is actually maintained and exacerbated. Several studies have found correlations between high levels of rumination and increased suicidality.[8] Indeed, it has been suggested that suicidal thoughts can be conceptualised as a form of rumination.[9]

Of course, the fact that people with a history of suicidal ideation or DSH (deliberate self-harm) display excessive use of one prominent marker of a ruminative/avoidant mode of processing – over-general autobiographical memory, i.e. difficulty in retrieving specific instances of past events in their lives – only adds to their problems. As we have seen in Chapter Nine, such over-general memory reduces problem-solving and impairs specific plans for the future.[10] This over-generality has been suggested as a critical aspect of the mind-lock that shifts a person from mild to severe feelings of entrapment.

What implications do these ideas have for the therapist who suspects a person is feeling suicidal? It will be important to assess how defeated and (especially) how trapped the person feels, as well as assessing how strong the urge is to escape and how much of the person's temperament, habits and life circumstances (for example, an impulsive temperament, alcohol habit and living alone or having easy access to dangerous means of self-harm) increase the risk.[11] These aspects require a therapist to spend time with a person in crisis to help clarify feelings.

In addition, it is necessary to know what *images* go through the person's mind when they feel that they cannot stand any more. It is important to ask gently for actual sensory detail (this may never have been disclosed before because it is so distressing, but the relief from sharing this with someone sympathetic is palpable). And then, critically, when disturbing thoughts or images of suicide or self-harm come, how does the person relate to them? (The simplest question is: 'What happens next?') Does it trigger ruminative brooding; or attempts at suppressing it? And then what happens? This is a sketch of a *process*, not the content of the thinking.

The discovery that the damaging effects of intrusive thoughts and images are actually maintained by the very attempts to control them is now prompting the search for new forms of therapy that focus on these exacerbating processes. These include Rumination-focused Cognitive Therapy for depression,[12] Acceptance and Commitment Therapy (ACT)[13] and Mindfulness-based Cognitive Therapy.[14] All of these approaches aim to teach patients how to recognise when they are getting stuck in ruminative brooding and avoidance, and to see such mind-lock (sometimes called 'cognitive fusion' because a person seems 'fused' to their thoughts) as a warning sign that tells them that their mood is deteriorating. The next step is to teach people to cultivate decentring or 'cognitive de-fusion' – seeing thoughts and images as temporary mental events. This helps people not only to see this mode of thinking for what it is, but also to stand back from it.[15] These treatments have been shown to be helpful for other diagnoses, but it is only recently that research has examined whether such an approach is specifically useful for suicidal patients.

Clinically, this means that although it may not be possible to control the extent to which suicidal thoughts and feelings arise, we can do something about what happens next. Since depression remains the most important final common pathway to suicide, the quest for new and better treatments to prevent depression itself is an important part of the agenda in attempting to deal with suicide.

Inspired by Marsha Linehan's use of mindfulness for people with serious personality and interpersonal problems, John Teasdale, Zindel Segal and I have been developing a mindfulness-based cognitive approach to help people stay well after recovery from depression. Using Jon Kabat-Zinn and colleagues' work with mindfulness for chronic pain at the University of Massachusetts Medical Center, we evaluated whether an eight-week programme that teaches patients a range of mindfulness meditation practices could reduce the risk of relapse in serious recurrent depression. Six studies have now found that for those who had experienced three or more episodes of major depression in the past, the relapse rate (over the next twelve months) is considerably reduced: from 66 per cent to 37 per cent in one study, and from 78 per cent to 36 per cent in another, averaging a 43 per cent reduction across all studies.[16]

MBCT was developed specifically to target the processes that keep people trapped in mind-lock. It teaches as its core skill the ability 'to recognise and to disengage from mind states characterised by self-perpetuating patterns of ruminative, negative thought' and to adopt a stance towards experience which is characterised by openness, curiosity and acceptance, rather than avoidance. Like Cognitive Therapy, MBCT aims to give patients the ability to see thoughts as mental events rather than facts, to decouple the occurrence of negative thoughts from the responses they would usually elicit and, eventually, to change their implicit meaning. However, while Cognitive Therapy maintains a strong focus on the *content* of thoughts and the re-evaluation of their meaning, the main aim in MBCT is to teach patients to take a different perspective on thinking itself. By consistently practising bringing awareness to present-moment experience, participants shift into a mode of functioning that is incompatible with the self-focused and analytical cognitive processes that perpetuate the sense of being trapped in depression. Segal, Williams and Teasdale describe this as a change from a 'driven–doing' mode, in which the main focus is on a desperate attempt to reduce the gap between 'how I feel now' and ideas of 'how I should be feeling' by ruminating or avoidance, to a mode of 'being', in which the individual is in immediate and intimate contact with present-moment experience, whatever that might be.[17] How, one might ask, could this be helpful? Surely people need to *reduce* awareness of their present-moment experience?

The transformation seems to come when participants, having learned first to focus their attention so it is not hijacked all the time by emotion, then learn to 'decentre' as a means of becoming *aware* of their thoughts, feelings and bodily sensations. Gradually, they discover a way to bring a sense of perspective and a spirit of 'allowing', kindness and compassion to their inner experience of suffering. Negative thoughts are viewed as mental events that can be seen clearly in the mental landscape, then let go of. This increased awareness reduces the automatic tendency to get entangled in habitual ruminative thinking. It ultimately leads to a profound shift towards seeing things more clearly, moment by moment. Across the eight sessions of MBCT different guided meditation practices – including an eating meditation, 'body scan', yoga stretches, walking meditation and sitting meditations – are introduced to participants. Towards the end of the treatment participants are encouraged to develop a home practice which fits their needs and which can be maintained in the longer term.[18]

In our research in Oxford, we have evaluated whether such Mindfulness-based Cognitive Therapy might be effective in reducing suicidal ideas and behaviour. We have found that MBCT reduces depression in those who have severe ongoing suicidality,[19] and reduces the risk of depression in those who are most vulnerable to recurrent depression with suicidal ideas and plans. Those with a history of trauma when they were children or adolescents showed a reduction in risk of having another episode of depression from 65 per cent (if they had only usual care) to 41 per cent after MBCT.[20] People were, on average, followed up for over a year, and the statistical analysis showed that the overall reduction in risk of depression for these high-risk patients averaged 57 per cent.

More details of the whole programme for therapists to develop mindfulness as an approach to suicidal behaviour can be found in *Mindfulness and the Transformation of Despair: Working with People at Risk of Suicide* (see Resources, page 272) and a detailed outline of the MBCT programme for those who wish to try it for themselves can be found in *The Mindful Way Workbook* (see Resources, page 271).

CONCLUDING REMARKS

Prevention of suicidal behaviour demands a multi-modal approach. Mental-health professionals need to remain mindful of the ease with which suicidal feelings may be missed in a therapy consultation. They must be aware of the preferred method by which clients would commit suicide if they had the chance, and able to estimate the lethality of the method as well as the probability of the action being carried out. But they also need to get a good sense of the reasons for living that still exist for the person, and how stable these factors are. They should be aware of the risk factors for repetition following episodes of deliberate self-harm, but also aware that half of the clients who have all these risk factors do not actually repeat within the following year.

The research reviewed by meta-analyses is pessimistic, but it helps us to understand why studies of treatment interventions are so difficult to carry out and often fail to show definitive results. Patients who respond well to treatment tend to be those who are less likely to repeat the attempted suicide episode anyway. That leaves those who have had a great many psychological, psychiatric and social problems in their lives, and only as studies have started to look at this more vulnerable sub-group have we begun to make advances. In particular, the structured psychological approaches of Greg Brown and Aaron Beck's Cognitive Therapy, and Marsha Linehan's Dialectical Behaviour Therapy, with its combination of firm structure and compassionate mindfulness, are inspiring many to think of new ways to help people with serious difficulties in finding a life worth living. These approaches prompted me and my colleagues to investigate whether mindfulness training might have a role to play in helping those who are trapped to find a way out. Our encouraging results with Mindfulness-based Cognitive Therapy in reducing the risk of recurrent depression in the most vulnerable people show that there are now a number of promising approaches that clinicians and suicidal people may explore.

CHAPTER THIRTEEN

Concluding Thoughts

Anguish is known to everyone since childhood, and everyone knows that it is often blank, undifferentiated. It rarely carries a clearly written label that also contains its motivation; when it does have one, it is often mendacious. One can believe or declare oneself to be anguished for one reason and be so due to something totally different: one can think that one is suffering at facing the future and instead be suffering because of one's past; one can think that one is suffering for others, out of pity, out of compassion, and instead be suffering for one's own reasons, more or less profound, more or less avowable and avowed; sometimes so deep that only the specialist, the analyst of souls, knows how to exhume them.

Primo Levi[1]

I have suggested that the key to understanding suicidal thoughts and behaviour is to view them as a cry of pain. Suicide comes out of mental anguish. It is a response to overwhelming stresses that arise from the environment, or from the uncontrollability of the mental anguish itself. When an individual first becomes aware that they lack control over important areas of their circumstances or of their mental life, the cry of pain may be one of anger and rage: a protest against the feelings of entrapment. As they become more and more convinced that they have failed, or that they have been rejected or abandoned, the anger becomes mixed with hopelessness and despair. A tunnel vision ensues, in which normal escape routes are not noticed. Offers of help are rejected or misinterpreted. The person feels more alienated, increasing his or her feelings of anger and hopelessness, and begins to seek alternative ways of escape. The likelihood of suicide at such times depends on how overwhelming such feelings are, whether there have been models among family or friends or in the media, whether a suitable method is readily available, how violent or impulsive the person is, and whether drugs or alcohol are to hand which reduce fear of death and impair judgement.

Completed suicide and non-fatal attempted suicide can be understood as different responses to these circumstances, occurring at different points in the downward spiral into hopelessness. For many years it was thought that suicide and attempted suicide had to be qualitatively different behaviours, partly because many who harm themselves say they do not want to die. Their motivation seemed much more complex than a simple wish to end their lives. But motivation for completed suicide is also complex. Because the tragedy of a death by suicide is so extreme, we tend to assume that, when death is the outcome, death has been the predominant motive.

Yet I have also suggested that the predominant motivation in suicidal behaviour is escape. The person feels trapped. They can see no way out of their prison, and take little account of the possibility that some of their feeling of entrapment comes from a constricted view of their own past life that feeds into their hopelessness about the future.

Getting away from seeing completed suicide as motivated only by a wish to die frees us from a punitive view of attempted suicide. In the past, we have allowed the question of how much a person wished to die to define the way in which we understand all who harm themselves. We ask ourselves, 'How suicidal was this behaviour really?' If we decide it was not, then we are inclined to dismiss it, get angry about it, see it as 'manipulative' and so on. The problem with the idea of the 'cry for help' is that it feeds this dismissive view of self-harm.

Of course, there were other reasons for thinking that suicide and attempted suicide were not the same thing, most importantly that those who completed suicide, on the one hand, and those who attempted it, on the other, seemed to differ in a number of respects. For example, while suicide, until recently, was primarily a feature of older males, attempted suicide seemed more a feature of younger females. Furthermore, while suicide rates were coming down in the 1960s in the United Kingdom, attempted suicide was rising. Such differences between suicide and attempted suicide seemed to suggest that each needed its own explanation. Yet, if we are to see age and sex differences as pointing to different underlying causes, what are we to make of the data from the United States and the United Kingdom that show male suicide rose while female suicide was falling? Here we had the same outcome, suicide deaths, moving in different directions in different sub-groups of the same population.

Instead, it is possible that the same underlying set of causes might produce the age and sex differences in suicidal behaviour that are sometimes observed. If suicidal behaviour is best seen as a cry of pain – a response to feeling trapped by uncontrollable external circumstances and internal anguish – then different types of people, older or younger, male or female, take action on these feelings at different points in the sequence of events as the trap is perceived to close. Internal and external stresses give rise to differences in perceived escape potential (i.e. the ability to see a way out). This, in turn, gives rise to stronger or weaker wishes to die.

A weaker wish to die may not be expressed as a wish to die at all, but rather as seeking temporary oblivion. But such people are best viewed as one end of a continuum of lethality that cannot be ignored. The protest and anger that most often produce non-fatal suicidal behaviour represent a response early in the sequence of events when escape still seems possible. The despair and apathy that produce more lethal suicidal behaviour represent the response to loss that comes later, when the person sees no hope in their situation at all. Even at this stage, however, the presence of social support can ameliorate the intensity of feelings of hopelessness. Men differ from women in the extent to which they perceive or make use of such supports. This is not simply a question of biology, but of the different ways in which boys and girls are taught to view emotional expression. Wherever children have developed the belief (from somewhere – it doesn't matter where) that it is shameful to display one's weaknesses, they will find it difficult later in life to seek support from others when in a crisis. Traditionally, boys were taught this attitude more than girls, but we need to guard against the possibility that increased employment opportunities for women require them to adopt this attitude in order to succeed.

Finally, we have seen that all the important contributors on the causal pathway from stress to suicidal behaviour involve a judgement by the individual. The person whose life is in crisis needs all the resources they can muster. But people most vulnerable to depression and suicide suffer an additional burden which makes their real problems seem even more aversive, uncontrollable and unsolvable. Biases in their memory prevent them from remembering positive aspects of their past and present life. Even worse, when they do recollect events, they do so in such non-specific ways as to suggest few ways of dealing with current problems. Furthermore, they induce a non-specific view of the future. Making concrete plans for the future (even for tomorrow or next week) is extremely difficult against a background of such vague and over-general recollection of the past. They are often perfectionist or rigid about their goals and plans, which makes them highly sensitive to real or imagined failure.

THE AFTERMATH OF SUICIDE

My aim in this book has been to explain something of what I understand of suicide and self-harm. Looking for unifying themes is important, but I do not deny that each individual circumstance will have some, perhaps many, elements that do not fit the overall pattern. In seeking an explanation of suicide, I have been conscious of the need to explain things not only to those in the helping professions, but also to the large number of people whose lives are touched by suicide and self-harm. My last word must be for them and those who care for them.

Clinicians who work with suicidal people and their families estimate that for every person who commits suicide there will be at least six who are deeply affected by the event – the bereaved family, friends and close workmates. For the survivors enormous problems follow in the aftermath of such a death. Even if the deceased has been depressed, even if they have talked of suicide, the actual death comes as a huge shock. And, of course, suicide sometimes comes right out of the blue with no warning at all.

The huge trauma of any sudden death is compounded in a suicide by a number of factors: many still feel a social stigma about suicide, and there is often a 'conspiracy of silence'. This is especially true where children are involved, and a child whose parent or brother or sister has committed suicide may have to deal with little support and with their own misconceptions and guilt about what has happened.

Even when social support is available, those bereaved by suicide are less likely to use it than those bereaved by other kinds of sudden death because of the social stigma and the presence of feelings of personal guilt and shame surrounding the event.[2] They have to cope with their own grief against the background of many 'Why?' questions: 'Why did they not ask me for help?', 'Could I have done more?', 'Why did I (or someone else) not see it coming, or take what signs there were more seriously?' Some will blame themselves for not intervening, and find themselves brooding endlessly on what they could have done to prevent it happening. In addition, many feel extremely angry with the deceased: 'Why couldn't they understand the effect of their death on those left behind?' Then they feel guilty for feeling angry, and the anguish deepens.

No answers to these questions can be completely satisfactory, but it may be helpful at some point for survivors to know how suicidal despair reduces a person's ability to ask for help, to accept help if offered or to understand the effect their action would have on others. We have seen that suicide arises from an overwhelming urge to escape feelings of being trapped, and that such entrapment is closely linked with feelings that one has failed. In such states, a person feels shame and humiliation, so is highly sensitive to anything that might increase such shame. Asking for or accepting help from others will seem to many just such a shameful situation. Even the thought of receiving help from others may increase suicidal thoughts in such circumstances. Further, the deficit in memory exacerbates the situation even more by blocking recollection of previous times when things were good or help was available.

But how can we understand the way a suicidal individual appears to take such little account of the effect of their action on others? Like someone trying to flee from a blazing house fire, the suicidal person is focused on escape. He or she has tunnel vision, which prevents them imagining what their act would do to others. They live in two worlds: the public world, in which they may pretend all is okay, and a private one in which they are completely self-absorbed, and where the feelings of other people do not figure.

Such catastrophic failure of empathy – the complete breakdown in understanding how others will react – is not well understood. Research in developmental psychology shows that empathy is something that depends on specific networks in the brain that develop rapidly in children at 3–4 years of age, but which goes on developing during later childhood and adolescence. These networks help all of us to understand other people's beliefs and intentions, as well as how others will be affected by things that happen in the world – including our own actions.

I believe that the radical loss of empathy that accompanies suicidal impulses in some people results from impairment of these same psychological mechanisms. Suicidal despair switches off the brain processes that are normally responsible for understanding the beliefs, intentions and feelings of others. Though this will often appear to be a callous disregard for others' feelings (especially close family and friends), it is more likely to be something over which the suicidal person has little control.

MAKING PEACE WITH DESPAIR

The quotation from Primo Levi with which this short chapter began is taken from his last book, *The Drowned and the Saved*. Levi had survived Auschwitz, and wrote of his experiences in his books *If This Is a Man* and *The Truce*. He was found dead at the bottom of the stairwell of his house in Turin in 1987, and is presumed to have committed suicide. In the quotation, Levi speaks of an anguish sometimes so deep that only the specialist, the analyst of souls, knows how to exhume it.

But what help can an analyst of souls provide? We cannot opt out of trying to answer such questions, no matter how much we would wish to remain silent. When therapies bring hope to those in despair, what is it that they are doing? Of course, they are offering support. They are helping the person to see that perhaps some of their problems are solvable. And they are helping the person to gain some distance from the constant propaganda of their mind that would persuade them they are a failure. But I believe these therapies are helpful only to the extent that they allow the person to give up wanting things to be different. As Marsha Linehan points out in her therapy, it is about balancing acceptance and change. For when people are in such distress, they become trapped by the idea that if things were different, then all would be well: if their partner were different; if their job were different; if their house were different; if they themselves were different.

Often, then, the anguish is exacerbated by the search for an escape. In the same way as an animal caught in a trap will only tighten the trap with its struggles, so the desperate search for a way out drives the suicidal person deeper into despair. The first step in dealing with anguish is, therefore, to make peace with despair; to take a step back and take stock of the situation; to give permission to oneself to feel whatever it is that one is feeling. This reflects the important insight that it is not the initial feelings of depression and anxiety that cause people the most problems, but how they react to them: if a person becomes depressed, they may see it either as a temporary mood which will pass or as evidence that they are worthless. In the former case, the depression may well lift; but in the latter, the self-denigration will cause further depression. There is the danger of a vicious spiral downward into despair.

Some, such as Buddhist teacher Ajahn Sucitto, have seen this as a profoundly spiritual question:

> It's one that cannot be resolved by trying to make the world into a different place – which tends to be the normal approach. To make peace with despair is a matter of understanding not just where difficulties such as sickness and violence arise, but also how the feeling of being bound to and oppressed by those problems occurs.[3]

Therapies that are helpful are those which allow the individual to see their moods as normal, rather than as evidence of their inherent deficiency as a person. They encourage them to ask not, 'How can I make everything different?' but rather, 'How can I take care of myself right now?' In short, they encourage people to be gentle with themselves.

NOTES AND REFERENCES

INTRODUCTION

1. For example, Sue Chance, *Stronger than Death*, W. W. Norton, New York, 1992. The author is a psychiatrist and a columnist for the *New York Times*, and the book is based on her own experiences from when her son committed suicide. It contains extracts from her journal, starting one week after his death, together with poems and other reflections.
2. E. Stengel, *Suicide and Attempted Suicide*, revised edition, Penguin Books, Harmondsworth, 1964.
3. Ibid., p. 115 (1975 edition). Other authors also used the 'cry for help' idea as a description of deliberate self-harm (see N. L. Farberow and E. S. Schneidman (eds), *The Cry for Help*, McGraw-Hill, New York, 1961), adding urgency to the need for clarification.
4. Many authors used to refer to any non-fatal suicidal behaviour as 'parasuicide' (with its deliberate agnosticism about motive), since most who deliberately harm themselves say they do not want to die. In this book I use the terms 'attempted suicide' and 'self-harm' interchangeably; 'parasuicide' may also be used in the same way.

CHAPTER ONE

1. H. G. Morgan, *Suicide Prevention: The Assessment and Management of Suicide Risk*, Health Advisory Service, Bristol, 1993.
2. For the data in this chapter I am grateful for Michael MacDonald and Terence Murphy's fascinating study, *Sleepless Souls: Suicide in Early Modern England*, Oxford University Press, Oxford, 1990, which shows how attitudes and responses to suicide have shifted over the past 2000 years. I have attempted to summarise their review as faithfully as possible, but the interested reader should refer to their book for the data and the careful analysis on which their conclusions are based.
3. M. T. Brancaccio, E. J. Engstrom and D. Lederer, 'The politics of suicide: historical perspectives on suicidology before Durkheim: an introduction', *Journal of Social History,* 46 (2013), pp. 607–19, doi: 10.1093/jsh/shs110.
4. MacDonald and Murphy, op. cit., p. 21.
5. See discussion of Marsha Linehan's research on p. 211.
6. *Diary of Samuel Pepys*, vol. 3, Swan Sonnenschein, London, 1906, pp. 344–5.
7. M. Montaigne, *Essayes*, vol. 2, pp. 26–8, 41.

CHAPTER TWO

1. E. Durkheim, *Le Suicide*, Alcan, Paris, 1897; *Suicide*, trans. by John A. Spaulding and George Simpson, Free Press, New York, 1951.
2. P. Sainsbury, J. Jenkins and A. E. Baert, *Suicide Trends in Europe*, World Health Organization, Copenhagen, 1981.
3. Until the 1960s it remained possible that the different overall rates merely reflected levels of stringency on the part of the authorities in different countries. In an important paper, P. Sainsbury and B. M. Barraclough showed this was not the case: see 'Differences between suicide rates', *Nature*, 220 (1968), p. 1252. They examined the suicide rates of immigrants to the United States from eleven countries and found that such immigrant populations retained the suicide rate from their countries of origin.

4. S. Platt, 'Epidemiology of suicide and parasuicide', *Journal of Psychopharmacology*, 6 (1968), pp. 291–9.
5. The only exception to this is in China, India and Sri Lanka, where there are reports of higher rates in women than men, especially younger women in the more rural areas. See A. T. A. Cheng and C. S. Lee, 'Suicide in Asia and the Far East', in K. Hawton and K. van Heeringen (eds), *International Handbook of Suicide and Attempted Suicide*, John Wiley, Chichester, 2000, pp. 29–48.
6. J. Harry, *Sexual Identity Issues*, Report of the Secretary's Task Force Report on Youth Suicide, vol. 2, DHHS publication No. (ADM) 89–162, Department of Health and Human Services, Washington, DC, 1989, pp. 131–42.
7. See S. Platt and K. Hawton, 'Suicidal behaviour and the labour market', in Hawton and van Heeringen (eds), op. cit., pp. 309–34.
8. Stuckler, Basu, Suhrcke, Coutts and McKee, 'Effects of the 2008 recession on health: a first look at European data', *Lancet*, 378 (9786) (2011), pp. 124–5.
9. K. Hawton, J. Faggs, S. Simkin, L. Harriss and A. Malmberg, 'Methods used for suicide by farmers in England and Wales', *British Journal of Psychiatry*, 173 (1998), pp. 320–4.
10. S. Fazel, M. Grann, B. Kling and K. Hawton, 'Prison suicide in 12 countries: an ecological study of 861 suicides during 2003–2007', *Social Psychiatry and Psychiatric Epidemiology*, 46 (2011), pp. 191–5, doi: 10.1007/s00127-010-0184-4.
11. S. Fazel and R. Benning, 'Suicides in female prisoners in England and Wales, 1978–2004', *British Journal of Psychiatry*, 194 (2009), 183–4, doi: 10.1192/bjp.bp.107.046490.
12. E. N. Stenager and E. Stenager, 'Physical illness and suicidal behaviour', in Hawton and van Heeringen (eds), op. cit., pp. 405–20.
13. N. K. Tang and C. Crane, 'Suicidality in chronic pain: a review of the prevalence, risk factors and psychological links', *Psychological Medicine*, 36 (2006), pp. 575–86.
14. B. Gjelsvik, F. Heyerdahl and K. Hawton, 'Prescribed medication availability and deliberate self-poisoning: a longitudinal study', *Journal of Clinical Psychiatry*, 73 (2012), pp. e548–54, doi:10.4088/JCP.11m07209.

15. A case illustrating how important it is not to ignore depression and other accompaniments of terminal illness is cited in J. Scott, 'Cancer patients', in J. Scott, J. M. G. Williams and A. T. Beck (eds), *Cognitive Therapy in Clinical Practice*, Routledge, London, 1989, pp. 103–26.
16. For a study of psychiatric diagnoses as they differed according to age in suicide victims, see C. L. Rich, R. C. Fowler, L. A. Fogarty et al., 'San Diego Suicide Study III: relationships between diagnosis and stressors', *Archives of General Psychiatry*, 445 (1988), pp. 589–92. See also A. Apter, D. Gothelp, I. Orbach et al., 'Correlates of suicidal and violent behaviour in different diagnostic categories in hospitalised patients', *Journal of the American Academy of Child and Adolescent Psychiatry*, 34 (1995), pp. 912–18.
17. G. Murphy, 'Psychiatric aspects of suicidal behaviour: substance abuse', in Hawton and van Heeringen (eds), op. cit., pp. 135–46.
18. For detailed statistics, see M. Shafii, J. Steltz-Lenarsky, A. M. Denick et al., 'Co-morbidity of mental disorders in the post-mortem diagnosis of completed suicides in children and adolescents', *Journal of Affective Disorders*, 15 (1988), pp. 227–33; Rich, Fowler, Fogarty et al., op. cit.; and, for a British follow-up survey in Edinburgh (1968–85), K. Hawton, S. Platt, J. Fagg and M. Hawkins, 'Suicide following parasuicide in young people', *British Journal of Psychiatry*, 152 (1993), pp. 359–66.
19. G. E. Murphy and R. D. Wetzel, 'Suicide risk by birth cohort in the United States, 1949–1974', *Archives of General Psychiatry*, 37 (1980), pp. 519–23; M. J. Solomon and C. P. Hellon, 'Suicide and age in Alberta, Canada, 1951–1977: a cohort analysis', *Archives of General Psychiatry*, 37 (1980), pp. 511–13; R. D. Goldney and M. Katsikitis, 'Suicide Rates in Australia', *Archives of General Psychiatry*, 40 (1983), pp. 71–4.
20. Charlton, Kelly, Dunnell et al., 'Trends in suicide deaths in England and Wales', *Population Trends*, 69 (1992), pp. 10–16.
21. See U. Bille-Brahe, 'Sociology and suicidal behaviour' in Hawton and van Heeringen (eds), op. cit., pp. 193–208. Bille-Brahe discusses evidence suggesting that cohort size is not always associated

with suicide, but only in those countries that have poorer welfare provision, so cannot make up for limited resources when a large cohort competes for them (pp. 24–5).

22. Charlton, Kelly, Dunnell et al., op. cit.
23. N. Kreitman, V. Carstairs and J. Duffy, 'Association of age and social class with suicide among men in Great Britain', *Journal of Epidemiology and Community Health*, 45 (1991), pp. 195–202.
24. For the Cross-National Collaborative Group reference, see 'The changing rate of major depression: cross-national comparisons', *Journal of the American Medical Association*, 268 (1992), pp. 355–73.
25. S. Zisook, I. Lesser, J. W. Stewart, S. R. Wisniewski, G. K. Balasubramani, M. Fava, M. et al., 'Effect of age at onset on the course of major depressive disorder', *American Journal of Psychiatry*, 164(10) (2007), pp. 1539–46; J. M. G. Williams, T. Barnhofer, C. Crane, D. S. Duggan, D. Shah, K. Brennan et al., 'Pre-adult onset and patterns of suicidality in patients with a history of recurrent depression', *Journal of Affective Disorders*, 138(1–2) (2012), pp. 173–9.
26. P. Cuijpers, A. T. F. Beekman and C. F. Reynolds, 'Preventing depression: a global priority', *Journal of the American Medical Association*, 307 (2012), pp. 1033–4.
27. For a discussion of factors that might account for rising rates of suicide in young people and declining rates in older people, see D. Gunnell et al., 'Why are suicide rates rising in young men but falling in the elderly?', *Social Science and Medicine*, 57 (2003), pp. 595–611.

CHAPTER THREE

1. Durkheim, op. cit.
2. B. Barraclough, J. Bunch, B. Nelson and P. Sainsbury, 'A hundred cases of suicide: clinical aspects', *British Journal of Psychiatry*, 25 (1974), pp. 355–73.
3. K. Hawton et al., 'Schizophrenia and suicide: systematic review of the risk factors', *The British Journal of Psychiatry*, 187 (2005),

pp. 9–20, doi: 10.1192/bjp.187.1.9, L. R. Wulsin, G. E. Vaillant and V. E. Wells, 'A systematic review of the mortality of depression. *Psychosomatic Medicine*, 61 (1999), pp. 6–17; J. Powell, J. Geddes, J. Deeks, M. Goldacre and K. Hawton, 'Suicide in psychiatric patients: risk factors and their predictive power', *British Journal of Psychiatry*, 176 (2000), pp. 266–72; J. K. Lonnqvist, 'Psychiatric aspects of suicidal behaviour: depression', in Hawton and van Heeringen (eds), op. cit., pp. 107–20.

4. G. W. Blair-West, G. W. Mellsop and M. L. Eyeson-Annan, 'Down-rating lifetime suicide risk in major depression', *Acta Psychiatrica Scandinavica*, 95 (1997), pp. 259–63.
5. A. L. Beautrais, P. R. Joyce, R. T. Mulder, D. M. Fergusson, B. J. Deavoll and S. K. Nightingale, 'Prevalence and comorbidity of mental disorders in persons making serious suicide attempts: a case-control study', *American Journal of Psychiatry*, 153 (1996), pp. 1009–14.
6. J. M. G. Williams, C. Crane, T. Barnhofer, A. J. W. Van der Does and Z. V. Segal, 'Recurrence of suicidal ideation across depressive episodes', *Journal of Affective Disorders*, 91 (2006), pp. 189–94, doi: 10.1016/j.jad.2006.01.002.
7. NICE, 'Antisocial personality disorder: the NICE guideline on treatment, management and prevention', 2010.
8. D. J. Gunnell, T. J. Peters, R. M. Kammerling and J. Brooks, 'Relation between parasuicide, suicide, psychiatric admissions, and socioeconomic depression', *British Medical Journal*, 311 (1995), pp. 226–30.
9. S. Platt, R. Micciolo and M. Tansella, 'Suicide and unemployment in Italy: description, analysis and interpretation of recent trends', *Social Science Medicine*, 34 (1992), pp. 1191–201.
10. P. Sainsbury, J. Jenkins and A. Levey, 'The social correlates of suicide in Europe', in R. Farmer and S. Hirsch (eds), *The Suicide Syndrome*, Croom Helm, London, 1980, pp. 38–53.
11. S. Evans-Lacko et al., 'The mental health consequences of the recession: economic hardship and employment of people with mental health problems in 27 European countries, *PLoS One*, 8(7) (2013), p.e69792; D. Stuckler et al., 'The public health effect of economic

crises and alternative policy responses in Europe: an empirical analysis', *Lancet*, 374 (9686) (2009), pp. 315–23.

12. For definitions of 'social support', see G. Brown and T. Harris, *The Social Origins of Depression – a Study of Psychiatric Disorder in Women*, Tavistock, London, 1978.
13. P. J. Taylor, P. A. Gooding, A. M. Wood et al., 'Defeat and entrapment in schizophrenia: the relationship with suicidal ideation and positive psychotic symptoms', *Psychiatric Research*, 178 (2010), pp. 244–8, doi: 10.1016/j.psychres.2009.10.015; M. Panagioti, P. Gooding, P. J. Taylor et al., 'Negative self-appraisals and suicidal behaviour among trauma victims experiencing PTSD symptoms: the mediating role of defeat and entrapment', *Depression and Anxiety*, 29 (2012), pp. 187–94, doi: 10.1002/da.21917; Z. Iqbal, M. Birchwood, P. Chadwick and P. Trower, 'Cognitive approach to depression and suicidal thinking in psychosis: 2. Testing the validity of a social ranking model', *British Journal of Psychiatry*, 177 (2000), pp. 522–8.
14. See K. Hawton and J. Fagg, 'Suicide, and other causes of death, following attempted suicide', *British Journal of Psychiatry*, 152 (1988), pp. 359–66; and D. L. Zahl and K. Hawton, 'Repetition of deliberate self-harm and subsequent suicide risk: long-term follow-up study of 11,583 patients', *British Journal of Psychiatry*, 185 (2004), pp. 70–5.
15. J. K. Lonnqvist, 'Psychiatric aspects: depression', in Hawton and van Heeringen (eds), op. cit., pp. 107–20.
16. See Iqbal et al., op. cit., in which the authors consider the evidence for an entrapment model of depression and suicidal thinking in schizophrenia.

CHAPTER FOUR

1. A. Alvarez, *Savage God: A Study of Suicide*, Random House, New York, 1972, p.291.
2. Although true in the individual case, studies of larger numbers have discovered a correlation between suicide intent and the number of pills taken: more than twenty has been found to indicate higher

suicide intent. See R. D. Goldney, 'Attempted suicide in young women: correlates of lethality', *British Journal of Psychiatry*, 147 (1981), pp. 382–90; K. G. Power, D. J. Cooke and J. S. Gibbons, 'Life stress, medical lethality and suicidal intent', *British Journal of Psychiatry*, 147 (1985), pp. 655–9; and D. J. Pallis, J. S. Gibbons and D. W. Pierce, 'Estimating suicide risk among attempted suicides', *British Journal of Psychiatry*, 144 (1984), pp. 139–48.

3. H. Bergen, K. Hawton, K. Waters, J. Ness, J. Cooper, S. Steeg and N. Kapur, 'Premature death after self-harm: a multicentre cohort study', *Lancet,* 380 (2012), pp. 1568–74, doi: 10.1016/s0140-6736(12)61141-6.
4. S. Platt, U. Bille-brahe, A. Kerkhof, A. Schmidtke, T. Bjerke, T. P. Crepet et al., 'Parasuicide in Europe – the WHO/EURO multicenter study on parasuicide. 1. Introduction and preliminary analysis for 1989', *Acta Psychiatrica Scandinavica,* 85 (1992), pp. 97–104, doi: 10.1111/j.1600-0447.1992.tb01451.x.
5. M. M. Silverman (2011), 'Challenges to classifying suicidal ideations, communications, and behaviours', in R. C. O'Connor, S. Platt and J. Gordon (eds), *The International Handbook of Suicide Prevention: Research, Policy and Practice*, Wiley-Blackwell, Chichester, pp. 9–26.
6. H. Hjelmeland, K. Hawton, H. Nordvik, U. Bille-Brahe, D. De Leo, S. Fekete et al., 'Why people engage in parasuicide: a cross-cultural study of intentions', *Suicide and Life-Threatening Behaviour,* 32 (2002), pp. 380–93, doi: 10.1521/suli.32.4.380.22336; M. Straiton, K. Roen, G. K. Dieserud and H. Hjelmeland (2013), 'Pushing the boundaries: understanding self-harm in a non-clinical population', *Archives of Psychiatric Nursing,* 27, pp. 78–83, doi: 10.1016/j.apnu.2012.10.008.
7. D. De Leo, 'DSM-V and the future of suicidology', *Crisis,* 32 (2011), pp. 233–9, doi: 10.1027/0227-5910/a000128.
8. K. E. A. Saunders, K. Hawton, S. Fortune and S. Farrell, 'Attitudes and knowledge of clinical staff regarding people who self-harm: a systematic review', *Journal of Affective Disorders,* 139 (2012), pp. 205–16, doi: 10.1016/j.jad.2011.08.024.
9. A. B. Norheim, T. K. Grimholt and O. Ekeberg, 'Attitudes towards

suicidal behaviour in outpatient clinics among mental health professionals in Oslo', *BMC Psychiatry,* 13 (2013), p. 90, doi: 10.1186/1471-244x-13-90.

10. J. Norrie, K. Davidson, P. Tata and A. Gumley, 'Influence of therapist competence and quantity of CBT on suicidal behaviour', *Psychology and Psychotherapy*, 86 (2013), pp. 280–93.
11. T. Joiner, *Why People Die by Suicide*, Harvard University Press, Cambridge, MA, 2007.
12. K. Hawton, H. Bergen, N. Kapur, J. Cooper, S. Steeg, J. Ness and K. Waters, 'Repetition of self-harm and suicide following self-harm in children and adolescents: findings from the multicentre study of self-harm in England', *Journal of Child Psychology and Psychiatry,* 53 (2012), pp. 1212–19, doi: 10.1111/j.1469-7610.2012.02559.x.
13. I am grateful to Bergljot Gjelsvik for information and discussion about these important issues of intent and lethality. See W. C. Myers, T. A. Otto, E. Harris, D. Diaco, and A. Moreno, 'Acetaminophen overdose as a suicidal gesture – a survey of adolescents knowledge of its potential for toxicity', *Journal of the American Academy of Child and Adolescent Psychiatry,* 31 (1992), pp. 686–90. doi: 10.1097/00004583-199207000-00016; J. L. Stumpf, A. J. Skyles, C. Alaniz and S. R. Erickson, 'Knowledge of appropriate acetaminophen doses and potential toxicities in an adult clinic population', *Journal of the American Pharmacists Association,* 47 (2007), pp. 35–41, doi: 10.1331/1544-3191.47.1.35. D. M. Wood, E. English, S. Butt, H. Ovaska, F. Garnham and P. I. Dargan, 'Patient knowledge of the paracetamol content of over-the-counter (OTC) analgesics, cough/cold remedies and prescription medications', *Emergency Medicine Journal,* 27 (2010), pp. 829–33, doi: 10. 1136/emj.2009.085027.
14. R. C. O'Connor, 'The integrated motivational-volitional model of suicidal behaviour', *Crisis,* 32 (2011), pp. 295–8, doi: 10.1027/0227-5910/a000120; see also R. C. O'Connor, 'Suicidal behaviour as a cry of pain: test of a psychological model', *Archives of Suicide Research,* 7 (2003), pp. 297–308.
15. M. K. Nock, G. Borges, E. J. Bromet, J. Alonso, M. Angermeyer, A. L. Beautrais et al., 'Cross-national prevalence and risk factors for

suicidal ideation, plans and attempts', *British Journal of Psychiatry,* 192 (2008), pp. 98–105, doi: 10.1192/bjp.bp.107.040113.

16. M. K. Nock, G. Borges, E. J. Bromet, C. B. Cha, R. C. Kessler and S. Lee, 'Suicide and suicidal behaviour', *Epidemiologic Reviews,* 30 (2008), pp. 133–54, doi: 10.1093/epirev/mxn002.
17. E. Arensman, T. Fitzgerald, T. Bjerke, J. Cooper, P. Corcoran, D. De Leo et al., 'Deliberate self-harm and suicide: gender-specific trends in eight European regions', *Journal of Epidemiology and Community Health,* 62 (2008), pp. A3–A4.
18. A. Schmidtke, U. Bille-Brahe, D. DeLeo et al., 'Attempted suicide in Europe: rates, trends and sociodemographic characteristics of suicide attempters during the period 1989–1992. Results of the WHO/EURO multicentre study on parasuicide', *Acta Psychiatrica Scandinavica,* 93 (1996), pp. 327–38, doi: 10.1111/j.1600-0447.1996.tb10656.x; A. Schmidtke, U. Bille-Brahe, D. DeLeo et al., 'Sociodemographic characteristics of suicide attempters in Europe – combined results of the monitoring part of the WHO/EURO multicentre study on suicidal behaviour', in A. Schmidtke, U. Bille-Brahe, D. DeLeo et al., eds, *Suicidal Behaviour in Europe: Results from the Who/Euro Multicentre Study on Suicidal Behaviour*, pp. 29–43, Hogrefe & Huber, Göttingen.
19. D. Buglass and J. Horton, 'A scale for predicting subsequent suicidal behaviour', *British Journal of Psychiatry*, 124 (1974), pp. 573–8.
20. J. Bancroft, K. Hawton, S. Simkin et al., 'The reasons people give for taking overdoses', *British Journal of Medical Psychology*, 52 (1979), pp. 353–65.
21. J. M. G. Williams, 'Differences in reasons for taking overdoses in high and low hopelessness groups', *British Journal of Medical Psychology*, 59 (1986), pp. 269–77.
22. A. T. Beck, D. Schuyler and J. Herman, 'Development of suicidal intent scales', in A. T. Beck, H. L. P. Resnick and D. J. Lettieri (eds), *The Prediction of Suicide*, Charles Press, Maryland, 1974.
23. D. W. Pierce, 'Suicidal intent in self-injury', *British Journal of Psychiatry*, 130 (1977), pp. 377–85.
24. R. Plutchik, H. M. Van Praag, S. Picard, H. R. Conte et al., 'Is there

a relationship between the seriousness of suicidal intent and the lethality of the suicidal attempt?', *Psychiatry Research*, 27 (1989), pp. 71–9.

25. D. W. Pierce, 'Predictive validation of a suicide intent scale', *British Journal of Psychiatry*, 139 (1981), pp. 445–6; C. Haw, K. Hawton, K. Houston and E. Townsend, 'Correlates of relative lethality and suicidal intent among deliberate self-harm patients', *Suicide and Life-Threatening Behaviour*, 33 (2003), pp. 353–64.
26. J. Suokas and J. Lonnqvist, 'Outcome of attempted suicide and psychiatric consultation: risk factors and suicide mortality during a five-year follow-up', *Acta Psychiatrica Scandinavica*, 84 (1991), pp. 545–9.
27. J. Sapyta, D. B. Goldston, A. Erkanli, S. S. Daniel, N. Heilbron, A. Mayfield et al., 'Evaluating the predictive validity of suicidal intent and medical lethality in youth', *Journal of Consulting and Clinical Psychology*, 80 (2012), pp. 222–31.
28. M. R. Phillips and H. G. Cheng, 'The changing global face of suicide', *Lancet,* 379 (2012), pp. 2318–19, doi: http://dx.doi.org/10.1016/S0140-6736(12)60913-1; M. Eddleston and M. R. Phillips, 'Self poisoning with pesticides', *British Medical Journal,* 328 (2004), pp. 42–4, doi: 10.1136/bmj.328.7430.42; F. Konradsen, W. van der Hoek and P. Peiris, 'Reaching for the bottle of pesticide – a cry for help: self-inflicted poisonings in Sri Lanka', *Social Science & Medicine,* 62 (2006), pp. 1710–19, doi: 10.1016/j.socscimed.2005.08.020.

CHAPTER FIVE

1. R. W. Maris, 'Deviance as therapy: the paradox of the self-destructive females', *Journal of Health and Social Behaviour*, 12 (1981), pp. 113–24.
2. See K. Hawton and J. Catalan, *Attempted Suicide*, second edition, Oxford University Press, Oxford, 1987.
3. R. D. Goldney, 'Parental representation in young women who attempt suicide', *Acta Psychiatrica Scandinavica*, 72 (1985), pp. 230–2.

4. G. Parker, H. Tupling and L. B. Brown, 'A parental bonding instrument', *British Journal of Medical Psychology*, 52 (1979), pp. 1–10.

5. S. Goschin, J. Briggs, S. Blanco-Lutzen, L. J. Cohen and I. Galynker 'Parental affectionless control and suicidality', *Journal of Affective Disorders*, 151 (2013) pp. 1–6, doi: 10.1016/j.jad.2013.05.096.

6. M. van Egmond, N. Garnefski, D. Jonker and A. Kerkhov, 'The relationship between sexual abuse and female suicidal behaviour', *Crisis*, 14 (1993), pp. 129–39.

7. S. D. Easton, L. M. Renner and P. O'Leary, 'Suicide attempts among men with histories of child sexual abuse: Examining abuse severity, mental health, and masculine norms', *Child Abuse & Neglect*, 37 (2013), pp. 380–7; N. Soylu and A. H. Alpaslan, 'Suicidal behaviour and associated factors in sexually abused adolescents', *Children and Youth Services Review*, 35 (2013), pp. 253–7, doi: 10.1016/j.childyouth.2012.11.002.

8. J. Brezo et al., 'Predicting suicide attempts in young adults with histories of childhood abuse', *British Journal of Psychiatry*, 193 (2008), pp. 134–9, doi: 10.1192/bjp.bp.107.037994.

9. T. Foster, 'Adverse life events proximal to adult suicide: a synthesis of findings from psychological autopsy studies', *Archives of Suicide Research*, 15 (2011), pp. 1–15.

10. A. Milner, A. Page and A. D. LaMontagne, 'Long-term unemployment and suicide: a systematic review and meta-analysis', *PLoSOne*, 8 (2013), p. e51333.

11. B. Barr, D. Taylor-Robinson, A. Scott-Samuel, M. McKee and D. Stuckler, 'Suicides associated with the 2008–10 economic recession in England: time trend analysis', *British Medical Journal,* 345 (2012), p. e5142.

12. K. Hawton, J. Fagg, S. Platt and M. Hawkins, 'Factors associated with suicide after parasuicide in young people', *British Medical Journal*, 306 (1993), pp. 1641–4.

13. R. C. O'Connor, S. Rasmussen, J. Miles and K. Hawton, 'Self-harm in adolescents: self-report survey in schools in Scotland', *British Journal of Psychiatry*, 194 (2009), pp. 68–72.

14. C. L. Bagge , C. R. Glenn and H. J. Lee, 'Quantifying the impact of

recent negative life-events on suicide attempts', *Journal of Abnormal Psychology*, 122 (2013), pp. 359–68.

15. S. M. Davonport, 'Association between parasuicide and St Valentine's Day', *British Medical Journal*, 300 (1990), pp. 783–4.
16. H. Bergen et al., 'Variations in time of hospital presentation', *Journal of Affective Disorders*, 98 (2007), pp. 227–37.
17. S. J. Cullum et al., 'Deliberate self-harm and public holidays: is there a link?' *Crisis*, 14 (1993), pp. 39–42; H. Bergen and K. Hawton, 'Variation in deliberate self-harm around Christmas and New Year', *Social Science and Medicine*, 65 (2007), pp. 855–67; R. A. Sansone et al., 'The Christmas effect on psychopathology', *Innovations in Clinical Neuroscience*, 8 (2011), pp. 10–13.
18. K. Hawton, L. Harriss, L. Appleby et al., 'The effect of the death of Diana, Princess of Wales, on suicide and deliberate self-harm', *British Journal of Psychiatry*, 177 (2000), pp. 463–6.
19. For further discussion of these difficulties, see A. K. MacLeod, J. M. G. Williams and M. M. Linehan, 'New developments in the understanding and treatment of suicidal behaviour', *Behavioural Psychotherapy*, 20 (1992), pp. 193–218.
20. J. J. Platt, G. Spivack and W. Bloom, *Manual for the Means–Ends Problem-solving Procedure (MEPS): A Measure of Interpersonal Problem-solving Skill*, Hahnemann Community MH/MR Center, Department of Mental Health Services, Hahnemann Medical College and Hospital, Philadelphia, 1987.
21. D. E. Schotte and G. A. Clum, 'Problem-solving skills in suicidal psychiatric patients', *Journal of Consulting and Clinical Psychology*, 55 (1987), pp. 49–54. Similarly poor problem-solving ability has also been found in younger suicidal people; see M. J. Rotheram-Borus, P. D. Trautman, S. C. Dopkins and P. E. Shrout, 'Cognitive style and pleasant activities among female adolescent suicide attempters', *Journal of Consulting and Clinical Psychology*, 58 (1990), pp. 554–61.
22. M. M. Linehan, P. Camper, J. A. Chiles, K. Strohsal and E. N. Shearin, 'Inter-personal problem solving and parasuicide', *Cognitive Therapy and Research*, 11 (1987), pp. 1–12.
23. I. Orbach, H. Bar-Joseph and N. Dror, 'Styles of problem solving in

suicidal individuals', *Suicide and Life Threatening Behaviour*, 20 (1990), pp. 56–64.

24. L. Pollock and J. M. G. Williams, 'Problem solving in suicide attempters', *Psychological Medicine*, 34 (2004), pp. 163–7.
25. J. M. G. Williams, T. Barnhofer, C. Crane and A. T. Beck, 'Problem solving deteriorates following mood challenge in formerly depressed patients with a history of suicidal ideation', *Journal of Abnormal Psychology*, 114(3) (2005), pp. 421–31.
26. R. C. O'Connor, S. Rasmussen and K. Hawton, 'Predicting depression, anxiety and self-harm in adolescents: the role of perfectionism and acute life stress', *Behaviour Research and Therapy*, 48(1) (2010), pp. 52–9.
27. A. K. MacLeod, G. Rose and J. M. G. Williams, 'Components of helplessness about the future in parasuicide', *Cognitive Therapy and Research*, 17 (1993), pp. 441–55.
28. A. K. MacLeod and C. Conway, 'Well-being and positive future-thinking for the self versus others', *Cognition and Emotion*, 21 (2007), pp. 1114–24.
29. J. F. Simonds, T. McMahon and D. Armstrong, 'Young suicide attempters compared with a control group', *Suicide and Life Threatening Behaviour*, 21 (1991), pp. 134–51.
30. A. K. MacLeod, B. Pankhania, M. Lee and D. Mitchell, 'Parasuicide, depression and anticipation of positive and negative future experiences', *Psychological Medicine*, 27 (1997), pp. 973–7.
31. R. C. O'Connor, L. Fraser, M.-C. Whyte, S. MacHale and G. Masterton, 'A comparison of specific positive future expectancies and global hopelessness as predictors of suicidal ideation in a prospective study of repeat self-harmers', *Journal of Affective Disorders*, 110(3) (2008), pp. 207–14.
32. M. M. Linehan, J. L. Goodstein, S. L. Neilsen and J. A. Chiles, 'Reasons for staying alive when you are thinking of killing yourself: the reasons for living inventory', *Journal of Consulting and Clinical Psychology*, 51 (1983), pp. 276–86.
33. S. Hepburn, T. Barnhofer and J. M. G. Williams, 'Effects of mood on how future events are generated and perceived', *Personality and Individual Differences*, 41 (2006), pp. 801–11.

34. C. L. Danchin, A. K. MacLeod and P. Tata, 'Painful engagement in deliberate self-harm: the role of conditional goal setting', *Behaviour Research and Therapy*, 48 (2010), pp. 915–20.
35. R. C. O'Connor, R. E. O'Carroll, C. Ryan and R. Smyth, 'Self-regulation of unattainable goals in suicide attempters: a two year prospective study', *Journal of Affective Disorders*, 142(1–3) (2012), pp. 248–55.
36. See A. Apter and O. Freusenstein, 'Adolescent suicidal behaviour', in Hawton and van Heeringen (eds), op. cit., pp. 261–74.
37. K. Hawton, K. E. Saunders and R. C. O'Connor, 'Self-harm and suicide in adolescents', *Lancet*, 379(9834) (2012), pp. 2373–82, doi: 10.1016/S0140-6736(12)60322-5.
38. N. Kapur, J. Cooper, R. C. O'Connor and K. Hawton, 'Non-suicidal self-injury v. attempted suicide: new diagnosis or false dichotomy?', *British Journal of Psychiatry.* 202(5) (2013), pp. 326–8. doi: 10.1192/bjp.bp.112.116111.
39. K. Hawton, H. Bergen, N. Kapur, J. Cooper, S. Steeg, J. Ness and K. Waters, 'Repetition of self-harm and suicide following self-harm in children and adolescents: findings from the multicentre study of self-harm in England', *Journal of Child Psychology and Psychiatry,* 53 (2012), pp. 1212–19, doi: 10.1111/j.1469-7610.2012.02559.x.

CHAPTER SIX

1. D. Humphry, 'Rational suicide among the elderly', *Suicide and Life Threatening Behaviour*, 22 (1992), pp. 125–9, see p. 127; D. Humphry, *Final Exit: The Practicalities of Self-deliverance and Assisted Suicide*, Carol Publishing, Secaucus, NJ, 1991.
2. Humphry, 'Rational suicide among the elderly', op. cit.
3. J. H. Groenewoud, P. J. van der Maas, G. van der Wal et al., 'Physician-assisted death in psychiatric practice in the Netherlands', *New England Journal of Medicine*, 336 (1997), pp. 1795–801.
4. A. Koestler, *Arrow in the Blue*, Collins and Hamish Hamilton, London, 1952.
5. R. D. Goldney, 'Arthur Koestler: was his suicide rational?', *Crisis*, 7 (1986), pp. 33–53.

6. J. Richman, 'A rational approach to rational suicide', *Suicide and Life-Threatening Behaviour*, 22 (1992), pp. 130–41.
7. Scott, op. cit.
8. Richman, op. cit.

CHAPTER SEVEN

1. S. Freud, *Mourning and Melancholia* [1917], standard edition, vol. 14, Hogarth Press, London, 1957, p.248.
2. Ibid, p.252.
3. S. Freud, *The Ego and the Id* [1923], standard edition, vol. 19, Hogarth Press, London, 1961, p53.
4. For psychoanalytic observations on suicide as a 'reversible' and 'magical' act, see K. A. Menninger, 'Psychoanalytic aspects of suicide', *International Journal of Psychoanalysis*, 14 (1933), p. 376; C. W. Wahl, 'Suicide as a magical act', *Bulletin of the Menninger Clinic*, 21 (1957), p. 91.
5. M. Klein, 'A contribution to the psychogenesis of manic-depressive states' [1935], in *Contributions to Psycho-Analysis 1921–1945: Melanie Klein*, Hogarth Press, London, 1948.
6. S. Asch, 'Suicide and the hidden executioner', *International Review of Psychoanalysis*, 7 (1980), pp. 51–60.
7. J. Bowlby, *Maternal Care and Mental Health*, Columbia University Press, New York, 1951.
8. J. T. Maltsberger, *Suicide Risk: The Formulation of Clinical Judgement*, New York University Press, New York and London, 1986.
9. P. W. Gold, F. K. Goodwin and G. P. Chrousos, 'Clinical and biochemical manifestation of depression', *New England Journal of Medicine*, 319 (1988), pp. 348–420.
10. M. Asberg, P. Thoren, L. Traskman et al., 'Serotonin depression: a biochemical subgroup within the affective disorders?', *Science*, 191 (1986) pp. 478–80.
11. See also E. F. Coccaro, L. J. Siever, H. M. Klar et al., 'Serotonergic studies in patients with affective and personality disorders', *Archives of General Psychiatry*, 46 (1989), pp. 587–99; K. M.

Malone, E. M. Corbitt, L. Shuhua and L. Mann, 'Prolactin response to Fenfluramine and suicide attempt lethality in major depression', *British Journal of Psychiatry*, 168 (1996), pp. 324–9; G. N. Pandey, S. C. Pandey, Y. Dwivedi et al., 'Platelet serotonin-2A receptors: a potential biological marker for suicidal behaviour', *American Journal of Psychiatry*, 152 (1995), pp. 850–5.

12. See R. M. Winchel, B. Stanley and M. Stanley, 'Biochemical aspects of suicide', in S. J. Blumenthal and D. J. Kupfer (eds), *Suicide over the Life Cycle: Risk Factors, Assessment and Treatment of Suicidal Patients*, American Psychiatric Association Press, Washington, DC, 1990.
13. M. Linnoila, M. Virkkunen, M. Scheinin et al., 'Low cerebral-spinal fluid 5-HIAA concentration differentiates impulsive from nonimpulsive violent behaviour', *Life Science*, 33 (1983), pp. 2609–14.
14. M. Rajalin, T. Hirvikoski and J. Jokinen, 'Family history of suicide and exposure to interpersonal violence in childhood predict suicide in male suicide attempters', *Journal of Affective Disorders*, 148(1) (2013), pp. 92–7, doi: 10.1016/*j*.jad.2012.11.055.
15. A. Roy, D. Nielson, G. Rylander and M. Sarchipione, 'The genetics of suicidal behaviour', in Hawton and van Heeringen (eds), op. cit., pp. 209–21. For the relationship with personality and mood variable, see A. Apter, H. van Praag, R. Plutchik et al., 'Interrelationships among anxiety, aggression, impulsivity and mood: a serotonergically linked cluster?', *Psychiatry Research*, 32 (1990), pp. 191–9.
16. A. Roy, et al., 'Suicide in twins', *Archives of General Psychiatry*, 48 (1991), pp. 29–32.
17. F. Schulsinger, S. S. Kety, D. Rosenthal and P. H. Wender, 'A family study of suicide', in M. Schou and E. Stromgren (eds), *Prevention and Treatment of Affective Disorders*, Academic Press, New York, 1979, pp. 277–87.
18. A. Dumais, A. D. Lesage, M. Alda et al., 'Risk factors for suicide completion in major depression: a case-control study of impulsive and aggressive behaviours in men', *American Journal of Psychiatry*, 162 (2005), pp. 2116–24, doi: 10.1176/appi.ajp.162.11.2116; G. Turecki, 'Dissecting the suicide phenotype: the role of impulsive–aggressive

behaviours', *Journal of Psychiatry and Neuroscience*, 30(6) (2005), pp. 398–408.

19. S. Kety, 'Genetic factors in suicide: family, twin and adoption studies', in Blumenthal and Kupfer (eds), op. cit., p.132.
20. Joiner, op. cit.

CHAPTER EIGHT

1. J. MacCartney,'Internet shame is killing our children', *Daily Telegraph,* 17 August 2013, http://www.telegraph.co.uk/technology/internet/10248675/Internet-shame-is-killing-our-children.html.
2. R. M. Post, 'Transduction of psychosocial stress into the neurobiology of recurrent affective disorder', *American Journal of Psychiatry*, 149 (1992), pp. 999–1010.
3. G. L. Engel, 'Anxiety and depression-withdrawal: the primary effects of unpleasure', *International Journal of Psychoanalysis*, 43 (1962), pp. 89–97.
4. R. D. Goldney, 'Attempted suicide: an ethological perspective', *Suicide and Life-Threatening Behaviour*, 10 (1980), pp. 131–41.
5. E. S. Schneidman, 'Orientations towards death: a vital aspect of the study of lives', *International Journal of Psychiatry*, 2 (1966), pp. 167–200.
6. P. Gilbert, J. Prince and S. Allan, 'Social comparison, social attractiveness and evolution: how might they be related?', *New Ideas in Psychology*, 13 (1995), pp. 149–65.
7. R. G. Wilkinson, 'Income distribution and life expectancy', *British Medical Journal*, 304 (1992), pp. 165–8.
8. P. Gilbert, *Depression: The Evolution of Powerlessness*, Lawrence Erlbaum Associates, Hove and Guilford, New York, 1992.
9. T. Schjelderup-Ebbe, 'Social behavior in birds' in C. Murchison, *A Handbook of Social Psychology* (1935), p.966; P. Gilbert, *Human Nature and Suffering*, Lawrence Erlbaum Associates, Hove and London, 1989. See also J. S. Price and L. Sloman, 'Depression as yielding behaviour: an animal model based on Schjelerup-Ebbe's pecking order', *Ethology and Sociobiology*, 8 (1987), pp. 85–98.
10. See P. Gilbert and S. Allan, 'The role of defeat and entrapment

(arrested flight) in depression: an exploration of an evolutionary view', *Psychological Medicine*, 28 (1998), pp. 585–98. There is now increasing evidence that biological processes are triggered by the perception and expectation of inescapability and that a vicious circle involving biological, social and psychological factors can occur. See K. van Heeringen, K. Hawton and J. M. G. Williams, 'Pathways to suicide: an integrative approach', in Hawton and van Heeringen (eds), op. cit., pp. 223–36 and O'Connor, 'Suicidal behaviour as a cry of pain, op. cit.

11. R. J. R. Blair, 'A cognitive approach to morality: investigating the psychopath', *Cognition*, 57 (1995), pp. 1–29.
12. Farberow and Schneidman (eds), op. cit.
13. Alvarez, op. cit., p.293.
14. MacDonald and Murphy, op. cit. see note 2, Chapter One.
15. See Joiner, op. cit.

CHAPTER NINE

1. J. D. Teasdale and S. J. Fogarty, 'Differential effects of induced mood on retrieval of pleasant and unpleasant events from episodic memory', *Journal of Abnormal Psychology*, 88 (1979), pp. 248–57; G. G. Lloyd and W. A. Lishman, 'Effect of depression on the speed of recall of pleasant and unpleasant experiences', *Psychological Medicine*, 5 (1975), pp. 173–80.
2. J. M. G. Williams and K. Broadbent, 'Autobiographical memory in attempted suicide patients', *Journal of Abnormal Psychology*, 95 (1986), pp. 144–9; J. M. G. Williams and B. H. Dritschel, 'Emotional disturbance and the specificity of autobiographical memory', *Cognition and Emotion*, 2 (1988), pp. 221–34.
3. J. M. G. Williams, T. Barnhofer, C. Crane, D. Hermans, F. Raes, E. Watkins and T. Dalgleish, 'Autobiographical memory specificity and emotional disorder', *Psychological Bulletin,* 133 (2007), pp. 122–48.
4. J. M. G. Williams, 'Depression and the specificity of autobiographical memory', in D. C. Rubin (ed.), *Remembering Our Past: Studies in Autobiographical Memory*, Cambridge University Press, Cambridge, 1996.

5. J. Evans, J. M. G. Williams, S. O'Loughlin and K. Howells, 'Autobiographical memory and problem solving strategies of para-suicide patients', *Psychological Medicine*, 22 (1992), pp. 399–405.
6. J. M. G. Williams, S. Chan, C. Crane, T. Barnhofer, J. Eade and H. Healy, 'Retrieval of autobiographical memories: the mechanisms and consequences of truncated search', *Cognition and Emotion*, 20 (2006), pp. 351–82.
7. For the work that led to these conclusions, see J. M. G. Williams, N. Ellis, C. Tyers, H. Healy, G. Rose and A. K. MacLeod, 'The specificity of autobiographical memory and imageability of the future', *Memory and Cognition*, 24 (1996), pp. 116–25.
8. A. D. Brittlebank, J. Scott, J. M. G. Williams and I. N. Ferrier, 'Autobiographical memory in depression: state or trait marker?', *British Journal of Psychiatry*, 162 (1993), pp. 118–21.
9. For example, see A. Rawal and F. Rice, 'Examining overgeneral autobiographical memory as a risk factor for adolescent depression', *Journal of the American Academy of Child and Adolescent Psychiatry*, 51 (2012), pp. 518–27.

CHAPTER TEN

1. Durkheim, *Le Suicide*, op. cit.
2. D. P. Phillips, 'The influence of suggestion on suicide: substantive and theoretical implications of the Werther effect', *American Sociological Review*, 39 (1974), pp. 340–54.
3. Suicides receiving media attention tend to involve violent and highly lethal methods, and are often carried out in public places.
4. B. Barraclough, D. Shepherd and C. Jennings, 'Two newspaper reports of coroners' inquests incite people to commit suicide?' *British Journal of Psychiatry*, 131 (1977), pp. 528–32.
5. K. A. Bollen and D. P. Phillips, 'Imitative suicides: a national study of the effects of television news stories', *American Sociological Review*, 47 (1982), pp. 802–9.
6. For evidence of suicide by burning as an imitative phenomenon, see J. R. Ashton and S. Donnan, 'Suicide by burning as an epidemic phenomena [sic]: an analysis of 82 deaths and inquests in England

and Wales in 1978–9', *Psychological Medicine*, 11 (1981), pp. 735–9.

7. T. Niederkrotenthaler, K. Fu, P. S. F. Yip et al., 'Changes in suicide rates following media reports on celebrity suicide: a meta-analysis', *Journal of Epidemiology and Community Health*, 66 (2012), pp. 1037–42; A. T. A. Cheng, K. Hawton, C. T. C. Lee et al., 'The influence of media reporting of the suicide of a celebrity on suicide rates: a population-based study', *International Journal of Epidemiology*, 36 (2007), pp. 1229–34.
8. D. P. Phillips, 'The impact of fictional television stories on American adult fatalities', *American Journal of Sociology*, 87 (1982), pp. 1340–59.
9. S. J. Ellis and S. Walsh, 'Soap may seriously damage your health' (letter), *Lancet* 1(8482) (1986), p. 686.
10. J. M. G. Williams, C. Lawton, S. Ellis, S. Walsh and J. Reed, 'Imitative parasuicide by overdose', *Lancet*, 8550 (1987), pp. 102–3 (report of findings of research commissioned by the Independent Broadcasting Authority).
11. A. Schmidtke and H. Hafner, 'The Werther effect after television films: new evidence from an old hypothesis', *Psychological Medicine*, 18 (1988), pp. 665–76.
12. K. Hawton, S. Simkin, J. Deeks et al., 'Effects of drug overdose in a television drama on presentations to the hospital for self-poisoning: time series and questionnaire study', *British Medical Journal*, 318 (1999), pp. 972–9.
13. R. C. Kessler and H. Stipp, 'The impact of fictional television suicide stories on US fatalities: a replication', *American Journal of Sociology*, 90 (1984), pp. 151–67.
14. D. P. Phillips and L. L. Carstensen, 'Clustering teenage suicides after television news stories about suicides', *New England Journal of Medicine*, 315 (1986), pp. 685–9.
15. A review from nine different countries showed that their guidelines are very similar, although they differ in the way they were developed (e.g. the degree to which media experts were involved): see J. Pirkis, R. W. Blood, A. Beautrais, P. Burgess and J. Skehan, 'Media guidelines on the reporting of suicide', *Crisis*, 27 (2006), pp. 82–7.

16. J. Pirkis, R. W. Blood, J. Skehan et al., 'Suicide in the news: informing strategies to improve the reporting of suicide', *Health Communication*, 25 (2010), pp. 576–7, doi: 10.1080/10410236.2010.496771; M. Gould, 'Suicide clusters and media exposure', in Blumenthal and Kupfer (eds), op. cit.
17. L. D. Biddle, K. Hawton, N. Kapur and D. Gunnell, 'Suicide and the internet', *British Medical Journal*, 336 (2008), p. 800.
18. J. Pirkis and R. W. Blood, 'Suicide and the news and information media: a critical review', Hunter Institute of Mental Health, New South Wales, 2010. Available from http://www.mindframe.media.info.
19. J. Pirkis, L. Neal, A. Dare, R. W. Blood and D. Studdert, 'Legal bans on pro-suicide websites: an early retrospective from Australia', *Suicide and Life-Threatening Behaviour,* 39(2) (2009), pp. 190–3.

CHAPTER ELEVEN

1. D. W. Coombs, H. L. Miller, R. Alarcon, C. Herlinhy, J. M. Lee and D. P. Morison, 'Presuicide attempt communications between parasuicides and consulted caregivers', *Suicide and Life-Threatening Behaviour*, 22 (1992), pp. 289–302.
2. Asking about people's reactions to their own suicidal feelings: see E. A. Holmes, C. Crane, M. J. V. Fennell and J. M. G. Williams, 'Imagery about suicide in depression – "flash-forwards"?', *Journal of Behaviour Therapy and Experimental Psychiatry,* 38 (2007), pp. 423–34, doi: 10.1016/j.jbtep.2007.10.00; C. Crane, D. Shah, T. Barnhofer and E. A. Holmes, 'Suicidal imagery in a previously depressed community sample', *Clinical Psychology & Psychotherapy,* 19 (2012), pp. 57–69, doi: 10.1002/cpp.741. For evidence of bias in clinicians, see K. E. A. Saunders, K. Hawton, S. Fortune and S. Farrell, 'Attitudes and knowledge of clinical staff regarding people who self-harm: a systematic review', *Journal of Affective Disorders,* 139 (2012), pp. 205–16, doi: 10.1016/j.jad.2011.08.024.
3. J. Motto, 'Suicide prevention for high-risk persons who refuse treatment', *Suicide and Life-Threatening Behaviour*, 6 (1976), pp. 223–30.

4. An Office of Population Census and Surveys report found that one in seven people in Britain between 16 and 64 has some sort of 'neurotic health problem' at any one time: see H. Meltzer, B. Gill and M. Pettigrew, *OPCS Survey of Psychiatric Morbidity in Great Britain*, OPCS, London, 1994.
5. *Sensitivity* of a test is defined as the number of true positives divided by the sum of true positives plus false negatives, then multiplied by 100. The numerator is the 'positive hit rate' (suicides successfully predicted) and the denominator is the total number of such hits that are possible – the total number of actual suicides in the population being studied. *Specificity* of a test is defined as the number of true negatives divided by the sum of false positives and true negatives, then multiplied by 100. The numerator is the negative 'hit rate' (lack of suicide successfully predicted) and the denominator is the total number of such hits that are possible – the total number of people who do not commit suicide in the population being studied.
6. A. D. Pokorny, 'Prediction of suicide in psychiatric patients: report of a prospective study', in R. W. Maris, A. L. Berman, J. T. Maltsberger and R. I. Yufit (eds), *Assessment and Prediction of Suicide*, Guilford Press, New York, 1992.
7. R. W. Maris, 'The prediction of suicide' in M. J. Kelleher (ed.), *Divergent Perspectives on Suicidal Behaviour*, Report of Fifth European Symposium on Suicide, Cork, 1994, pp. 28–41.
8. L. Appleby, J. Shaw, J. Amos et al., *Safer Services: Report of the National Confidential Inquiry into Suicide and Homicide by People with Mental Illness*, HM Stationery Office, London, 1999. See NCI's latest report, *National Confidential Inquiry into Suicide and Homicide by People with Mental Illness*, July 2013, University of Manchester, which reports a rise in suicides in the UK, and a continued increase in the proportion of people using hanging as a method of suicide in the first decade of the twenty-first century.
9. L. Appleby, J. A. Dennehy, C. S. Thomas et al., 'Aftercare and clinical characteristics of people with mental illness who commit suicide: a case control study', *Lancet*, 353 (1999), pp. 1397–400.
10. J. A. Dennehy, L. Appleby and B. Faragher, 'A case control study of

suicide by discharged psychiatric patients', *British Medical Journal*, 312 (1996), p. 1580.

11. Maris, 'The prediction of suicide', op. cit.
12. R. C. O'Connor, S. Rasmussen and K. Hawton, 'Predicting depression, anxiety and self-harm in adolescents: the role of perfectionism and acute life stress', *Behaviour Research and Therapy,* 48 (1) (2010), pp. 52–9.
13. D. Lester and K. Abe, 'The effect of restricting access to lethal methods for suicide: a study of suicide by domestic gas in Japan', *Acta Psychiatrica Scandinavica,* 80 (1989), pp. 180–2, doi: 10.1111/j.1600-0447.1989.tb01324.x; D. Lester, 'The effects of detoxification of domestic gas on suicide in the United States', *American Journal of Public Health,* 80 (1990), pp. 80–1.
14. T. Amos, L. Appleby and K. Kiernan, 'Changes in rates of suicide by car exhaust asphyxiation in England and Wales', *Psychological Medicine,* 31 (2001), pp. 935–9; R. E. Kendell, 'Catalytic converters and prevention of suicides', *Lancet,* 352 (1998), p. 1525, doi: 10.1016/s0140-6736(05)60332-7; J. A. Mott, M. I. Wolfe, C. J. Alverson, S. C. Macdonald, C. R. Bailey, L. B. Ball et al., 'National vehicle emissions policies and practices and declining US carbon monoxide-related mortality', *Journal of the American Medical Association*, 288 (2002), pp. 988–95, doi: 10.1001/jama.288.8.988.
15. D. Gunnell, O. Bennewith, K. Hawton, S. Simkin and N. Kapur, 'The epidemiology and prevention of suicide by hanging: a systematic review', *International Journal of Epidemiology*, 34 (2) (2005), pp. 433–42, doi: 10.1093/Ije/Dyh398.
16. V. Ajdacic-Gross, M. G. Weiss, M. Ring, U. Hepp, M. Bopp, F. Gutzwiller and W. Rossler, 'Methods of suicide: international suicide patterns derived from the WHO mortality database', *Bulletin of the World Health Organization,* 86 (2008), pp. 726–32, doi: 10.2471/blt.07.043489.
17. A. L. Beautrais, D. M. Fergusson and L. J. Horwood, 'Firearms legislation and reductions in firearm-related suicide deaths in New Zealand', *Australian and New Zealand Journal of Psychiatry,* 40 (2006), pp. 253–9, doi: 10.1080/j.1440-1614.2006.01782.x.

18. R. D. Goldney, 'Suicide in Australia: some good news', *Medical Journal of Australia,* 185 (2006), p. 304. But conflicting evidence: S. McPhedran and J. Baker, 'Suicide prevention and method restriction: evaluating the impact of limiting access to lethal means among young Australians', *Archives of Suicide Research,* 16 (2012), pp. 135–46, doi: 10.1080/13811118.2012.667330.
19. C. L. Rich, J. G. Young, R. C. Fowler, J. Wagner and N. A. Black, 'Guns and suicide – possible effects of some specific legislation', *American Journal of Psychiatry,* 147 (1990), pp. 342–6.
20. N. D. Kapusta, E. Etzersdorfer, C. Krall and G. Sonneck, 'Firearm legislation reform in the European Union: impact on firearm availability, firearm suicide and homicide rates in Austria', *British Journal of Psychiatry,* 191 (2007), pp. 253–7, doi: 10.1192/bjp.bp.106.032862.
21. A. R. Andres and K. Hempstead, 'Gun control and suicide: the impact of state firearm regulations in the United States, 1995–2004', *Health Policy,* 101 (2011), pp. 95–103, doi: 10.1016/j.healthpol.2010.10.005.
22. D. Gunnell, N. Middleton and S. Frankel, 'Method availability and the prevention of suicide – a re-analysis of secular trends in England and Wales 1950–1975', *Social Psychiatry and Psychiatric Epidemiology,* 35 (2000), pp. 437–43, doi: 10.1007/s001270050261.
23. For further discussion of this work, see D. Lester, *Can We Prevent Suicide?*, AMS Press, New York, 1989.
24. I am grateful to Bergljot Gjelsvik for these data. M. Aitken, E. R. Berndt and D. M. Cutler, 'Prescription drug spending trends in the United States: looking beyond the turning point', *Health Affairs,* 28 (2009), pp. W151–W160, doi: 10.1377/hlthaff.28.1.w151; 'Prescription drug trends, 2010', retrieved 13 March 2013 from http://www.kff.org/rxdrugs/upload/3057-08.pdf.
25. M. A. Caudill-Slosberg, L. M. Schwartz and S. Woloshin, 'Office visits and analgesic prescriptions for musculoskeletal pain in US: 1980 vs. 2000', *Pain,* 109 (2004), pp. 514–19, doi: 10.1016/j.pain.2004.03.006.
26. M. King and C. Essick, 'The geography of antidepressant, antipsychotic, and stimulant utilization in the United States', *Health &*

Place, 20 (2013), pp. 32–8, doi: http://dx.doi.org/10.1016/j.healthplace.2012.11.007; Y. Hsia and K. Maclennan, 'Rise in psychotropic drug prescribing in children and adolescents during 1992–2001: a population-based study in the UK', *European Journal of Epidemiology,* 24 (2009), pp. 211–16, doi: 10.2307/40284112.

27. King and Essick, op. cit.
28. A. Mercier, I. Auger-Aubin, J. P. Lebeau, P. Van Royen and L. Peremans, 'Understanding the prescription of antidepressants: a qualitative study among French GPs', *BMC Family Practice*, 12 (2011), p. 99, doi: 9910.1186/1471-2296-12-99.
29. S. Sakshaug, H. Strøm, C. Berg, H. S. Blix, I. Litleskare and T. Granum, 'Drug consumption in Norway 2008–2012' [2013], retrieved 19 April 2013 from http://www.legemiddelforbruk.no/english/.
30. B. Gjelsvik, F. Heyerdahl and K. Hawton, 'Prescribed medication availability and deliberate self-poisoning: a longitudinal study', *Journal of Clinical Psychiatry*, 73(4) (2012), pp. e548–e554, doi:10.4088/JCP.11m07209.
31. B. Gjelsvik, F. Heyerdahl, D. Lunn and K. Hawton, 'Change in access to prescribed medication following an episode of deliberate self-poisoning: a multi-level approach' [2013] (manuscript submitted).
32. For data on knowledge of toxicity of medication, see D. I. R. Jones, 'Self-poisoning with drugs', *British Medical Journal*, 282 (1977), pp. 28–9. For data on the effects of repackaging of analgesics in the UK, see K. Hawton et al., 'UK legislation on analgesic pack sizes: before and after study of long-term effects on poisonings', *British Medical Journal,* 329 (2004), pp. 1076–9; K. Hawton, H. Bergen, S. Simkin, S. Dodd, P. Pocock, W. Bernal, D. Gunnell and N. Kapur, 'Long term effect of reduced pack sizes of paracetamol on poisoning deaths and liver transplant activity in England and Wales: interrupted time series analyses', *British Medical Journal*, 7 (February 2013), p. 346:f403, doi: 10.1136/bmj.f403.
33. K. Hawton, S. Simkin and J. Deeks, 'Co-proxamol and suicide: A study of national mortality statistics and local non-fatal self

poisonings', *British Medical Journal,* 326 (2003), pp. 1006–8, doi: 10.1136/bmj.326.7397.1006326/7397/1006.

34. K. Hawton, H. Bergen, S. Simkin, A. Brock, C. Griffiths, E. Romeri et al., 'Effect of withdrawal of co-proxamol on prescribing and deaths from drug poisoning in England and Wales: time series analysis', *British Medical Journal,* 338 (2009), p. b2270, doi: 10.1136/bmj.b2270bmj.b2270 [pii].
35. S. E. Roberts, B. Jaremin and K. Lloyd, 'High-risk occupations for suicide', *Psychological Medicine*, 43 (2013), pp. 1231–40.
36. S. Greer and M. Alderson, 'Samaritan contact among 325 parasuicide patients', *British Journal of Psychiatry*, 135 (1979), pp. 263–8.
37. C. Jennings, B. M. Barraclough and J. R. Moss, 'Have the Samaritans lowered the suicide rate: a controlled study', *Psychological Medicine*, 8 (1978), pp. 413–27.
38. For sceptical evaluations, see *Suicide and Parasuicide*, MRC Topic Review, Medical Research Council, London, 1995; D. Shaffer, M. A. Garland, M. Gould et al., 'Preventing teenage suicide: a critical review', *Journal of the American Academy of Childhood and Adolescent Psychiatry*, 27 (1988), pp. 675–87.
39. D. Shaffer, A. Garland, V. Vieland et al., 'The impact of curriculum-based suicide prevention programs for teenagers', *Journal of the American Academy of Childhood and Adolescent Psychiatry*, 30 (1991), pp. 588–96.
40. http://www.nice.org.uk/niceMedia/documents/suicidePO.pdf (2004); https://www.gov.uk/government/uploads/system/uploads/attachment_data/file/216928/Preventing-Suicide-in-England-A-cross-government-outcomes-strategy-to-save-lives.pdf (2012).

CHAPTER TWELVE

1. For further reading, see these three excellent books: *Why People Die by Suicide* by Thomas Joiner; *Treating Suicidal Behaviour: An Effective, Time-Limited Approach* by David Rudd, Thomas Joiner, and Hasan Rajab; *The Interpersonal Theory of Suicide: Guidance for Working with Suicidal Clients* by Thomas Joiner, Kim Van Orden, Tracy Witte and David Rudd.

2. National Institute for Health and Clinical Excellence, 'Self-harm: longer-term management' (2011), Clinical Guideline CG133.
3. Ten studies have evaluated the efficacy of DBT for suicidal BPD patients, nine of which are discussed in the NICE's 'Borderline Personality Disorder' (2009), Clinical Guideline 78.
4. G. K. Brown, T. T. Have, G. R. Henriques, S. X. Xie, J. E. Hollander and A. T. Beck, 'Cognitive Therapy for the prevention of suicide attempts: a randomized controlled trial', *JAMA* (2005), 294(5), pp. 563–70. See also B. Stanley, G. Brown, D. Brent et al., 'Cognitive Behaviour Therapy for Suicide Prevention (CBT-SP): treatment model, feasibility and acceptability', *Journal of the American Academy of Child and Adolescent Psychiatry*, 48(10) (2009), pp. 1005–13, doi: 10.1097/CHI.0b013e3181b5dbfe.
5. See David Jobes, *Managing Suicidal Risk: A Collaborative Approach*, Guilford Press, New York, 2006.
6. M. Gould, F. A. Marrocco, M. Kleinman, J. G. Thomas, K. Mostkoff, J. Cote and M. Davies, 'Evaluating iatrogenic risk of youth suicide screening programs: a randomized controlled trial', *JAMA*, 293(13) (2005), pp. 1635–43, doi:10.1001/jama.293.13.1635.
7. E. Dunmore, D. M. Clark and A. Ehlers, 'A prospective investigation of the role of cognitive factors in persistent posttraumatic stress disorder (PTSD) after physical or sexual assault', *Behaviour Research and Therapy*, 39 (2001), pp. 1063–84, doi: 10.1016/s0005-7967(00)00088-7; E. Dunmore, D. M. Clark and A. Ehlers, 'Cognitive factors involved in the onset and maintenance of posttraumatic stress disorder (PTSD) after physical or sexual assault', *Behaviour Research and Therapy,* 37 (1999), pp. 809 –29, doi: 10.1016/s0005-7967(98)00181-8; R. Ehlers, A. Mayou and B. Bryant, 'Psychological predictors of chronic posttraumatic stress disorder after motor vehicle accidents', *Journal of Abnormal Psychology,* 107 (1998), pp. 508–19, doi: 10.1037//0021-843x.107.3.508; R. Stei and A. Ehlers, 'Dysfunctional meaning of posttraumatic intrusions in chronic PTSD', *Behaviour Research and Therapy,* 38 (2000), pp. 537–58, doi: 10.1016/s0005-7967(99)00069-8.
8. R. Morrison and R. C. O'Connor, 'A systematic review of the

relationship between rumination and suicidality', *Suicide and Life-Threatening Behaviour,* 38 (2008), pp. 523–38, doi: 10.1521/suli.2008.38.5.523.

9. A. Kerkhof and B. van Spijker, 'Worrying and rumination as proximal risk factors for suicidal behaviour', in O'Connor, Platt and Gordon (eds), op. cit., pp.199–210.
10. J. M. G. Williams, T. Barnhofer, C. Crane and A. T. Beck, 'Problem solving deteriorates following mood challenge in formerly depressed patients with a history of suicidal ideation', *Journal of Abnormal Psychology,* 114 (2005), pp. 421–31.
11. R. C. O'Connor, 'Towards an integrated motivational-volitional model of suicidal behaviour', in O'Connor, Platt and Gordon (eds), op. cit. pp. 181–98.
12. E. R. Watkins, 'Dysregulation in level of goal and action identification across psychological disorders', *Clinical Psychology Review,* 31 (2011), pp. 260–78, doi: 10.1016/j.cpr.2010.05.004.
13. S. C. Hayes, 'Acceptance and Commitment Therapy, Relational Frame Theory, and the third wave of behavioural and cognitive therapies', *Behaviour Therapy,* 35 (2004), pp. 639–65, doi: 10.1016/s0005-7894(04)80013-3.
14. Z. V. Segal, J. M. G. Williams and J. D. Teasdale, *Mindfulness-based Cognitive Therapy for Depression*, second edition, Guilford Press, New York, 2013.
15. E. Hargus, C. Crane, T. Barnhofer and J. M. G. Williams, 'Effects of mindfulness on meta-awareness and specificity of describing prodromal symptoms in suicidal depression', *Emotion,* 10 (2010), pp. 34–42, doi: 10.1037/a0016825.
16. J. Piet and E. Hougaard, 'The effect of Mindfulness-based Cognitive Therapy for prevention of relapse in recurrent major depression', *Clinical Psychology Review,* 31 (2011), pp. 1032–40, doi: 10.1016/j.cpr.2011.05.002; Z. V. Segal, J. M. G. Williams and J. D. Teasdale, *Mindfulness-based Cognitive Therapy for Depression: A New Approach to Preventing Relapse*, Guilford Press, New York, 2002. For other research findings see: Z. V. Segal, J. D. Teasdale and J. M. G. Williams (2004), 'Mindfulness-based Cognitive Therapy: theoretical rationale and empirical status', in S. Hayes et al.

(eds), *Mindfulness and Acceptance: The New Behaviour Therapies*, Guilford Press, New York, 2010 (pp.45–6).

17. Segal, Williams and Teasdale, op.cit.
18. Further details of MBCT can be found in the following (see Resources for details):
    a) *The Mindful Way through Depression*
    b) *Mindfulness: A Guide to Finding Peace in a Frantic World*
    c) *The Mindful Way Workbook: An Eight-week Program to Free Yourself from Depression and Emotional Distress*
19. T. Barnhofer, C. Crane, E. Hargus, M. Amarasinghe, R. Winder and J. M. G. Williams, 'Mindfulness-based Cognitive Therapy as a treatment for chronic depression', *Behaviour Research & Therapy*, 47 (2009), pp. 366–73.
20. J. M. G. Williams, et al., 'Mindfulness-based Cognitive Therapy for preventing relapse in recurrent depression: a randomized dismantling trial', *Journal of Consulting and Clinical Psychology*, online, 2 December 2013, doi: 10.1037/a0035036.

CHAPTER THIRTEEN

1. P. Levi, *The Drowned and the Saved*, trans. R. Rosenthal, Abacus, London, 2005 (p.53).
2. N. L. Farberow, 'Adult survivors after suicide: research problems and needs', in A. A. Leenaars (ed.), *Life Span Perspectives of Suicide*, Plenum Press, New York, 1991.
3. Ajahn Sucitto, 'Making peace with despair', in *Peace and Kindness*, Amaravati Publications, Hemel Hempstead, 1990 (p.11).

RESOURCES

This section provides some points of contact if you wish to explore any of the issues in this book further.

For those in a suicidal crisis

Crisis centres

If you need to contact a suicide crisis centre, and do not know how to access one, go to the International Association for Suicide Prevention website resources page, http://www.iasp.info/resources/, where you will find links to centres all over the world. You will also see links to how best to help someone you are worried about (follow the link: *Helping Someone*). Here are some specific sources of support that you may find useful.

UK

Samaritans: www.samaritans.org/

Centre for Suicide Prevention, Manchester: www.bbmh.manchester.ac.uk

Centre for Suicide Research, Oxford: cebmh.warne.ox.ac.uk/csr
The Alliance of Suicide Prevention Charities (TASC): www.tasc-uk.org

Ireland
National Office for Suicide Prevention: www.nosp.ie

South Africa
South Africa Suicide Hotlines: www.suicide.org/hotlines/international/south-africa-suicide-hotlines.html

Australia
Suicide Prevention Australia: www.suicidepreventionaust.org

New Zealand
Suicide Prevention Information New Zealand: www.spinz.org.nz

For those bereaved by suicide

This is probably the hardest thing you have ever faced. It often feels so overwhelming that it can feel that nothing could ever help relieve the pain. If you need support and don't know where to turn, you may wish to contact others who have been through the same experience, and it is best to search online for local groups of others who have been through it too. Search for 'bereaved by suicide' or 'suicide survivors'. You'll find groups such as Survivors of Bereavement by Suicide and Papyrus – both UK-based organisations that are there to help.

Sometimes it is enormously helpful simply to hear other people's experiences, and you can do this by going to www.healthtalkonline.org and following the A–Z link to suicide. There are interviews with those who have been through it, covering issues and reactions about the time before the suicide, the time soon after; the funeral, inquest, burial or cremation; and the sources of help that people found helpful.

For those who wish to learn more about the Mindfulness approach to depression and suicide

Mindfulness is an integrative, mind–body-based training that enables people to change the way they think and feel about their experiences, especially physical or mental pain. Rooted in ancient meditation practices but drawing on neuroscientific advances, it creates an effective means for people to learn how to deal effectively with stress and depression. It uses meditation as a form of mental training to develop sustained attention – attention that is purposeful, in the moment and non-judgemental, releasing the mind from habitual patterns in order to meet new challenges.

An 8-week training programme known as Mindfulness-based Cognitive Therapy (MBCT) has been shown to have a profound impact on sufferers of depression, reducing the chances of relapse back into depression by 40 to 50 per cent, and is now recognised by the UK's National Institute for Health and Care Excellence (NICE) as an effective treatment for recurrent depression.

If you want to try the full eight-week MBCT course, as the patients in our clinical trials have done, the best way is to work through *The Mindful Way Workbook* (see below) using the CD/downloads of guided meditation instructions that are included with it. If you wish to 'taste' mindfulness to see if you find it helpful, you may find *Mindfulness: Finding Peace in a Frantic World* (see below) helpful. In both cases, the week-by-week guidance will help you establish a regular practice of mindfulness meditation that so many have found transformational.

The Mindful Way Workbook: An Eight-Week Program to Free Yourself from Depression and Emotional Distress by John Teasdale, Mark Williams and Zindel Segal (Guilford, 2014)

This has been written specifically to accompany you as you work your way through the full eight-week MBCT programme. Along with describing the content in each session, you will see the rationale for the different exercises and helpful hints for how to practise.

Mindfulness: Finding Peace in a Frantic World by Mark Williams and Danny Penman (Piaktus, 2011)

This offers another option for you if you wish to taste shorter meditation practices to see if this is something that you wish to explore. It includes meditations narrated by Mark Williams.

The Mindful Way through Depression by M. Williams, M. Teasdale, Z. Segal and J. Kabat-Zinn (Guilford, 2007)

This book is proving very helpful for people who are interested in reading about how the practice of mindfulness can be broadened to deal with milder, but more ubiquitous, mental states, such as worry and unhappiness. It features guided meditations narrated by Jon Kabat-Zinn and provides the reader with more extensive background to these practices than would typically be provided in an MBCT class.

For further information, look at www.oxfordmindfulness.org, where there are many links to resources to support your practice. You can also sign up for an online mindfulness course by visiting www.bemindfulonline.com.

Free podcast on depression

The New Psychology of Depression is a series of six free podcasts by Mark Williams available for download from iTunes U. See https://itunes.apple.com/gb/itunes-u/new-psychology-depression/id474787597?mt=10.

For therapists

Mindfulness-based Cognitive Therapy for Depression, second edition, by Z.V. Segal, J.M.G. Williams and J.D. Teasdale (Guilford, 2013).

This is the MBCT manual, essential reading for those who wish to teach MBCT to people suffering from mental health problems, but also providing helpful advice to many other teachers of mindfulness who wish to understand the psychological theory that underlies and motivates the modern applications of mindfulness to emotional problems.

Mindfulness and the Transformation of Despair: Working with People at Risk of Suicide by J.M.G. Williams, M.J.V. Fennell, T. Barnhofer, R.S. Crane, S. Silverton (Guilford, 2014)

This book is written for therapists and mindfulness teachers who wish to offer MBCT to those who are suicidal and despairing. Divided into four parts, it includes (a) the theoretical and research background, (b) practical steps to assess risk and week-by-week adaptations to the clinical programme for the highly vulnerable person, (c) implications for training of teachers, and (d) the outcomes of the ten-year Wellcome Trust research programme that established the effectiveness of mindfulness both in reducing risk of further depression and for breaking the link between recurring depression and suicidal hopelessness.

INDEX

Abbot, George 6
Acceptance and Commitment Therapy 222
Addam, Agnes 156
alcohol 37–8, 144–5
Alvarez, Al 64–5, 77–8, 155, 198
and firearms 28
Andrewes, Lancelot 6–7
anomie 45, 54, 56, 158
Appleby, Prof. Louis 193
Aquinas, Thomas 104
arbitrary inference 215
Aristotle 104
Arrow in the Blue (Koestler) 114
assisted suicide xiv, xviii–xix, 101–4
  arguments against euthanasia and 110–17
    consent, question of 110–11
    no-man-is-an-island 113–14
    slippery-slope 111–12
  as compulsory euthanasia 103
  at Dignitas 109–10
  in European countries 109
  historical background to 104–10
  legal support for 107
  in Netherlands 107, 112
  in Oregon 102
    and other American states 109
  rational 113
  and religion 102, 105
  UK illegality of 109
attempted suicide 64–100
  causes of 79–100
  commonness of 70–3
  definitions of 66–70
  and Diana, Princess of Wales 86
  and emotions 95–9
  and employment status 83
  and events as precipitating factors 86–7
  and external circumstances 74–5, 76–7
  and future-directed thinking 90–2

attempted suicide *cont.*
  and hopelessness 90–2
  and ideas and behaviour 72
  and intent 74–7
  and interpersonal problems 87–90, 141–2
  motivations for 72–4
  'parasuicide' 66
  and parenting 80–1
  precipitating factors in 85–6
  premeditation of 76
  and reasons-for-living inventory 92–5
  and 'reasons for overdose', listed 73
  and self-harm 96–9, 154–5
    risk of repeating, assessment of 217
    see also under suicide
  self-reported 75–7
  and sexual abuse 81
  and special dates 85
  and substance abuse 37–8, 84
  and suicide, as cry of pain xv, xvi, 143, 154–5, 231
  and suicide, as two responses to same circumstances 229
  and suicide notes 75
  and vulnerability factors 80–4
    long-term 80–3
    short-term 83–4
Auschwitz 235

Beck, Prof. A. T. 215, 226
Biathanatos (Donne) 12, 13, 113
Blood, Warwick 185
Blount, Charles 104
Blumenthal, Susan 44, 45
Bowlby, John 142
Brown, Prof. Greg 215, 226
bullying 140, 151

Casualty 181
catastrophising 215
Cobain, Kurt 176, 186
Cognitive Therapy 69, 210, 214, 215
conservation-withdrawal 144–5

Death on Request 107
Death with Dignity Act 102
deliberate self-harm (DSH), *see* attempted suicide
depression 41, 46–7, 61, 142, 161–2, 187–8
  persistence of 173–4
  Rumination-focused Cognitive Therapy for 222
despair, making peace with 235
Dialectical Behaviour Therapy (DBT) 211–12, 220, 226
Diana, Princess of Wales 86
Diaries (Pepys) 10–12
dichotomous thinking 214
Dignitas 109–10
Dignity in Dying (formerly Exit; Voluntary Euthanasia Society) 103, 108, 109, 114
divorce 27, 38, 56
DNA 142
Doctor Faustus (Marlowe) 7
Donne, John 12–14, 113
dopamine 130–1
Drowned and the Saved, The (Levi) 228, 235
Durkheim, Émile 25, 44–5, 51–4, 118, 158, 177
  critiques of 57–9

EastEnders 179–80
employment status 31–2, 55–6, 83
Engel, G. L. 144
entrapment 59, 61, 143, 152–7, 159, 221, 230

and alcoholics 62
historical evidence for 155–7
ethology 142, 144
euthanasia, *see under* assisted suicide
Exit, *see* Dignity in Dying

family cohesion, decrease in 40–1
Fein, Esther 103
Final Exit (Humphry) xiv
firearms 199–201
and farmers 33, 200
restrictive legislation on 200
US availability of 43, 199
Five Dissertations (Hume) 105
5-HIAA 131
Freud, Sigmund 123–6

gender 26, 29, 50–1
Gentleman's Companion, The 15
Gilbert, Prof. Paul 145–6, 147, 152
Gilden, Charles 104–5
Gilpin, John 8
Gjelsvik, Bergljot 202–3
Goethe, Johann 176–7
Goldney, Prof. Robert 115, 144
grief and mourning 123–5
Guide to Self-deliverance 114

hara-kiri 54
see also kamikaze
Hargus, Emily 95
Hawton, Keith 181
Hemlock Society 103
Hepburn, Silvia 93
Hippocrates 130
Hippocratic Oath 107
Hume, David 4, 105–6
Humphry, Derek xiv, 112

If This Is a Man (Levi) 235
interpersonal problems 87–90, 141–2, 151

Japan, high student suicide rate in 140
see also hara-kiri; kamikaze pilots
Joiner, Thomas 138
Jones, Jim 118–19
Jonestown 118–19
Joyce, Anthony 10
Jung, Carl 165

Kabat-Zin, Jon 223
kamikaze pilots 54, 119–21
see also hara-kiri
Ker, Sir Robert 13
Kety, Seymour 136–7
Klein, Melanie 127
Koestler, Arthur 114–15
Koestler, Cynthia 114, 115
Koresh, David 119

Lamm, Richard 112
Lancet 179–80
Lennard, T. B. 20
Levi, Primo 228, 235
Linehan, Prof. Marsha 92, 95, 211, 223, 226
Lishman, Prof. Alwyn 164
Lou Gehrig's disease 107–8

MacDonald, Michael 156
MacIntosh, Sir James 20
MacLeod, Prof. Andrew 91, 92, 94, 173
Magnyficence (Skelton) 7
Maltsberger, John 128–9
Marlowe, Christopher 7
martyrdom 117–21
and religion 118

Means–End Problem Solving test (MEPS) 87–8
Menninger, Karl 126
mind-lock 169–74, 223
  and problem-solving 171–2
Mindful Way Workbook, The (Teasdale, Williams, Segal) 225
Mindfulness-based Cognitive Therapy (MBCT) 222, 223–5
  see also Cognitive Therapy
Mindfulness and the Transformation of Despair (Williams et al.) 225
Mood Induction Procedure 164
More, Thomas 9, 13
Morgan, Prof. Gethin 1–2
mourning and grief 123–5
'Mourning and Melancholia' (Freud) 123–5
Multicentre Study of Self-Harm 69
Murphy, Terence 156

National Confidential Inquiry into Suicide and Homicide by People with Mental Illness 193–4
National Institute for Health and Care Excellence (NICE) 207
negative rumination 46, 220–1
neurons 130–1
norepinephrine 131

O'Connor, Prof. Rory 70, 94
On Sacred Disease (Hippocrates) 130
'On Suicide' (Hume) 105
over-the-counter medication 66, 202
Oxford Centre for Suicide Research 26, 70

'painful engagement' 94
'parasuicide' 66
parenting 80–1
Pepys, Samuel 10–12
Philips, David 177–8, 179, 182, 184
Pirkis, Jane 185
Pollock, Leslie 88
post-traumatic stress disorder 220
Purdy, Debbie 110
Pythagoras 3, 104

Ramesay, William 15
reasons-for-living inventory 92–5
reincarnation 118
religion 30, 102, 105, 118
Richman, Prof. Joseph 115
RNA 142
Rose, Daniel 156
Rumination-focused Cognitive Therapy 222
  see also Cognitive Therapy
rural areas 32–3, 55

St Augustine 12–13
Samaritans 205
Savage God (Alvarez) 64–5, 198
Schmidtke, Arnold 181
Science 136
Segal, Zindel 223, 224
selective abstraction 214–15
self-esteem 80, 143
self-harm, deliberate, *see* attempted suicide
Seneca 198
serotonin 131, 132–3, 136
sexual abuse 50, 81, 81–3
Skelton, John 7
Sleepless Souls (MacDonald, Murphy) 156
Sorrows of Young Werther, The (Goethe) 177

Stengel, Irwin xiv–xv
substance abuse 37–8, 84, 144–5
Sucitto, Ajahn 236
suicidal signs and symptoms 213–16
suicide 147
  aftermath of 232–4
  and age 50–1
  and alcohol 37–8, 48, 144–5
  among young males, rise in 38–42
  assisted, *see* assisted suicide
  attempted, *see* attempted suicide
  and attempted, as cry of pain xv, xvi, 143, 154–5, 231
  and attempted, as two responses to same circumstances 229
  behaviour, non-fatal 54–5
  biological approaches to 130–7
  brain's role in 58, 130–2
  brief history of 1–23
    and Christianity 3–5, 6–7, 12–13, 18–20
    classical and medieval attitudes to 3–5
    decriminalisation of (UK) 21
    and insanity 5, 18, 19
    and law 20–1
    and *non compos mentis* verdict 5, 6, 9, 15–16
    in other countries 17–18
    in seventeenth century 10–14
    in Tudor times 5
  and bullying 140, 151
  and causation, Durkheim's view of 51–2
  as causes 59–62
  cohort and period effects on 39–40, 41
  and conservation-withdrawal 144–5
  in contemporary society 24–43
  and depression 41, 46–7, 61, 142, 161–2, 187–8
    persistence of 173–4
  and deprivation 55
  and despair, making peace with 235
  and divorce 27, 38, 56
  in *EastEnders* 179–80
  and employment status 31–2, 55–6
  and entrapment 59, 61, 62, 143, 152–7, 159, 221, 230
    historical evidence for 155–7
  and ethnicity 29–30
  evolutionary approach to 145–51
  exploring signs and symptoms of 213–16
  factors affecting risk of 29–38
  and family cohesion, decrease in 40–1
  and firearms 28
  and gender 26, 29, 50–1, 159
  genetic influences on 134–7
  and grief and mourning 123–5
  hara-kiri 54
    see also kamikaze
  Hume's view of 105–6
  and imitation 177–82
    criticisms of research into 181–2
    mechanisms of 184
  and imprisonment 33
  increase in, among young people xiv
  and insanity 5, 18, 19, 44–5, 51
    see also suicide: psychiatric vs social

suicide *cont.*
  and intent 74–7
    external circumstances 74–5, 76–7
    self-report 75–7
  and interpersonal problems 179–80
  in Japan 140
    see also hara-kiri; kamikaze pilots
  kamikaze 54, 119–21
    see also hara-kiri
  and lifespan issues 35–7
  and martyrdom 117–21
  mass 118–20
  means to commit, availability of 196–205
    dangerous jobs 204–5
    medication 201–3
    weapons 199–201
    see also attempted suicide: and substance abuse; firearms; suicide: and substance abuse
  media's influence on 176–86
    and fiction 178–81
    and guidelines 183–4
    Internet incitement 185
  and medical illness 34–5
  and memory 162, 163–74
    and hopelessness 172–3
    over-general 169, 170–4
    searching our past 167–70
  Menninger's three elements of 126
  methods of 28
  and mind-lock 169–75, 223
    and persistence of depression 173–4
    problem-solving 171–2
  and mourning and grief 123–5
  object-relations approach to 127–30
  in other countries 26–7
  and personality disorder 49–50
  predicting, problems with 192–205
    means, availability of 196–205
    sensitivity and specificity 192–3
    timing 193–6
    see also suicide: means to commit, availability of
  preventing 187–208
    by keeping in touch 190
    and primary care, some cautions 191
    and Samaritans 205
    school-based intervention 206–7
    see also suicide: therapy to avert
  and psychiatric illness, evidence for 45–50
  psychiatric vs social 44–62
  psychoanalytic perspectives on 123–30
  rational 34, 113
    vs depressive 114–15
    and irrational, distinction between 115–17
  and religion 30, 118
  renewed debate into xiv
  in rural areas 32–3, 55
  and schizophrenia 48–9, 61
  and school grades 139–40
  and self-harm:
    connections between 157–9
    see also under attempted suicide
  and sexual orientation 30
  and shoplifting 141

and social class 31
and social facts, Durkheim's view of 52–4
and social facts and the individual 57–9
social theory, evidence to support 54–6
and substance abuse 144–5
therapy to avert 209–27
  Acceptance and Commitment Therapy 222
  appropriateness of 218
  Cognitive Therapy 69, 210, 214, 215
  and confidentiality barriers 217–18
  Dialectical Behaviour Therapy (DBT) 211–12, 220, 226
  existing evidence, reviewing 210–13
  exploring signs and symptoms 213–16
  Mindfulness-based Cognitive Therapy (MBCT) 222, 223–5
  possibly precipitating a suicide attempt 219
  psychological barriers to 216–19
  and risk of repetition after self-harm 217
  Rumination-focused Cognitive Therapy 222
  towards new understanding of 219–25
  Usual Care 210–11, 225
and 'Thou shalt not kill' 3, 12–13
world wars' effects on 27
Suicide and Attempted Suicide (Stengel) xiv–xv
suicide bombers 117–18
suicide notes 75, 140

Teasdale, John 164, 223, 224
Truce, The (Levi) 235

Usual Care 210–11, 225
Utopia (More) 9, 13

van Oyjen, Dr Wilfred 107, 108
Voluntary Euthanasia Society, *see* Dignity in Dying

Waco 119
Wallington, Nehemiah 8
WHO World Mental Health Survey initiative 70
Williams, J. M. G. 224
World Health Organization 25, 26
World Medical Association 103, 111